Teacher Learning in the Digital Age

Teacher Learning in the Digital Age

Online Professional Development in STEM Education

Edited by

CHRIS DEDE
ARTHUR EISENKRAFT
KIM FRUMIN
ALEX HARTLEY

HARVARD EDUCATION PRESS
Cambridge, Massachusetts

Library of Congress Control Number 2015952937

Paperback ISBN 978-1-61250-897-9
Library Edition ISBN 978-1-61250-898-6

Published by Harvard Education Press,
an imprint of the Harvard Education Publishing Group
Harvard Education Press
8 Story Street
Cambridge, MA 02138

This project was supported, in part, by the National Science Foundation under
grant number 0733268. Opinions expressed are those of the authors and not
necessarily those of the National Science Foundation.

Cover Design: Saizon Design
Cover Photo: © Romas_Photo/Shutterstock.com

The typefaces used in this book are Sabon for text and Myriad Pro for display.

Contents

Online and Blended Teacher Learning and Professional Development

CHRIS DEDE AND ARTHUR EISENKRAFT

Professional development is the chief means for improving classroom instruction and, in turn, student achievement.[1] Professional development comprises all of a teacher's opportunities for growth after the formal work associated with getting certified and securing a job. Although many teachers enter the teaching profession because of the high value they place on learning, too few engage in professional development on a regular, extended basis throughout their career. Almost all teachers participate in some professional development annually, but it is often superficial in both time and content. Whether expenditures provide a good return on investment and how to improve the cost/benefit ratio of professional development experiences are important educational and policy questions.

As teacher development moves online to take advantage of the scale and other affordances of the web, it's important to ask what works and what doesn't and for whom. To seek answers to these questions, the editors of this volume sought to highlight many of the best models in this rapidly changing field by identifying top developers of online professional development—with an emphasis on science, technology, engineering, and mathematics (STEM) education, where much exciting innovation has taken place—and inviting them to write about what they have learned in the process of designing and implementing their professional development models.

This resulting volume is intended to serve as an overview of online teacher professional development (sometimes referred to as oTPD) to help researchers and developers understand the range of effective models and their conditions for success. It will also help teachers, funders, and policy makers to better understand alternative options for professional development and to make more informed decisions regarding professional development. Educators are eager to understand more about what is promising and what is still in need of investigation. We think that readers will share the excitement of the authors featured in this volume.

CONTRASTING PROFESSIONAL DEVELOPMENT WITH TEACHER LEARNING

The title of this book includes the terms *professional development* and *teacher learning,* the key distinctions of which are agency and formality. Professional development may be mandated for teachers and is generally a formal experience with a fixed duration, curriculum, and instructional strategy and expected outcomes. Teacher learning, by contrast, is typically begun by an educator as a voluntary activity and may be informal, with duration, content, form of learning, and eventual impact uncertain at its inception. The various models described in the following chapters fall on a continuum, with mandated, formal professional development at one end and voluntary, informal teacher learning at the other, and many approaches somewhere in between.

These models that combine professional development and teacher learning may use a specific, commercial curriculum as the focus of professional development. There is an inherent tension between the goals of the developers and the users, however, and this is often denoted as a lack of consistency between the *intended* curriculum as envisioned by the developers and the *enacted* curriculum as implemented by the teacher.[2] This tension often leads to different perceived goals of professional development. For example, in communities of practice based primarily on peer learning but enriched by experts, giving teachers what they need (e.g., strategies for promoting scientific inquiry) as opposed to what they want (e.g., a worksheet to check if students can balance equations) is sometimes a challenge. That said, the richest forms of professional learning lie toward the middle of the continuum, combining theoretical and research-based insights with the wisdom of practice. These can foster teacher ownership by providing some autonomy while accomplishing lasting impacts via expert modeling of innovative practices and teacher-led discussions about overcoming challenges in implementation.

In discussing almost any form of innovation in schooling, the dialogue inevitably turns to how teachers can be helped to effectively adapt a new approach to the particular constraints of their own classroom settings. Despite attempts to develop "teacher-proof" instructional strategies or "teacher-in-a-box" standalone education technologies, enabling students to achieve deep motivation and learning requires personalized guidance from a skilled, knowledgeable educator. Many a promising instructional innovation has failed because its implementation did not include adequate methods for professional development and teacher learning.

Professional development is very important for shifts in teachers' practices because participants must not only learn new skills but also "unlearn" almost unconscious beliefs, assumptions, and values about the nature of teaching, learning, and schooling.[3] Professional development that requires unlearning necessitates high levels of emotional/social support in addition to mastering the intellectual and technical dimensions involved. In order for teachers of STEM subjects to transform from presentational, assimilative instruction to active inquiry-based forms of student learning, teachers must unlearn their own mental models, which include emotional investments developed over decades of, first, being a student receiving traditional instruction and then years of building skills in conventional instruction. Without unlearning, teachers teach as they themselves were taught.

Recent research on how people learn and how to better assess students has led to new curriculum and new teaching strategies. The present landscape of teaching in the United States is dominated by the Common Core State Standards, the National Research Council's Framework for K–12 Science Education, and the Next Generation Science Standards (NGSS).[4] Although these can be viewed as political documents, in that states may or may not adopt them, all states are being influenced by the changes in emphasis that these documents recommend. Teachers must be able to compare and contrast what they are presently doing in their classrooms with the vision of what could be done as articulated in these documents.

Since both Common Core (math) and NGSS (science) speak to how students will be assessed, teachers must increase their familiarity with these new assessment approaches and teaching methods, which lead to students understanding STEM knowledge and skills more deeply and increasing their ability to apply these in real-world situations. Teachers also need opportunities to discuss the limitations of the Common Core and NGSS, as some people are confounding the Common Core and NGSS assessments with limitations on the curriculum. For example, NGSS recommends that testing be limited to Newton's Second Law at the high school level, but some teachers misinterpret this to mean that only one of Newton's three laws should be included in the course. Overall, teachers need to understand that the tests are limited in scope and represent only a sampling of what students need to know, with items biased toward what can easily be measured.

Beyond these transformative shifts in STEM teaching, educational approaches must change dramatically to prepare students for work and life (as opposed to further schooling) in the modern era.[5] Rather than moving into stable industrial jobs, young people now must compete in a rapidly shifting, global, knowledge-based, innovation-centered economy. And in order to secure a reasonably comfortable lifestyle, they now must go beyond a high school diploma and acquire not just academic knowledge but also character attributes such as intrinsic motivation, persistence, and flexibility. Moreover, mastery now requires the ability to apply knowledge and skills in real-world contexts, not just in academic settings, by demonstrating proficiency via effective, authentic performances.

In its landmark report *Education for Life and Work*, the National Research Council describes "deeper learning" as the instructional strategy needed to achieve these ambitious goals.[6] The approaches recommended by advocates of deeper learning are not new, and historically these instructional strategies have been described under a variety of terms; until now, however, they have been rarely practiced within schools.

- *Case-based learning* helps students master abstract principles and skills through the analysis of real-world situations.
- *Multiple, varied representations* of concepts provide different ways of explaining complicated things, showing how those depictions are alternative forms of the same underlying ideas.
- *Collaborative learning* enables a team to combine its knowledge and skills in making sense of a complex phenomenon.
- *Apprenticeships* involve working with a mentor who has a specific real-world role and, over time, enables mastery of knowledge and skills.
- *Self-directed, life-wide, open-ended learning* is based on a student's passions and connected to a student's identity in ways that foster academic engagement, self-efficacy, and tenacity.

- *Learning for transfer* emphasizes that the measure of mastery is application in life rather than simply in the classroom.
- *Interdisciplinary studies* help students see how different fields can complement each other, offering a richer perspective on the world than any single discipline can provide.
- *Personalized learning* ensures that students receive instruction and supports that are tailored to their needs and responsive to their interests.
- *Connected learning* encourages students to confront challenges and pursue opportunities that exist outside of their classrooms and schools.
- *Diagnostic assessments* are embedded into learning and are formative for further learning and instruction.

These approaches to deeper learning entail very different teaching strategies than the familiar, lecture-based forms of instruction characteristic of industrial-era schooling, with its one-size-fits-all processing of students. Rather than requiring rote memorization and individual mastery of prescribed material, they involve in-depth, differentiated content; authentic diagnostic assessment embedded in instruction; active forms of learning, often collaborative; and learning about academic subjects linked to personal passions and infused throughout life. Active research in these desired strategies is complex, and professional development is essential as a component of this research. Teacher learning is vital for achieving the transformation in practice emerging from this shift.

CHALLENGES AND OPPORTUNITIES IN PROFESSIONAL DEVELOPMENT

A precursor to this book, Chris Dede's edited volume *Online Professional Development for Teachers*, published in 2006, provides a dismal picture of professional development at that time:

> Unfortunately, at present most teacher professional development programs are not of high quality, offering "fragmented, intellectually superficial" seminars (Borko, 2004, 3). In addition, face-to-face, pull-out programs are unable to provide ongoing daily guidance for teachers as they attempt to implement novel curricula or pedagogies. This problem of just-in-time support is exacerbated when teachers attempt to implement new strategies in environments made hostile by reluctant peers or administrators who see those innovations as undercutting the

current school culture. Further, conventional approaches to professional development typically fail to provide day-to-day professional mentoring for entry-level teachers; this lack of guidance is a major factor underlying the high attrition rate among new teachers within their first five years in the classroom. As a result of all these factors, teachers often become frustrated with professional development, at times because it is ineffectual, and at times because it requires sacrifices disproportionate to the enhancement it provides.[7]

This situation has not substantially improved in the past decade. Most teacher professional development is one-size-fits-all (despite dramatic differences among individual teachers), just-in-case rather than just-in-time (so forgotten when the opportunity finally arises for application), and focused on superficial improvements rather than needed major shifts, such as transforming STEM instruction based on the Common Core and NGSS.[8]

The failure to provide universal, high-quality professional development in education is in sharp contrast to other professions (e.g., law, medicine), and this shortfall is in part responsible for continuing difficulties in both attracting strong people to teaching and keeping them in classroom instruction for more than a few years.[9] Moreover, few forms of professional development have been studied using strong methods of evaluation and research, so improvement is difficult given a lack of findings about what strategies are working well and why.[10]

The chapters comprising this book delineate insights about the process of professional development and teacher learning that have emerged in the last decade. While advances in theory and empirical research have enriched the field, the most profound change during this period has been the evolution of digital technology, particularly the rise of mobile devices, wireless broadband, and social media. A mobile infrastructure is now in place that allows educators to access professional learning experiences life-wide, regardless of place and time, using ubiquitous devices that have become part of everyone's personal activities.

Further, this infrastructure supports a broad range of peer-based capabilities for sharing educational artifacts, thinking together, and cocreating learning resources. The following list is illustrative of a much richer array of social media, digital tools on which the models in this book draw:

- *sharing:* social bookmarking, photo/video sharing, social networking, writers' workshops and fanfiction

- *thinking:* blogs, podcasts, online discussion forums, Twitter
- *cocreating:* wikis/collaborative file creation, mashups/collective media creation, collaborative social change communities.

Technological constraints that plagued professional development models in 2006 are largely gone, creating exciting opportunities for rich interaction and universal access. This book features models of professional development and teacher learning that go well beyond what was possible a decade ago, although, to date, achieving scale and sustainability for these approaches has been difficult.

THE GENESIS AND DESIGN OF THIS BOOK

A decade has passed since the workshop at Harvard leading to the publication of *Online Professional Development for Teachers*.[11] During that time, the publication and adoption of Active Physics, an innovative project-based high school curriculum, generated a need to provide high-quality online professional development that received National Science Foundation (NSF) support.[12] A related project, also supported by NSF, studied the professional development choices that teachers are making to teach the revised Advanced Placement (AP) curriculum.[13] That project brought Chris Dede, Arthur Eisenkraft, Kim Frumin, Alex Hartley, and others together.

Based on these intersecting interests, it seemed time for another synthesis of how digital media are shaping professional development and teacher learning. Gerhard Salinger, in one of his final acts in a long, illustrious, productive, and inspiring career with NSF, authorized remaining funding from one of these grants to be allocated for supporting an Online Teacher Professional Development Summit that was held November 14–16, 2014, at the University of Massachusetts Boston. The event was organized by the four coeditors of this book to focus on innovative models of online professional development and teacher learning in STEM subjects because substantial investment in the last decade has produced novel, powerful approaches. The organizers asked colleagues and others working in the field for recommendations for people to invite who represented the top developers of online teacher professional development for STEM instruction. They received approximately one hundred recommendations and from that group selected twenty-two participants representing a range of experiences. Criteria for selection included published research articles and/or funded projects by NSF or similar organizations. (For economic reasons, they did not select international participants.)

Authors were asked to provide a description of the model's strategy for educational improvement, audience, balance of content and skills, primary method of teacher learning, and discussion of whether the model is a face-to-face, online, or blended program. (The terms *hybrid* and *blended* are used interchangeably in this book.) They were also asked to provide information about

- the types of infrastructure and technology required by the model
- the degree of commitment required of participants
- how the model ensures high-quality enactment
- research and evaluation of the model and the results
- the intended versus enacted models by participants
- whether the model is intended for local professional development or the larger education community (or both).

In addition, authors were asked to consider the adaptability (how readily a model can be modified to fit local conditions without losing its effectiveness), scalability (the extent a model can be implemented in many types of settings with varying levels of resources), inclusivity (accessibility across cultures, technical divides, diversity, physical challenges, and a host of other equity issues), and sustainability (over time in terms of resources) of the model. During the summit, authors presented papers that were then discussed in small groups and revised.

The book is designed so that it need not be read cover to cover, although certainly that is the best way to achieve an overall perspective on the current state of professional development and teacher learning for STEM education. The chapters are grouped into four parts: "Courses," "Curriculum Support," "Resources and Strategies," and "Summary Insights." In the appendix, we provide discussion questions for readers and those who may be using this book as part of a course.

As part of the introductory section of the book, in chapter 1 Barry Fishman considers possible futures for online teacher professional development and connects these trends and the latest research into what makes for more effective professional development in general with models presented in this volume. Often, a look forward is included as the last chapter in a book such as this, but we have decided to place it first so that readers can consider the models in relation to Fishman's forecast. His chapter concludes with comments on the research methods commonly employed to examine outcomes related to online teacher professional development and how a shift in these methods may lead to more scalable and sustainable designs to support teacher learning online.

Part I, "Courses," presents four exemplary models of courses designed for teacher professional development. In chapter 2, Susan Doubler and Katherine Paget describe Talk Science, a web-based professional development course that helps teachers support strategic and purposeful classroom discussions in which students build coherent lines of reasoning based on their own ideas. The course, which uses four types of videos, takes place over a three-month period as participating teachers implement the Inquiry Curriculum, a multigrade study of concepts and practices key to understanding the particulate model of matter.

In chapter 3, Glenn Kleiman and Mary Ann Wolf discuss how the MOOCs for Educators (MOOC-Eds) initiative has achieved impact and scale. This initiative was designed to explore whether MOOC-like approaches could be adapted to address the professional development needs of many educators, including teachers, instructional coaches, and school and district administrators; incorporate research-based principles of effective professional development; and provide scalable, accessible, cost-effective professional development.

Ruth Schoenbach, Cynthia Greenleaf, Willard Brown, and Heather Howlett describe in chapter 4 an online course designed for high school science teachers by WestEd, a nonpartisan nonprofit research, development, and service agency based in San Francisco. The iRAISE (Internet-based Reading Apprenticeship Improving Science Education) course, which is focused on disciplinary literacy, is based on the Reading Apprenticeship instructional framework, a pedagogical approach that has been developed over a twenty-plus-year history of iterative research and development with communities of practitioners. The chapter addresses the aims and questions that guided the "translation" of a sixty-five-hour, yearlong, ten-day face-to-face professional development sequence into an all-online, mostly synchronous course, as well the strengths and challenges of this approach.

In chapter 5, Robert Steiner and his colleagues from the American Museum of Natural History describe the professional development program Seminars on Science, which began in 1998 as the development of hybrid offerings that take advantage of in-person opportunities at the museum and elsewhere. The authors also discuss the development of MOOC versions of the courses as well as the future prospects for online and blended teacher professional development at the museum.

Part II, "Curriculum Support," begins with chapter 6, by Abigail Levy and Arthur Eisenkraft, who write about the Active Physics Teacher Community formed to help teachers using the Active Physics curriculum. This professional development model assists teachers in preparing for their classes each day by providing them with formal instruction directly related to the lessons they are teaching; in sharing their knowledge, experiences, successes, and challenges with other teachers using the same lesson plans and curriculum; and with comparing the effectiveness of their teaching with the effectiveness of others' teaching, thereby allowing them to use data to inform their instruction and modify their strategies appropriately.

In chapter 7, Jacqueline Miller and Katherine Paget discuss the Electronic Teacher Guide (eTG), a professional development model that was developed as a proof-of-concept exemplar to determine whether a print guide for an inquiry-based, educative curriculum could be redesigned as a cybertool that would have the potential to transform and improve teacher learning. The eTG prototype can also provide a model for science curriculum developers and publishers for supporting teachers' "move" into the digital classroom.

Barbara Zahm and Ruta Demery describe in chapter 8 CyberPD, a cyber-learning professional development model readily and inexpensively distributed to districts implementing Project-Based Inquiry Science, an NSF-funded middle school science curriculum. The pedagogical elements in CyberPD include driving questions, learning by design, sustained inquiry, and engagement in scientific reasoning and practices. These key elements are not separate but are synergistic and common across all thirteen units and facilitate science learning at scale.

In Part III, "Resources and Strategies," chapter 9, by Al Byers and Flavio Mendez, provides an overview of the resources available through the NSTA Learning Center, where more than 170,000 teachers spend many hours completing self-directed on-demand web modules, take formal online courses with university partners, participate in web seminars and virtual conferences, and share online digital resource collections and professional insights through moderated discussion forums. This model currently has more than 90,000 personally uploaded resources, 14,000 teacher-generated public collections, and 60,000 user-generated posts on more than 5,800 topics across its public and private forums. The chapter shares the center's challenges and successes and offers insights into how NSTA's platform may be configured for the needs of individuals as well as for entire school districts and institutions of higher education.

In chapter 10, Kim Frumin and Chris Dede describe the important role of moderators in online professional learning communities, as documented by research on the College Board's online AP Teacher Communities (APTCs) in high school biology and chemistry. Of the many forms of professional development that the College Board offers, participation in the APTCs has the largest positive, direct, and statistically significant association with both teacher practice and student outcomes.[14] The value of an online community lies in its ability to enable the rich and open exchange of ideas, experiences, and resources among its members. Based on theory and research, seven guidelines and other methods are presented that moderators can use to support the changes in behavior and knowledge sharing to which an online community aspires.

Raymond Rose details in chapter 11 strategies and resources that can help providers of online and blended teacher professional development meet their legal obligations for accessibility by people with disabilities, including existing standards for quality and accessibility and a course review process against these published standards.

In the final part of the book, "Summary Insights," Steven Schneider and his colleagues discuss in chapter 12 five cases of online professional development approaches designed at WestEd. The authors recount the multi-threaded story of how WestEd's traditional, face-to-face delivery is evolving into a variety of online approaches, summarized in a conceptual framework that spans various types of professional development. The details help articulate how these approaches evolved, lessons learned in their implementation, the role of facilitators, and why online or blended formats were considered most advantageous.

Finally, to close the volume, Chris Dede and Arthur Eisenkraft delineate core tensions in improving the models described in this volume, set out an aspirational vision for the next five years, and recommend next steps for various stakeholders.

As coeditors, we've learned much from each of the author's contributions, as well as from their participation in and interactions at the Online Teacher Professional Development Summit. We hope you find this book an equally rewarding experience in terms of the enthusiasm and insights it offers.

CHAPTER 1

Possible Futures for Online Teacher Professional Development

BARRY FISHMAN

> It's hard to make predictions—especially about the future.
> —*Danish proverb*

> The only way you can predict the future is to build it.
> —*Alan Kay, computer scientist*

What is the future of online teacher professional development? This chapter explores potential answers to this question by considering: (1) shifting goals for teacher professional development, (2) the ongoing evolution of pedagogical approaches employed in teacher professional development, and (3) shifts in technologies available to support teacher professional development. It also previews the exemplary models included in this volume by connecting them with these trends as well as the latest research into what makes for more effective professional development in general. The chapter concludes with comments on the research methods commonly employed to examine outcomes related to online teacher professional development and how a shift in these methods may lead to more scalable and sustainable designs to support teacher learning online. But first, it is important to examine just what we mean when we talk about online teacher professional development.

WHAT WE TALK ABOUT WHEN WE TALK ABOUT ONLINE PROFESSIONAL DEVELOPMENT

First and foremost, *online* teacher professional development is *professional development*. As with any topic in education involving technology, the quality or success of an online teacher professional development program is not primarily a function of the technology employed. It is a function of the context for the professional development, its pedagogical design, who the participants are, its duration, and so forth. The term *professional development* itself encompasses a broad range of activities with a commensurately broad range of purposes. Generally, the term describes learning activities related to the profession of teaching pursued after the conclusion of pre-service training. Professional development can thus be used to describe teacher enhancement activities from the early (induction) years of teaching through retirement and encompasses mentoring, self-study, study groups, organized workshops, and so forth, all of which might be conducted as one-time, short-term, long-term, or ongoing engagements. When the word *online* is added, it generally refers to activities that are conducted via the Internet. These activities can be synchronous, with all participants interacting in real time, or asynchronous, where participants work with materials at their own pace for submission and later feedback. Activities can be conducted completely online or in a hybrid (blended) format that mixes face-to-face interaction with online activity. The range of potential designs for online professional development is vast, and it is important to avoid essentializing the concept when discussing its quality, characteristics, or effects.

There is broad agreement in policy and practitioner circles that high-quality professional development is key to the successful improvement of schools and the implementation of productive curricular reforms.[1] But there is also broad agreement that much professional development is either ineffective or not as effective as it might be for a variety of reasons, such as lack of sufficient time or lack of a strong connection between what teachers study in professional development and the contexts where that new knowledge is to be employed.[2] As Dede and colleagues argue, online professional development is perceived as having a range of potential advantages, such as greater flexibility to accommodate teachers' schedules, the ability to aggregate resources and expertise from disparate locations, and the promise of creating "a path toward providing real-time, work-embedded support" for teachers, something that Fullan argues for in calling for schools to become learning organizations with a focus on continual improvement in order to embrace continuous change.[3] For these reasons and others, policy makers have advocated for more teacher professional development to be delivered online.[4]

The use of technology, in general, does not lead to desired outcomes or even improvement simply by its presence, though what is done with the technology can make a difference in how the overall sociotechnical system functions.[5] The outcomes produced by interactions with systems are a product of design. Though the authors are not talking about professional development, Roschelle and colleagues argue that there are essentially two directions one can go in designing with technology: do existing things better, or do better things.[6] The first approach is the more common, whereby technology is applied in order to make common practices more efficient, more effective, or more widely available. The second approach is about rethinking the activity and taking a different approach that is facilitated by the introduction of technology. For example, the idea of asynchronous distance learning has existed in the form of lessons by postal mail since at least the mid-1800s. Introducing electronic communication technologies (i.e., online tools) to this process may make the exchange of lessons and responses faster and perhaps less expensive, but it does not alter the basic mechanics of the process whereby people teach and learn at a distance. However, tools such as audio and video conferencing, text chats, screen sharing, collaborative document editing, and so forth offer the opportunity to change the dynamic. Using these tools, synchronous communication becomes possible, allowing distance participants to teach and learn with each other in real time. That's doing something different and potentially (though not necessarily) better.

As Vrasidas and Glass document, the early years of network-enabled distance education were based primarily on objectivist or behaviorist pedagogies, emphasizing an information transmission approach, and the same was true for early instances of online professional development.[7] As technologies evolved, some projects began to explore more interactive approaches that encouraged teachers to observe new practices and try them out in their own classrooms. Tinker and Haavind document a range of such programs in the early 1990s, which were built around technologies such as email, listservs, and bulletin boards.[8] In the late 1990s, many prominent examples of online professional development environments moved even more strongly toward socioconstructivist approaches such as communities of practice or problem-based learning.[9] These environments included:

- TAPPED-IN from SRI, which created a persistent virtual space to facilitate the work of teachers engaged in communities of practice by blending components of a synchronous MOO (multiuser domain object-oriented) environment with asynchronous web-based resources[10]
- WIDE World from the Harvard Graduate School of Education, which provided online courses around topics (e.g., teaching for understanding) organized according to constructivist principles[11]
- the Math Forum, which provided teachers access to a range of mathematics teaching materials, access to consulting experts ("Ask Dr. Math"), and a forum for discussions of mathematics materials and instruction.[12]

These examples notwithstanding, much online learning in general, and online teacher professional development in particular, remains organized as interactive courses using a learning management or content management environment such as Moodle or Blackboard.

SHIFTING GOALS FOR TEACHER PROFESSIONAL DEVELOPMENT

There are many possible goals underlying teacher professional development, but one of the most important is the improvement of student learning.[13] Desimone presents a straightforward logic model to depict the manner in which professional development engagement by teachers leads to improved student outcomes. In that model, the core features of professional development—content focus, degree of active learning, coherence with other initiatives, duration, and collective participation of teachers from the same school or district—lead to increases in teachers' knowledge and skills and changes in their attitudes or beliefs, which in turn lead to changes in instruction and then improvements in student learning.[14] All of this is constrained by the broader context for the professional development, including characteristics of teachers, students, schools, and the policy environment. For this book's purposes, the nature of the professional development—online, hybrid, or face-to-face—is another contextual constraint that may impact how different components of Desimone's logic model interact.

In the fifth edition of the American Education Research Association *Handbook of Research on Teaching,* Dede and Fishman explore a broad range of emerging social and cultural shifts that may—arguably *should*—impact the goals for teacher professional development.[15] The National Research Council's *Gathering Storm* reports and Thomas Friedman's "flat world" argument describe ongoing changes and challenges in the world

TABLE 1.1   Twenty-first-century knowledge and skills

Cognitive outcomes	Intrapersonal outcomes	Interpersonal outcomes
Cognitive processes and strategies	Intellectual openness	Teamwork and collaboration
Knowledge	Work ethic and conscientiousness	Leadership
Creativity	Positive core self-evaluation	Communication
Critical thinking	Metacognition	Responsibility
Information literacy	Flexibility	Conflict resolution
Reasoning	Initiative	
Innovation	Appreciation of diversity	

economy, with suggestions about how education needs to change to meet these challenges.[16] Students must learn to communicate and collaborate across new (and old) media, to find and validate information from diverse sources, to transform information into new knowledge and ideas, to identify problems and develop paths to solutions, and to develop skills to support lifelong learning. These new types of knowledge and skills are part of a larger domain collectively described as "twenty-first century skills." The 2012 National Research Council report *Education for Life and Work* presents a consensus view of these skills arrayed across cognitive, intrapersonal, and interpersonal dimensions (summarized in table 1.1).[17] School, as currently designed, targets *some* of the cognitive outcomes in table 1.1. The majority of these outcomes, however, require retooling educational programs and the way(s) we prepare teachers to succeed in preparing students in these programs. It is also worth remembering that all of these changes take place against a backdrop of increased global mobility, creating populations of learners that are increasingly diverse in terms of socioeconomic status, cultural background, and native language. And all of this change takes place against a backdrop of constrained budgets and fragile national and local economies.

The 2010 National Education Technology Plan (NETP) includes a section focused on a new set of engagements for teachers—aligned with the demands identified by Friedman and the National Research Council—called "connected teaching."[18] There is a tradition that characterizes teaching as a solitary or isolating activity that happens behind closed doors.[19] But the

NETP argues that, in an increasingly fluid and interconnected world, it makes more sense for teachers to think of themselves as operating at the hub of an array of learning resources that begins with their own classroom but extends outward to include other classrooms, the surrounding community, and an entire world of online resources and information. The NETP cites research pointing to the "life-long" and "life-wide" nature of learning, where learning (and teaching) is enriched by connection across formal and informal learning environments and where learning is most engaging when it can unite academic content with peer culture and individual interests.[20] Becoming a "connected teacher" represents new skills for teachers that mirror the twenty-first-century skills depicted in table 1.1 and also dictates an expanded set of goals for teacher professional development. These are not new ideas, as notions of teachers learning together in collaborative professional networks, in particular online networks, have been around as long as the Internet. But the need for developing capacities for connected teaching is quickly becoming critical.[21]

These reflections on shifting goals for teacher learning may seem pie in the sky with respect to the future, and they must be tempered by the reality of an increasing emphasis on standardized testing and other forms of high-stakes assessments that continue to dictate the immediate agenda for teacher performance and thus teacher professional development. Indeed, in an environment where job security is linked to value-added measures based largely on test scores, it would be imprudent for teachers to select professional development pathways that do not include a focus on how to improve student performance on those tests.[22] However, a focus on *only* the immediate demands of testing misses the bigger picture and risks producing students who can perform well on a test but not in the world beyond. A challenge for professional development providers is to design teacher learning that addresses both needs. Organizations like WestEd (see chapter 12) and the National Science Teachers Association (NSTA; see chapter 9) offer a range of teacher learning options online to address these varying needs.

SHIFTING PEDAGOGIES FOR TEACHER PROFESSIONAL DEVELOPMENT

A comprehensive consideration of pedagogical approaches for teacher professional development is beyond the scope of this chapter, but there are trends that mirror the shifting goals described above. As Vrasidas and Glass note, early examples of distance education, including those mediated by technologies such as the Internet, embodied what can be characterized as instructivist pedagogical paradigms with a focus on knowledge transmission.[23] Lessons were organized into discrete units of information, and learners would interact with those lessons and then be tested for mastery before moving on to the next lesson. Similarly, there is a long history of teacher professional development organized as top-down information delivery sessions. Teachers have referred to this as "sit and get" professional development, and it is derided by teachers and scholars alike.[24] Though such approaches persist, alternative approaches with roots in sociocognitive or constructivist learning have been experimented with for decades and better reflect teaching and learning that is aligned with twenty-first-century skills and knowledge.[25] The core ideas in this shift are not new, but they are challenging to instantiate, which may explain the persistence of more straightforward and less demanding pedagogies.[26] Putnam and Borko characterize these "new views of knowledge" as organized around seeing cognition as situated, social, and distributed.[27] It can be argued that we are still working on instantiating these core ideas into current conceptions on online teacher professional development. It is possible that technology is enabling us to realize them in new ways.

Situative theorists view cognition as deeply embedded in context and goals and therefore emphasize *authenticity* as a key design element of learning environments, in terms of both activities and contexts.[28] For teacher professional development, this suggests the importance of focusing learning around what teachers must do in their own classrooms and working to reduce the amount of translation needed to transfer learning in professional development into practice. In this frame, professional development is about general topics for teachers from a range of settings. For example, a workshop on collaborative learning delivered to teachers of various subject areas drawn from across an entire district is likely to be less effective than professional development developed for teachers engaged in a shared practice activity, such as implementing new science curriculum materials by focusing on how to use collaborative learning techniques with those materials. Such alignment makes the connections in Desimone's logic model tighter and may explain why professional development that is actually embedded in practice, such as the lesson study approach, is viewed as so effective.[29] This book explores this idea in several chapters. For instance, Miller and Paget (chapter 7) describe an electronic teacher guide that serves as a tool for the customization of curriculum materials and makes curriculum an educative resource for teachers in the process.[30] Levy and Eisenkraft (chapter 6) describe how an online community designed to accompany the Active Physics curriculum helped teachers through an explicit model for preparing instruction, sharing experience about practice, and comparing results.[31] And Zahm and Demery (chapter 8) explore the role of online learning resources in supporting the sustainability of a specific problem-based inquiry curriculum in science.

A social and dialogical view of cognition focuses on how learners interact with others to construct knowledge. A key to learning is exposure to and engagement with practices and ways of understanding, interpreting, and communicating about the world that emerge from communities. This view is explored in Lave and Wenger's seminal work on learning through apprenticeship, Wenger's subsequent development of the communities of practice theory, and work around cognitive apprenticeship that focuses on how to bridge the gap between real-world practice and forms of practice that are attainable in classrooms.[32] In a science classroom, for instance, the goal would be to model scientific thinking, as opposed to having students act as "little scientists." Viewed from this perspective, it is important to design learning experiences for teachers that engage them with the communities of practice they are trying to model in their classroom and also to create opportunities for teachers to interact with and learn from one another in a professional community.

This was a central goal for teacher learning in the Center for Learning Technologies in Urban Schools (LeTUS). LeTUS professional development was situated in that all teachers were working together to implement a common and new inquiry-oriented curriculum. Teachers also shared a common context in that they were all teaching middle school science in the Detroit Public Schools. In LeTUS professional development design research, a highly valued element was time for teachers to share and reflect on their local experiences with the curriculum.[33] In essence, the teachers' contextualized knowledge was the final element of the curricular design, and one that could come only from peers. This same idea was at the heart of a more recent study in which online professional development was designed to accompany an inquiry-oriented high school environmental science curriculum.[34] This research focused on an experimental comparison of online and face-to-face professional development experiences for teachers, where the content of the professional development was held constant. The study found that the professional development conditions produced equivalent outcomes for changes in teacher knowledge, classroom practice, and student learning.[35]

Grounding learning in peer exchange was a core idea behind online teacher learning communities such as the Math Forum, TAPPED-IN, and LabNet, where opportunities to interact with colleagues is a crucial design feature.[36] Video is another tool that facilitates both situating cognition in context and fostering dialogue. Using a shared video prompt was a core technology in anchored instruction pedagogy.[37] The Jasper Woodbury series had students first watch a video together and then present a range of problems that could be solved by extracting and extrapolating information from the video.[38] This same basic idea is at the core of video- and case-based pedagogies for teacher professional development.[39] A challenge for the design of professional development cases has always been how authentic they should be. A general consensus has emerged that teachers have an easier time accepting and working with video that does not appear overproduced or staged.[40]

The third aspect of new views of cognition explored by Putnam and Borko is distributed cognition.[41] In this view, thinking is "stretched over" both people and artifacts or objects that they use as part of everyday practice.[42] Something as simple as writing down notes on paper helps to extend our memory, allowing more complex manipulations of information that might otherwise be difficult to remember. Yet, in many school learning situations, working with tools (e.g., calculators) or peers (e.g., collaboration) is framed as "cheating," even though the same activity is valued as a crucial skill for success in the real world (see table 1.1).[43] In thinking about professional development, distributed cognition recognizes both the importance of peers for thinking together and also materials, such as curriculum, for shaping how teachers think about practice. Distributed cognition also supports thinking about the creation of performance supports for teachers to use in practice, such as scientific instruments or discussion guides. If such resources are designed for use both in professional development *and* in practice, teacher learning can move fluidly from *learning about* to *learning with*, another key idea in socioconstructivist thinking and technology.[44]

SHIFTING TECHNOLOGIES FOR TEACHER PROFESSIONAL DEVELOPMENT

When compared to context, goals, or pedagogical design, technology is arguably the least important component of a learning environment. That being said, the affordances of different technologies enable new variations and forms of organizing activity. There are activities that are much easier to do with particular technologies when they are used well. Changes in technology are worth examining in order to understand new design possibilities to better support teaching and learning related to twenty-first century skills or challenging pedagogies.

To help identify potential trends in technology that may impact education and could also play a role in teacher professional development, a valuable resource with a good track record is the New Media Consortium's Horizon Reports. These reports employ a panel of experts to survey the landscape and nominate technology that is likely to impact education in the near term, the medium term, and the long term.[45] Blending the forecasts for both K–12 and higher education in this consideration makes sense, because teacher learning occupies a gray area that is sometimes about tools designed specifically for K–12 classroom use and sometimes about tools for use in graduate or postgraduate coursework. The latest versions of the Horizon Report emphasize "fast" (1–3 years) and "mid-range" trends (3–5 years) around the development and integration of hybrid learning environments, blending online with face-to-face learning. Another mid-range trend is the increasing use of games and "gamification," or the addition of game-like elements to learning environments. And in the long term, the Horizon Reports point to an increasing emphasis on what is being called "personalized learning," or the tailoring of teaching and learning to individual learners' needs. This trend dovetails with both big data and learning analytics and the rapid growth of personally owned computing devices, including smart phones, tablets, or laptops.

Development and Integration of Hybrid Learning Environments

Sometime around 2012, a form of online learning called a massive open online course (MOOC) appeared on the scene and threw higher education into a panic. Hailed in the media as "new," MOOCs, which offer university courses for free online, had actually been around for some time in different formats and employ a basic pedagogy that is largely lecture based and instructivist, harking back to the earliest forms of distance education.[46] MOOCs are now referred to as either cMOOCs or xMOOCs. cMOOCs (the c stands for the use of connectivist and social theories of learning) usually operate at a scale of hundreds of participants. Pedagogically, a cMOOC is designed to support collective knowledge building among participants.[47] In contrast, the form of MOOCs popularized by organizations such as EdX and Coursera are xMOOCs, designed to serve thousands or tens of thousands of students using pedagogies that are largely lecture based and top down. xMOOCs still depend on collective participation, as the theory of supporting so many students at scale is that learners will interact with each other in discussion forums to make sense of the lectures. The emphasis, though, is on processing the material as delivered by instructors as opposed to joint sense making and knowledge building.

Colleges and universities have seemed almost compelled to participate in the latest wave of MOOC expansion, perceiving a threat to their business model of tuition-based courses packaged into semesters and multi-course programs of study.[48] In response, some universities have been using MOOCs as a vehicle to experiment with ways of using online learning environments to extend traditional face-to-face learning. The idea of blending face-to-face and online learning has been called *blended* or *hybrid learning* and, in using the most productive affordances of each modality, has led to positive learning outcomes.[49] Most universities, however, are using MOOCs as a vehicle to reach new audiences of students in hopes of raising their institutional profile or reputation, even if the eventual benefits are hazy. There are already numerous MOOCs for teacher learning.[50] How well do existing MOOCs support teacher learning? What are effective designs for teacher learning MOOCs? The answers are not yet clear, but there are many efforts under way to answer these questions, including some described in this book.

Leaders in face-to-face teacher professional development are experimenting with MOOCs as a way to extend their research-based models for teacher learning. For instance, the Friday Institute has extensive experience with small-group online teacher learning and is now exploring how MOOCs can support larger-scale teacher learning that is self-directed, peer-supported, job-connected, and supportive of a broad range of participant voices (see chapter 3). NSTA offers a broad range of teacher learning options, including MOOCs offered by partners such as MIT, to connect teachers to content-area learning in areas such as biology (see chapter 9). NSTA in particular sees the future of teacher learning as blended and hybrid, and it is developing a range of learning options for science teachers across multiple modalities. Science museums such as the American Museum of Natural History are experimenting with MOOCs as a way to expand access to museum resources and as an extension of the core program Seminars on Science, designed to engage teachers in authentic science problems and practices (see chapter 5).

The Try Science online course, developed jointly by TERC and Lesley College, employed a hands-on inquiry approach for K–8 teachers and was designed to offer teachers activities they can use directly in their classroom.[51] A similar approach, described in chapter 2, is taken by a new project from TERC and Clark University called Talk Science, which employs video cases delivered online that are meant to be explored by teachers, who discuss the cases in local study groups, try out activities in their classrooms, and then hold discussions again with their colleagues in study groups. In chapter 4, Schoenbach, Greenleaf, Brown, and Howlett describe an extensive online course based around an apprenticeship model of reading instruction that also engages teachers in iterative cycles of online learning, practice, and reflection.

Helping teachers make a connection between professional development and their local needs is a challenge for all teacher professional development. As Schlager and Fusco note in reflecting on what worked well and what did not work in TAPPED-IN, the online activities and communities that leveraged local action were the most successful in terms of online activity and engagement.[52] This observation can be linked to the later findings about the importance of coherence in professional development, which Garet et al. describe as consistency with local reform efforts and Penuel et al. frame as the effort required to translate the professional development activities into local classroom practices.[53] Try Science, as the name implies, addresses this explicitly through its activity design, as does Talk Science. A new offering, NGSX, an online and hybrid professional development environment offered in conjunction with the new Next Generation Science Standards, addresses this gap by attempting to organize local science teachers to work on local problems face to face while using online tools to leverage broad-based knowledge building about practice around the new science standards from teachers nationwide.[54]

Games, Gamification, and Gameful Design

A persistent challenge in professional development is engagement—getting teachers to want to participate in professional learning activities of their own volition and driven by their personal goals. In exploring reasons why teachers "stay away" from professional development, Supovitz and Zeif conclude that there was often a mismatch between what teachers thought they wanted from professional development and what was offered.[55] In many cases, professional development is mandated by teachers' employment contract, and the options available are limited. And there is also the problem of coherence (or lack thereof): if the professional development does not feel relevant, a teacher is likely to avoid participating. Two related approaches to addressing problems of motivation are the use of games and the use of gamification or gameful design.

Games as tools for teaching K–12 content have been growing in popularity.[56] Growing more slowly is the idea of games for teaching teachers. Games can be defined broadly, and often the consideration of games in education also includes simulations, something that many teachers have participated in as part of practice teaching.[57] But literal games and digital games for professional development are a different matter. SimSchool is an online simulation environment designed to support preservice teacher self-efficacy by allowing them to "play" with a simulated classroom environment to try out different pedagogical practices.[58] An even more advanced environment is Quest2Teach, which is built on top of the same massively multiplayer online role-playing game platform as the Quest2Learn environment.[59] Quest2Teach is also aimed at preservice teachers, allowing them to explore and practice specific techniques around literacy instruction. But the plan is to build out a range of different scenarios that will be of value to both preservice and in-service teachers. The TeachLivE environment does something similar but uses kinesthetic interfaces like Microsoft Kinect and voice interaction.[60] These game-based and simulation environments all share common goals, such as enabling repeated practice both to build skills and increase teacher self-efficacy. The designers of these environments stress the ability to practice in safe spaces, where students are always available and where you can always go back and try something again from scratch.

Akin to the use of games for teaching and teacher learning is the use of gamification, which can be defined as the use of game-like features in order to encourage participation and increase engagement. There is a booming industry in gamification across practically all business sectors, including education. Elements familiar from games, such as avatars, badges, and points or stars, can easily be added to a learning environment in order to nudge participants in the desired direction. But gamification also has a broad range of detractors who argue that the changes are typically superficial and manipulative.[61] Even so, gamified tools for education are increasingly popular, such as Class Dojo, a tool that uses badges and points to help shape classroom behavior. One critic drily noted that administering electric shocks to students would have a similar effect.[62] Still, gamification is popular in corporate training and is gaining popularity in the world of teacher professional development. There are many blog posts on the topic (search for "gamified professional development"), and start ups are beginning to emerge, such as 3D GameLab, a tool that originated in the Boise State University preservice teacher education program and has branched out as its own company.[63]

A potentially deeper approach to engagement based on games is gameful design.[64] This approach focuses on the design of learning environments that increase intrinsic motivation and engagement by supporting feelings of autonomy, belonging, and competence, which are the core principles of self-determination theory.[65] Note that being gameful requires neither literally playing games nor using game metaphors. The design goal in these environments is to have learners engage in hard problems because they are interested in solving those problems and feel like the effort will result in some meaningful progress or result. NSTA is exploring this approach in their Learning Center (see chapter 9). The success of these designs is related to the area of personalized learning.

Personalized Learning and Learning Analytics

Collins and Halverson predict that the future will bring a stealthy or evolutionary change to education as a result of technology.[66] Furthermore, they argue that the seeds of this change are all around us, driven by the rise in interest-driven learning that we also label "connected learning" and what Thomas and Brown call "a new culture of learning."[67] When someone chooses to sign up for a MOOC, when they go to a maker space, when they form a local interest group to pursue a hobby—these are all self-directed choices that guide learning. This was what the NETP was moving toward with the idea of connected teachers.[68] Self-directed learning, coupled with a range of other emergent and rediscovered technologies, has the potential to drive a change in both what we learn and how we learn, and this change should and will extend to teacher professional development.

One area of rapid change is the growth of mobile and personal technologies that are enabling an always-connected mode of information exchange and access to knowledge and resources. Where online learning was once something we had to set aside special time and perhaps go to a special location (e.g., a computer lab) to engage in, now we can Skype or access YouTube videos anywhere and anytime on our smartphones.

A technology that has a long history and is also strongly associated with video games is digital badges.[69] These badges can be treated like micro-credentials to note accomplishments or used to map out a sequence of challenges to be accomplished along a pathway toward some higher-order goal. A unique feature of digital badges is that they can easily be shared or aggregated, much like a professional portfolio, and the evidence behind the badge, since it is often also digital, can be examined to verify the value of the badge. Compare the potential of this tool to the participation certificates that are often distributed at professional development sessions. Scholars like Hickey are exploring this area and helping develop the field's understanding of different contexts and purposes for these badges.[70]

Learning analytics is the purposeful use of data generated in the course of learning or learning-related activities in order to understand and optimize the learning process.[71] Digital badges, for example, because they have metadata that is available for aggregation and inspection, can inform learning analytics, as can teachers' interactions with online learning or professional development materials. In fact, online interactions are particularly ripe for data mining; because the interaction is digital, it is easily traced and analyzed. Some of the earliest examples of true learning analytics applications in education were intelligent tutoring systems such as the Cognitive Tutors, which trace learner activity in order to present optimal feedback and next steps to accelerate learning.[72] Similar analytics tools and technologies are important drivers in the personalized learning movement.[73]

What does all this imply for the future of online teacher professional development? One possibility is that teachers' personalized needs might drive more of the agenda for professional development. Rather than offer one-size-fits-all courses or workshops, teachers will be able to assemble materials online that precisely fit their local teaching needs. We might go even further, and emphasize the identification and mapping of professional learning pathways that start in preservice and grow and change as teachers' experiences expand or their teaching context shifts (see chapter 9).

Technologies such as badges and analytics can help teachers map their personalized learning pathways, identify their progress along them, and point to appropriate resources to support needed next steps. A common criticism of these approaches is that they are the opposite of the connected, social, and dialogical learning advocated by Putnam and Borko as well as so many of the successful digital environments named here.[74] But just as the NGSS professional development strives to help local groups of teachers connect to others with shared needs and interests, personalization does not have to mean isolation. Rather, in the spirit of connected learning, personalization is about finding others with whom you share interests so that individual strengths can be amplified.[75] This may explain why many online learning efforts still focus on building professional *community* rather than on the provision of focused courses or curricula. The NSTA and the College Board both operate online communities where teachers can ask questions and organize conversations around their own needs. It is notable that productive learning in such environments seems strongly related to the presence of a good moderator who can help organize individual's interests and provide support to individuals (see chapters 9 and 10).[76]

The shifting technologies for teacher professional development hold promise for new approaches for teachers across the professional continuum. Many challenges remain, however, not the least of which is the realization of demands that democratize and expand access to professional learning for all.

SHIFTS IN HOW WE STUDY (AND DESIGN) TEACHER PROFESSIONAL LEARNING

Whenever someone asks a question in the form, "Is technology *x* more effective or better than technology *y*?" the best answer is usually, "It depends." Whether something is effective or not is a product of the overall sociotechnical system, including how it is used across a variety of real-world contexts. This is certainly true for questions related to the efficacy of online teacher professional development. As Dede and colleagues argue, we will not make progress toward the professional development we need if we continually ask comparative questions.[77] What we need is an approach to research that can ask not only "whether a program design works well but also to provide evidence to explain why it works well."[78] The challenge moving forward is not to try and *discover* what the most effective approach to professional learning is. Rather, it is to *design* effective professional learning programs based on the best theories of learning and employing the most effective media and technology available.

The learning sciences have long pursued a research methodology called design-based research, which uses iterative and theory-driven design in real-world contexts to build interventions that allow for the development and testing of theory while at the same time (hopefully) improving the performance of learning environments.[79] Cobb and colleagues put this eloquently in arguing that design experiments take "small-t" theories and "place these theories in harm's way."[80] If the intervention fails to produce the theorized result, the researcher/designer needs to examine whether the theory is wrong, the intervention was inadequate, or both. Through rapid iteration, one hopes to develop interventions that work to the point where they help the field understand what might work best moving forward.

Design-based research is a valuable tool, but its main shortcoming is that there is rarely a focus on designing interventions that are scalable or sustainable after the research comes to an end. This has been a point of struggle for the field.[81] In response to this challenge, a methodological paradigm that is an evolution of design-based research has been proposed: design-based implementation research (DBIR).[82] A key tenet of DBIR is that the design/theory process begins with an eye toward sustainability, and to be considered DBIR, the research design needs to embrace four common elements:

- a focus on persistent problems of practice from multiple stakeholders' perspectives
- a commitment to iterative, collaborative design
- a concern with developing theory related to both classroom learning and implementation through systematic inquiry
- a concern with developing capacity for sustaining change in systems.[83]

Of these four commitments, the first and fourth are what distinguish DBIR from design-based research. If we are trying to design effective online professional development, perhaps the most important question is not what the designer is trying to accomplish but what teachers who participate in professional learning perceive as their needs. This is a negotiation, because designers and researchers will have perspectives about what is important in the design of professional learning that might be at odds with what teachers *think* they want. But to avoid the problem of teachers simply choosing not to participate, this gap must be closed through negotiation.[84] The fourth commitment asks, What in the environment would have to change in order for this professional learning offering to be sustainable? Without answers to this question, the professional learning offering has little chance of growing and reaching beyond the audience of its initial offering.

This chapter opens with two quotations. The first is a Danish proverb that muses on the challenge of making accurate predictions about the future. The second, from a computer scientist, advocates that we take action toward creating the future we want to see. There will undoubtedly be new tools and technologies that hold promise for changing the way we think about and practice professional learning in the future. If the past is any indicator, expecting the existence of these "things" to result in meaningful improvement is likely to be fruitless. There is a chance that new network technologies will enable us to do some of the things we currently do with greater efficiency and possibly even greater effectiveness. But our goal should be enabling better and more powerful approaches for teacher learning. And to reach that version of the future, we must actively engage in conversation, research, and design.

PART I

COURSES

Many organizations offer professional development in the form of courses that help teachers learn about a specific topic or improve some aspect of their practice. This section highlights four courses for teachers that take place online: Talk Science, a series supported by the National Science Foundation; the Friday Institute's MOOCs for Educators (MOOC-Eds) initiative; iRAISE, a course for science teachers based on the successful Reading Apprenticeship program; and the American Museum of Natural History's Seminars in Science.

Although these four courses have varied approaches and foci, they are similar in that they aim to provide comprehensive support to teachers rather than a series of on-demand resources and support materials. They were designed to support teachers in a variety of settings, grade levels, and subjects within the sciences. Teachers enroll in a course, are expected to meet the demands of the course, and receive an evaluation (grade) for their efforts. Given the nature of course enrollment, participants can be required to participate in the community by responding to discussions, critiquing posts, or posting a certain number of times per week. These differences set them apart from other models where participants are free to come and go, and incentives for participation are quite different.

CHAPTER 2

Professional Learning with Web-Based Videos

The Talk Science Experience

SUSAN J. DOUBLER AND KATHERINE F. PAGET

Supporting effective dialogue in the unpredictable flow of classroom discussions is difficult, but discussion is a critical part of learning, where students' ideas come together. Tackling this problem in the context of science learning is Talk Science, a National Science Foundation (NSF)–supported, web-based, video-rich professional development program.

In Talk Science, teachers learn to support strategic and purposeful classroom discussions in which students build coherent lines of reasoning based on their own ideas. The professional development program is comprised of eight sessions that take place over a three-month period as participating teachers teach the Inquiry Curriculum, a multigrade study of concepts and practices key to understanding the particulate model of matter. While Talk Science is about science talk, the strategies, skills, and professional development model are applicable to learning in other disciplines. The program is openly available on the web (inquiryproject.terc.edu) for schools and districts to use to advance teachers' professional learning in grades 3–5. The video-rich materials help teachers learn more about the science concepts they teach, the ideas students are likely to have about those concepts, and discussion strategies that will help students progress toward scientific understanding. Talk Science's collection of video cases provides just-in-time, contextualized support and is cross-linked and embedded in the NSF-supported

Inquiry Curriculum, providing ongoing encounters with the resources as the curriculum is taught. The power of video technology adopted by Talk Science helps teachers see and hear alternative patterns of interchange. Four types of videos serve as the cornerstone of the web-based professional development model: Classroom Cases, Scientist Cases, Talking Points, and Talk Strategies.

- *Classroom Cases* provide video examples of productive discussions, delineate four types of discussions, and provide opportunity for teachers to study discussions in action in the context of an authentic setting—the curriculum they teach. The cases assist teachers in seeing mediation strategies that help students co-construct scientific understanding through discussion.
- *Scientist Cases* provide interviews with seven academic scientists, each working in an area of physical science (e.g., physics, materials science, geology), as they engage in investigations from the Inquiry Curriculum. In dialogues concerning the ways each scientist approaches and tackles problems, the interviewer brings forward models of science as a knowledge-generating enterprise, revealing how the development of conceptual understanding blends with disciplinary practice.
- *Talking Points* explain the goals of productive talk and the rationale for establishing shared classroom norms and how to establish a culture of productive talk in the classroom.
- *Talk Strategies* introduce nine specific talk moves to help teachers lead productive science discussions.

The professional development program provides a working model of situative learning in which learning takes place in interactive systems where it is *distributed* across multiple individuals (i.e., teachers, students, virtual scientists, and a sociolinguist) as well as material artifacts in the social and physical environment (e.g., video, the classroom, and study group guides).[1] Distributed activity enables individuals to attain a higher level of functioning beyond what they could do on their own. In the case of Talk Science, professional learning is situated in virtual contexts with scientists, other teachers, and a sociolinguist in face-to-face social contexts of their classrooms and in study group meetings with colleagues.

The program supports teachers in (1) understanding science; (2) setting a clear goal, structure, and outcome for each discussion; (3) attending to, eliciting, and anticipating the range of ideas held by learners; and (4) establish-

FIGURE 2.1   Talk Science, a working model of situative learning

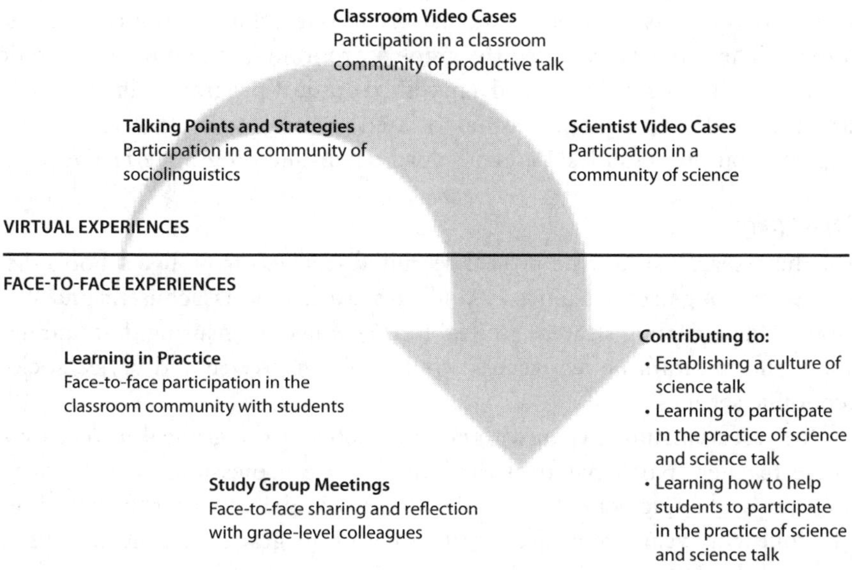

Classroom Video Cases
Participation in a classroom
community of productive talk

Talking Points and Strategies
Participation in a community of
sociolinguistics

Scientist Video Cases
Participation in a
community of science

VIRTUAL EXPERIENCES

FACE-TO-FACE EXPERIENCES

Learning in Practice
Face-to-face participation in the
classroom community with students

Contributing to:
• Establishing a culture of
  science talk
• Learning to participate
  in the practice of science
  and science talk
• Learning how to help
  students to participate
  in the practice of science
  and science talk

Study Group Meetings
Face-to-face sharing and reflection
with grade-level colleagues

ing a culture of productive talk in the classroom and using a set of strategies that keeps every discussion moving forward toward greater understanding.

As illustrated in figure 2.1, teachers engage in virtual and face-to-face learning experiences to meet these aims. Study begins with *virtual web-based study* in which teachers (1) increase their own understanding of the science by studying video cases of scientists engaged in the same investigations they do with their students; (2) develop a new vision of classroom interaction through study of classroom video cases in which they see other teachers leading the same discussions they will lead in the classroom; and (3) become familiar with the rationale behind productive talk and strategies for supporting productive talk. Study shifts to two *face-to-face contexts* in which teachers (1) try out ideas in the classroom, quickly exploring new pedagogical ideas in the safety of the classroom, getting feedback based on student reactions, and transferring new learning to practice; and (2) participate in grade-level meetings where they share and reflect on their experiences and hear about the experiences of colleagues, exchange feedback, and work toward establishing new norms for talk across the school.

DEVELOPMENT AND RESEARCH

The core development work of Talk Science took place over a three-year period as project staff worked intensively in one urban school (four classrooms). The project developed the grade 4 program first and then the grade 5 program. The staff later added a modified grade 3 program using the same structure and existing video. An associated research study that focused on implementation in grades 4 and 5 helped determine program effectiveness.

Participants

For the research study, the project recruited teachers from five schools distributed among urban, suburban, and rural areas in Massachusetts and Vermont. This sampling strategy (see table 2.1) aimed at ensuring that findings about the program's effectiveness would hold in diverse and varied socioeconomic settings.

The research study began with eleven teachers from grade 4 in year two. These teachers participated in the Talk Science professional development program and implemented the grade 4 Inquiry Curriculum for the first time. The following year, the project worked with nine grade 4 teachers, eight of whom had participated in the Talk Science program previously. In this third year, Talk Science staff also studied the program with eleven teachers from grade 5 from the aforementioned schools, who participated in the Talk Science program and implemented the Inquiry Curriculum for the first time.

Research Questions and Data Sources

The Talk Science project collected various kinds of information to address three research questions:

- How do teachers' awareness, understanding, and skills for supporting science talk change as they use Talk Science?
- How does student talk change as a result of changes in teachers' language-related actions?
- How do classroom discourse patterns change as a result of changes in the teachers' actions?

During the second year of the project, the staff interviewed grade 4 teachers prior to and on completion of the curriculum in order to explore their understandings of and strategies for supporting classroom talk, as well as their understandings of the science concepts in the curriculum. To explore patterns in teachers' facilitation of discussions and students' participation

TABLE 2.1   Pilot classrooms

Year 2	Grade 4	5 schools	11 teachers	Urban, suburban, and rural settings
Year 3	Grade 4	Same 5 schools	9 teachers	Urban, suburban, and rural settings
	Grade 5	Same 5 schools	9 teachers	Urban, suburban, and rural settings

in classroom discussions, they gathered audio recordings of a fifteen-minute pre- and post-concept cartoon discussion from each teacher's classroom and video recordings of two sets of early and late lesson discussions from three teachers. The staff also audio-recorded the teachers' study group meetings that took place in their respective schools.

During the third year of the project, the staff continued to collect data from the grade 4 teachers, who were now implementing the Inquiry Curriculum and participating in the Talk Science program for the second time. During this year, staff again interviewed teachers regarding their perspectives on and strategies for supporting classroom discussions, and the project collected audio recordings of fifteen-minute pre- and post-concept cartoon discussions in their classrooms. The project collected these data in order to draw comparisons and track teachers' progress over the two years of their participation in the professional development program.

The project also collected data in the third year from grade 5 teachers pertaining to their understandings, perspectives, practices, and participation in the program. Talk Science staff interviewed grade 5 teachers prior to and on completion of the curriculum regarding their perspectives on the role of classroom discussions in students' science learning, strategies for facilitating classroom discussions, and understanding of the core ideas in the curriculum. To examine patterns in classroom talk, the project audio recorded fifteen-minute pre- and post-concept cartoon discussions from all teachers and video-recorded two sets of early and late lesson discussions from three teachers. Finally, staff audio-recorded the teachers' study group meetings that were held in their respective schools.

USING VIDEO TO SUPPORT PRODUCTIVE SCIENCE TALK

Talk is essential to science inquiry. It enables students to compare and evaluate observations and data, raise questions, develop hypotheses and explanations, debate and explore alternative interpretations, develop insight into reasoning they may not have considered, and make meaning of inquiry experiences. Yet, established patterns of classroom talk seldom engage students in building new understanding based on evidence from their science experiences. Vivid images of science talk and classroom talk are needed. Talk Science embraced the power of video technology to help teachers see and hear alternative patterns of interchange.

Classroom Cases

The challenge. In science classrooms, instructional time often runs out before meaning-making discussions can take place. Ironically, this seems to be particularly true when students are engaged in firsthand exploration or data collection and the teacher is reluctant to bring a halt to productive activity. When discussions do take place, they commonly focus on recounting the procedures or reporting observations and measurements rather than on analyzing data, using evidence to support claims, or developing explanations.

Meaning-making discussions are part of the vision for science learning outlined in the National Research Council's (NRC) science framework.[2] Yet, conventional patterns for classroom discussion often do little to deepen student understanding. If these patterns are to change, alternative models are needed that convey expected changes in instructional planning, classroom organization, use of time, and student-to-teacher and student-to-student interactions. Before they invest in change, teachers need evidence that new practices will contribute to deeper student learning; to be convinced that this will work in their classroom with their students; and, once convinced, to see how to make significant and complex changes themselves.

In the Talk Science project, the first challenge was to help teachers perceive talk as an essential part of science inquiry, to understand that talk is where science understanding comes together and where the practices of science merge. The second challenge was to help teachers to see how roles shift—theirs and their students'—when discussions are productive, to see what it looks like to listen carefully to students' ideas, and to help students learn to elaborate their ideas and build on each others' ideas in order to move everyone's understanding forward.

Why use video? A cognitive apprenticeship model informed the development of the classroom video cases.[3] Apprenticeship provides opportunity to study the nuances of practice in action in an authentic setting. In the case of Talk Science, the authentic setting is the classroom. In an apprenticeship, learners use what they are learning and continue to learn on their own.[4] Participating teachers move from their independent web study to their classroom, where they incorporate their new learning as they enact the same discussion they observed in the video case. Teachers then have face-to-face meetings with grade-level colleagues to share and reflect on their classroom experiences.

The project has high expectations for apprenticeship through video. Video can reveal the split-second exchanges that take place in the classroom and bring forward effective patterns of student and teacher interaction. Video provides vivid images of skilled facilitation and helps the viewer understand not only what is said but how it is said, including the physical dimensions of the skill—the timing, the gesturing, the tone of voice. Video provides opportunities for teachers to see what productive discussion looks like in multiple and diverse classrooms. It can give the teacher a sense of the whole process—how the discussion is launched and sustained, how surprises and problems are handled, how the discussion is refocused when it begins to veer off course, and how it wraps up.

Building the Classroom Cases. The Talk Science program includes four Classroom Cases for each grade (3–5). Each case is intentionally set in the context of the Inquiry Curriculum and used in parallel with teaching the curriculum. Each case illustrates a discussion from beginning to end. This full view helps teachers envision how they will execute the discussion. While a case captures all phases of a discussion, it is much shorter than the actual classroom event. Illustrative video segments are spliced together into a cohesive story that focuses teacher attention on the most relevant aspects of the discussion. Each clip is short in order to help the viewer sustain attention and follow the story line.

The Classroom Cases not only help teachers to see effective discussion in action, they reveal general structures that help teachers understand the reasoning and thinking that expert facilitators employ as they plan and facilitate discussions. For example, the grade 3 cases focus on strategies for listening to and understanding children's ideas and reasoning, while the grades 4 and 5 cases are organized around four types of discussion—elicitation, explanation, data analysis, and consolidation. The role and characteristics of each discussion type are described in the introduction to the relevant Classroom Case. While all discussions share the overarching purpose of helping students make sense and meaning of their classroom work, this typology helps the teacher know what to emphasize as the discussion unfolds.

For example, the Classroom Case in Step 6 of the grade 5 Talk Science Pathway focuses on the facilitation of a data discussion. The video case captures a data discussion in Candace's classroom as her students investigate "What happens to weight and volume when water freezes?" The case begins with a narrated overview of the key components of data discussions, a description of the student investigation viewers will see, and a series of questions that are introduced to differentiate data discussions from other discussions: What question are we trying to answer? What information do we have to work with? What's the pattern or shape of the data? Based on the data, what claims can we support?

The discussion is then presented in four segments to illustrate different components of a data discussion. In the first segment, "Predicting Sets the Stage," Candace focuses attention on the investigation question and elicits students' predictions. She prompts all students to provide the thinking behind their prediction. In the second segment, "Revisiting Condensation," Candace and her students discuss a logistical issue related to accurate measurement: condensation has formed on the outside of their frozen bottles—will this affect their measurements? This issue provides opportunity for students to revisit their earlier learning experiences with condensation. In the next section, "Variation in the Data," some of the weight measurements taken before and after freezing vary by a degree. Is this change significant? Candace supports students as they use their collective data to make claims. In the final clip, "Comparing Results with Predictions," students compare their measured weight changes with their predictions. While all agree that the weight doesn't change, Candace has one more important question for her students before the discussion comes to an end: "Does this make sense that the weight doesn't change?" Discussion of this last question helps to consolidate students' learning.[5]

Rather than develop the cases with teachers who are experts at leading discussions, the researchers worked with teachers in one school over a two-year period and filmed there. The cases capture teachers who are in the process of developing discussion skills. Participants see teachers who are learners working to build their practice and sometimes making mistakes. These teachers see professional learning as an incremental process, and they recognize that the classroom interactions are authentic and unscripted. They also see change in students, as students become better at putting their ideas into words, listening to each other more carefully, and building on each other's ideas.

The project videotaped multiple classrooms at each grade level. Thus, participants observe more than one teacher and classroom. They see each teacher incorporating the discussion skills into her own style of teaching. This variety helps participants understand that there are multiple ways to support effective discussions. By sharing discussions from multiple classrooms, Talk Science hoped to provide evidence that productive talk is doable in all classrooms.

What did the project find? Research with the grade 4 teachers provides evidence of certain changes in their facilitation of classroom science discussions. After participating in the Talk Science program for one year, almost all teachers increased their use of academically productive Talk Strategies to guide students' science learning. Specifically, they more often used talk moves to deepen students' reasoning and to promote active listening to peers' ideas.

Furthermore, through a comparative analysis of a subset of teachers who participated in the Talk Science professional development program twice, project staff found that teachers increased their use of productive Talk Strategies during both years. In particular, teachers focused more frequently on deepening students' reasoning and fostering active listening that in turn supported students' co-construction of science understanding.

For grade 5, program staff observed changes in teachers' understandings of the role of classroom discussions as they began to recognize the value of science discussions not only for participation and sharing of individual ideas but also for developing ideas and making meaning together. After participating in the Talk Science program, teachers reported making discussions an integral part of their science lessons and described several shifts in the nature of their classroom discussions. Specifically, they increased their use of Talk Strategies to probe students' reasoning and to help students deepen their reasoning with the help of data and evidence from their classroom investigations.

Teacher study groups frequently discussed content pertaining to Classroom Cases, Talking Points, and Talk Strategies. Specifically, the rural and urban study groups focused most on Classroom Cases videos and their classroom discussions. Across the five rural study group meetings, 47.41 percent of the teachers' talk pertained to the videos and their own classroom science discussions. Similarly, across the urban and suburban study group meetings, 57.01 percent of the teachers' talk involved references to this resource.

Yet, the suburban study group focused most on content related to the Talking Points and Talk Strategies. The group discussed productive talk, norms, talk goals, and talk moves in connection with the resource. Across the five suburban study group meetings, 53.07 percent of teachers' talk pertained to this resource.

Scientist Cases

The challenge. The seemingly straightforward agenda for facilitating effective science discussions—to focus discussion on science learning goals, to know the science yourself, and to employ discussion strategies that engage students in the practices of science—masks the challenges teachers face in supporting productive discussions. This is in part because many teachers have had limited experience with science as a knowledge-building enterprise in their own learning.

Why use video? The Scientist Cases videos address this important challenge. They are designed to show teachers the science investigations their students will conduct through the eyes of a scientist; to see how the scientist uses the practices of science to observe, reason, talk about, and make sense of phenomena; and to see the questions the scientist asks, what the scientist attends to, and how the scientist thinks. Again, a cognitive apprenticeship model informs the case development; the authentic setting is the scientist's laboratory or office.[6] Teachers participating in the Talk Science Professional Development Pathway proceed from their vicarious experience with the scientist to their own classrooms, where they enact the same investigation they observed the scientist conducting in the video case. Then, teachers participate in their study group meeting, where they refer to the scientist's actions to clarify their own understanding of the science and to think about the science ideas of their students.

Building the Scientist Cases. Talk Science includes four Scientist Cases videos for grades 4 and 5. Each case is intentionally set in the context of the Inquiry Curriculum and used in parallel with teaching the curriculum (see table 2.2). Teachers observe how a scientist thinks about matter, the subject of the Inquiry Curriculum.

In each video, Sara Lacy, a TERC scientist, interviews a working scientist in a physical science discipline (e.g., physics, materials science, geology). Each case is based on the premise that knowing how a scientist tackles an investigation and how a scientist thinks and talks about the subject matter will help teachers listen to their students and support their learning.

TABLE 2.2   Scientist Cases videos by grade level

	Investigation	Scientist
Grade 4	What does a scientist think when he observes rocks?	Michael Haritos, Boston Latin School
	Heavy for size	Christopher Swan, Tufts University
	How does a scientist think about liquid volume?	Linda Grisham, Mass Bay Community College
	The mineral materials	Roger Tobin, Tufts University
Grade 5	Mini-lakes	Laurie Baise, Tufts University
	Water to vapor	Roger Tobin, Tufts University
	Water to ice	Hugh Gallagher, Tufts University
	Air, a gas	Lindley Winslow, MIT

In a series of dialogues concerning the ways the scientist approaches and talks about the same activities that the students do, Lacy brings forward models of science as a knowledge-generating enterprise, revealing the way the development of conceptual understanding blends with disciplinary practice. She asks each scientist questions that bring to the surface the big ideas and key concepts of the topic and the key challenges to student understanding.[7]

Lacy sets teacher learning in a broader conceptual context than the investigations themselves by asking the scientist questions such as: How do you think about density in your work? Why is measurement of density important? What are some of your benchmarks for density? For example, in the grade 5 curriculum "Investigating Water Transformations, Water to Ice" unit, the challenges to learning about freezing and melting are surfaced in the Scientist Case. In the video interview Lacy conducts with physicist Hugh Gallagher, she primes him to address questions like those raised in the aligned scientist essay by Roger Tobin: Are there properties that don't change when the material melts or freezes? The weight? The volume? Are the solid and the liquid different materials or the same? Gallagher also explains how he uses a microscopic perspective (matter is composed of discrete particles too small to see) to understand what he observes from a macroscopic perspective (similarities and differences in weight, volume, and temperature).[8]

The interviewer also probes ideas that teachers need to listen for, which are articulated by cognitive psychologist Carol Smith: "Children are not always sure that it is still the same kind of material. Children initially think that when something freezes or melts, its weight should change as well. When water freezes (unlike what happens when you pour it from one shaped container to another), its volume actually increases (as can be demonstrated dramatically when bottles of water 'explode' when put in the freezer). How can this be, especially if its weight (and mass) remains the same?" Lacy reports that she wanted the scientist to not only model ways of doing science and the procedures for conducting the investigation but also to provide language for teachers to use in answering children's questions during science discussions.

What did Talk Science find? Changes in both learning and instructional practice were anticipated outcomes for each of these ten-to-seventeen-minute Scientist Cases videos. In particular, project staff anticipated that teachers' understandings of core science concepts in the Inquiry Curriculum and their understanding of science practice would change. Results from two sources showed significant patterns of differences in conceptual understanding and in engagement.

Teachers' knowledge of core ideas regarding subject matter improved after they participated in the program. Analysis of a forty-one-question pre/post interview administered to all eleven grade 5 teachers indicated that they all obtained higher scores and presented more elaborate explanations of concepts within the curriculum in the post-interviews than in the pre-interviews. A careful examination of six content areas found in Talk Science Research findings showed that teachers increasingly drew on the particle model to explain processes of dissolving, evaporation, and condensation in the post-interviews.[9] Since these change scores are the result of both teaching the Inquiry Curriculum and participating in the Pathway, there is no way to disarticulate the source of the change, but it was a clear and significant effect.

Another important difference emerged when teacher study group talk was coded for content. Engagement with the resources revealed differences among teacher groups. The rural group showed a much higher frequency of engagement with the Scientist Cases than did the urban and suburban schools. The teachers in the rural schools spent 21.7 percent of the time in their five meetings discussing the scientist videos; in contrast, the urban group spent 7.48 percent and the second suburban group 4.47 percent of the time on the scientist videos. This suggests that the study guides provided were used flexibly at each site.

Talking Points

The challenge. While talk is a well-established part of classroom action, the conventional patterns of classroom talk may not be productive. Often, teachers rely heavily on discussion patterns they experienced in their own learning. For example, a common, well-engrained pattern is one in which the teacher asks a question, calls on a student to respond, and judges whether the answer is correct (i.e., initiation-response-evaluation, or IRE). This pattern is often counterproductive to building learning environments in which students elaborate on their thinking, listen to each other, and build ideas together.[10]

Why use video? Breaking away from this IRE pattern requires rethinking the purpose of discussion, setting new norms for classroom talk, and building a classroom culture of productive talk. In order to change deeply engrained interaction patterns, teachers need to see alternative models of interaction and to understand how investing in change will deepen student learning. They need help knowing how to begin to establish a culture of productive talk and to be reassured that their teaching expertise is relevant and provides a rich starting place for change. Talking Points serve this purpose.

Building the Talking Points. The Talk Science program includes three video-rich Talking Points. These cases appear early in the program and address the following questions: How is a culture of talk established? What is productive talk? Why is talk important? In each case, Sarah Michaels, a sociolinguist, discusses these questions with a teacher through videos of classroom discussions. Each case blends rationale with practical know-how and brings together outside-the-profession and inside-the-profession expertise to interpret the classroom interactions in the videos.

In the videos, the dual voices of linguist and teacher bring the theory behind productive talk to life, with the linguist providing the research perspective and the teacher offering the practical perspective of how the new vision works in action. Teachers' professional knowledge is valued and conveys the idea that what is proposed is both viable and worth doing.

Talk Strategies

Establishing a culture of classroom talk is essential. To address this need, the program uses video and multimedia resources to introduce a set of Talk Strategies.

The challenge. Effective scientific discourse is difficult to manage and requires improvising and facilitating dialogue in the unpredictable flow of classroom discussion.[11] Strategies are needed to offload some of the in-the-moment complexity teachers face, to help teachers attend to students' ideas, maintain focus, and aid learners in building understanding together.

Building the Talk Strategies. These needs are addressed in five cases that help teachers manage productive discussions. Each fifteen-to-seventeen-minute video case focuses on student-to-teacher and student-to-student interchanges within conversations, enabling the viewer to deconstruct teachers' facilitation of productive talk.

The first of the five cases introduces four goals for supporting effective discussion. These help students share, expand, and clarify their ideas; listen to each other; elaborate on their reasoning; and think with their own and other's ideas. In order to meet these goals, teachers begin using a set of nine facilitation moves. Moves that help students share, expand, and clarify their own thinking include (1) providing time for students to think, (2) encouraging students to say more, (3) asking students for clarification. A move that helps students listen to each other is (4) asking students to rephrase or repeat what another student said. Moves that help students elaborate on their reasoning are (5) asking students for evidence of their reasoning and (6) challenging an idea that has been put forward. Moves that help students to think with their own and others ideas are (7) asking students if they agree, (8) encouraging other students to add to what a student has said, and (9) asking a student to explain what another student said. These moves help teachers break free of well-entrenched patterns of interchange and develop new patterns that are more productive. The moves also help teachers manage the complexity of classroom talk. They help teachers "buy time" to listen to children's ideas and then decide how to support student learning. Teachers quickly realize that the nine talk moves can be used in any discussion context.

The moves can be readily incorporated into practice but come with a caution, because they may be viewed as all that is needed by teachers. While the four goals and associated moves are essential, they are not enough. To facilitate productive discussions, teachers must also have goals in mind, must provide a focus for the discussion, must understand the science, and must establish classroom norms for productive discussions. For example, students must learn to direct their comments to each other as well as to the teacher.

Developing a culture of productive talk in the classroom is a significant change in practice that requires change in teacher beliefs. Unless teachers view their role and that of their students differently, change in discussion patterns may be superficial and at risk of falling back to earlier patterns of interchange. To help facilitate change, a teacher who uses the nine talk moves may see the effect on students, and this in turn may provide the teacher with the needed evidence to revise her belief system.[12]

What did Talk Science find? In order to study changes in the culture of classroom science talk, project staff examined pre- and post-concept cartoon discussions from grades 4 and 5 and meaning-making discussions in grade 5. They also observed shifts in teachers' perspectives on the role of classroom discussions. Before the program, teachers mainly viewed discussions as opportunities for students to share their individual ideas and hear ideas from peers and as a means to assess students' understanding. After the program, teachers increasingly viewed discussions as opportunities to co-construct ideas with peers, think collectively, and develop understandings together.

Teachers' facilitation of discussions changed. Teachers utilized the nine talk moves more often in the post-discussions than in pre-discussions. Specifically, they drew prominently on moves to elicit students' thinking and made a greater use of moves to probe and deepen students' reasoning with data and evidence from their investigations. Although focus on these resources in all groups was high, the suburban study group focused most on content related to the Talking Points and Talk Strategies and discussed productive talk, norms, talk goals, and talk moves in connection with the resource. Across the five suburban study group meetings, 53.07 percent of teachers' talk pertained to these resources.

LESSONS LEARNED

The research suggests that the video models in Talk Science hold great promise for advancing professional learning. Video simulates cognitive apprenticeship and provides "legitimate peripheral participation" for teachers to observe scientists and other practitioners as well as their students.[13] Involvement with these video exemplars strengthens science understanding, develops pedagogical skills, and leads to new skills in their teaching.

Video plays a critical role in each phase of the Talk Science blended professional development model. Independent, video-rich, web-based study provides teachers with vivid examples from the classroom and from science, and its easy web accessibility allows self-paced learning. These video examples provide material for advanced planning for the practices teachers would like to enact.[14] The video cases also serve as "objects to think with" as teachers share insights, reflect on classroom experiences, and plan for teaching with their colleagues.

Through their study of video and study group discussions, teachers put their learning into practice. Seeing how the classroom is organized for effective discussion, learning what to say to facilitate academically productive talk, and having access to scientists conducting the same investigations their students will experience in class together provide a powerful platform for guided inquiry science instruction.

Video serves as a source of evidence to support shifts in teacher beliefs—beliefs about what science is and how it is practiced, shifts in beliefs about their role and the ways learning is supported in the classroom, and shifts in expectations for student learning. Video helps teachers envision alternatives to their current practice and provides evidence that alternatives are possible.

Video has a wide reach and can provide a great number of teachers with consistently high-quality professional development. Having all program resources (including the video cases) readily accessible on the web increases the flexibility of use and meets the varying needs of teachers in different school settings. Carefully aligning teachers' professional learning with the curriculum they teach, as reflected in the tight coupling of the Talk Science program with the Inquiry Curriculum, and drawing the scientist, classroom, and strategy case examples from the curriculum itself allow teachers to develop both relevant subject matter knowledge and instructional practice in order to promote students' reasoning through discussions.

The video-rich Talk Science cases provide vivid images of classroom and science practice that enable teachers to incorporate new instructional strategies, develop their knowledge of core scientific ideas, and begin to conceptualize classroom discussions in more dialogic terms. The findings suggest that changes in all three aspects of teachers' professional learning—knowledge of the science, underlying perspectives on classroom discourse, and instructional practice—collectively deepen.

CHAPTER 3

Going to Scale

The MOOCs for Educators Initiative

GLENN M. KLEIMAN AND MARY ANN WOLF

Beginning in 2012, the Friday Institute launched a set of massive open online courses (MOOCs) for district and school leaders and educators to explore whether MOOC-like approaches could be adapted to address the professional development needs of many educators, incorporate research-based principles of effective professional development, and provide scalable, accessible, cost-effective professional development.

This MOOC-Ed initiative builds on prior work designing, implementing, and researching small cohort, facilitated online workshops through the Education Development Center's EdTech Leaders Online program and online professional learning communities, cohorts, and courses at the Friday Institute. The MOOC-Eds incorporate four major design principles that reflect research-based practices for educators' professional learning: *multiple voices, self-directed learning, peer-supported learning,* and *job-connected learning.* The Friday Institute then developed *instructional elements*—specific things that participants use and do—that instantiate these principles in the courses. The Friday Institute's active research program uses the extensive data available to explore participants' *self-directed learning* paths, interaction patterns for *peer-supported learning,* the value of different types of resources and activities, and the impact of MOOC-Eds on participants' knowledge and practices. The importance of effective professional development stems from the many and ongoing changes in schools and demands placed on educators, as well as the reality that many educators do not have access to the professional development they want and need. In the past few years alone, educators have been facing changes in curriculum standards, student assessments, expectations for the uses of technology and the personalization of learning, diversity of students' cultural and linguistic backgrounds, and teacher evaluation processes, along with decreased funding leading to larger class sizes, fewer resources, and the need to make education more productive and cost-effective.

These changes raise two critical questions: How can the nearly 3.5 million K–12 educators in the United States (teachers and administrators in public and private schools) be prepared for the rapid changes facing our education system?[1] How can the next generation of educators be prepared to teach and to lead in an education system that is far different from the one they experienced as students?

While almost all educators have access to some professional development each year, over 50 percent of them express dissatisfaction with their professional development opportunities, finding that it is neither relevant nor personalized.[2] Effective professional development is ongoing, job embedded, relevant to one's professional needs, and a means of providing opportunities for collaboration with peers.[3] Some aspects of professional learning—such as coaching from more experienced educators, professional learning communities, and hands-on learning of technology tools—benefit from local person-to-person connections. However, based on prior experience and research in online professional development, the Friday Institute set out to learn more about the idea that some professional development needs could be met by scalable, cost-effective, online learning opportunities that take advantage of current technologies—that is, by programs that use MOOC-like approaches adapted specifically for education professionals.

This chapter summarizes the explorations of that hypothesis over the past two years through the MOOCs for Educators (MOOC-Ed) initiative at the Friday Institute for Educational Innovation at the North Carolina (NC) State University College of Education. The authors of this chapter and the large team of educators, designers, technologists, and researchers working on the MOOC-Ed initiative bring extensive experience that has informed these efforts. Evidence from the Edtech Leaders Online Program (ETLO) and the related eLearning for Educators project (funded by the US Department of Education) demonstrates the value of small-scale, facilitated online professional development courses and lessons learned about the resources, activities, and discussions that educators value.[4] Similarly, the eLearning for Educators project's large-scale randomized control studies show that cohort-based, facilitated online workshops can have positive impacts on teachers' professional knowledge and practices and, in turn, on their students' achievement.[5] National Science Foundation (NSF)–funded research also finds that both facilitated, cohort-based online courses and self-paced, individualized courses can lead to effective learning as well as provide information about the advantages and disadvantages of each type of course.[6] And research at NC State on online communities of practice for educators and on interaction patterns within MOOC-Ed discussions provides lessons about the types of online resources, activities, and discussions educators find to be of value and the instructional elements that support their productive engagement in online exchanges.[7]

This project set out to develop online professional learning experiences that are related to other MOOCs in that they can serve thousands of educators in one course, are open to all interested participants, are delivered online, and are structured like a course to provide content and activities in defined time periods. However, the Friday Institute MOOC-Eds have a set of characteristics that make them different from MOOCs designed for other audiences and purposes.

The MOOC-Eds are designed to help adult educators meet their professional learning needs, so it is assumed that participants are literate, motivated, and self-directed learners. The creators of MOOC-Eds value the experience and expertise of the participants and design ways in which they can share what they know and further the learning of others. Though the MOOC-Eds have defined requirements for participants who desire continuing education units (CEUs), they do not have grades or formal tests; therefore, they do not have to address concerns about test security and integrity that MOOCs providing course credit have to address. There is an emphasis on establishing professional connections among MOOC-Ed participants, who are identified in all their comments and projects; they are not allowed to post or give feedback anonymously. Further, participants are encouraged to participate in the MOOC-Eds with colleagues and engage in local discussions in order to relate the experience to their own context. The MOOC-Ed's focus is on participants reaching their own goals, which they articulate when registering for the course, not on goals set by the course creators or on completion rates. Another important factor is that this approach is designed in accordance with the research-based principles of effective professional development, which were incorporated into the four major design principles for MOOC-Eds.[8]

- *Multiple voices* allow participants to learn about the perspectives of other teachers and administrators and those of students, researchers, and experts in the field. MOOC-Eds are purposefully *not* designed around one or two experts who present online lectures. They are about a rich set of perspectives presented within the context of activities and exchanges that reflect specific design principles.
- *Self-directed learning* enables participants to personalize their experience by identifying their own goals, selecting among a rich array of resources, and deciding whether, when, and how to engage in discussions and activities to further their own learning and meet their goals.
- *Peer-supported learning* occurs when participants engage in online discussions, review each others' projects, rate posted ideas, recommend resources, crowdsource lessons learned, and participate in Twitter chats and other exchanges appropriate to the individual course.
- *Job-connected learning* takes place through the use of case studies and classroom- and school-related projects, developing action plans, and other activities that center participants' work on critical problems of practice and data-informed decision making in their own classrooms, schools, or districts.

The MOOC-Eds are designed for scalability and sustainability as they accommodate large numbers of participants at a minimal cost per person. They utilize *self-directed learning* to allow individuals to adapt their own learning experiences and *peer-supported learning* to provide interactions without the cost of a large number of facilitators. MOOC-Eds include *multiple voices*, such as educators, students, experts in the field, and administrators, and seek to provide personalized pathways, alternative models, and strategies to address different participants' needs and interests. The design includes multiple options, such as video, audio, and print versions of materials, to ensure accessibility.

THE FRIDAY INSTITUTE MOOC-EDS

As of 2015, the Friday Institute has run the MOOC-Ed courses listed in table 3.1, with more than 20,000 participants registered. The participants come from all fifty states as well as eighty other countries.

TABLE 3.1 Overview of the Friday Institute MOOC-Eds

Course information	Audience	Description
Digital Learning Transition *Partner:* Alliance for Excellent Education	District leaders, school leaders, instructional coaches, library media specialists, teacher leaders, consultants	This course helps school and district leaders understand how technology and the global information age impact what students need to know and how and when student learning can take place. Participants study the elements of a successful digital learning transition, develop goals for digital learning aligned to student outcomes, and create an action plan for their own district, school, or classroom.
Coaching Digital Learning: Cultivating a Culture of Change	Instructional coaches, library media specialists, teacher leaders, professional development providers	This course is for those who provide professional development and coaching to classroom teachers in the effective uses of digital learning. Participants enhance their digital learning content knowledge and further develop their strategies for working with teachers.
Fraction Foundations: Helping Students Understand Fractions *Funders:* William and Flora Hewlett Foundation and Oak Foundation	K–8 educators, teacher educators, professional development providers	This course helps educators teach fractions concepts and skills more effectively through understanding students' thinking and implementing research-based approaches in their classroom. It will help educators address rigorous curriculum standards for fractions, whether from the Common Core State Standards or from other up-to-date standards.
Disciplinary Literacy for Deeper Learning *Funder:* William and Flora Hewlett Foundation	Grades 6–12 teachers in ELA, science, social studies, history, and mathematics; professional development providers, teacher educators	This course explores what it means to read, write, speak, and listen for learning and creating knowledge within a discipline. It offers a model for inquiry-based disciplinary literacy to help promote deeper learning and foster personalized application to local contexts.
Learning Differences *Partners:* Big Brothers Big Sisters, New Teacher Center, Teach For All, Teach For America *Funder:* Oak Foundation	Teachers, instructional coaches, library media specialists, parents, professional development providers, teacher educators, administrators	This course helps teachers develop strategies that will support students who find learning in traditional classrooms to be challenging. The course considers findings from the learning sciences to help teachers understand the specifics of executive function, motivation, and working memory as a foundation for developing strategies to address the needs of their students with learning differences.
Teaching Statistics Through Data Investigations *Funder:* William and Flora Hewlett Foundation	Teachers of statistics and math (middle school–early college), teacher educators, professional development providers	This course enables educators to learn to use investigations to teach statistics and help students explore data to make evidence-based claims. It is designed to help teachers address the additional attention to statistics in the Common Core and other rigorous curriculum standards.

Through the work of designing, implementing, and evaluating MOOC-Eds, the Friday Institute is developing a set of *instructional elements* that help ensure that the four design principles are effectively incorporated into each MOOC-Ed. The instructional elements include conceptual frameworks, student scenarios, expert panels, participant projects with peer feedback, resource collections, asynchronous discussions, Twitter chats, and crowd-sourcing, along with other course-specific elements that enable participants to structure their experiences and guide their own learning. While these elements are the vehicles for translating the design principles into MOOC-Ed materials, there is not a one-to-one mapping between principles and elements. Ideally, each instructional element encompasses multiple principles. Figure 3.1 highlights the connection between the design principles and the instructional elements. The challenge for the designers of each MOOC-Ed is to select and organize a coherent, well-balanced set of instructional elements to instantiate all the principles while providing the flexibility required to address the different goals, contexts, roles, prior knowledge, and learning preferences of the many participants.

Conceptual Frameworks

Conceptual frameworks provided within each MOOC-Ed help participants see the big picture and understand the structure of the course so that they can better guide their own learning. The frameworks also help participants bridge what they are learning about research and practice and provide a common language to help them communicate about key ideas. These frameworks vary to reflect the goals, content, and audience of the MOOC-Ed.

For example, the Digital Learning Transition MOOC-Ed uses a framework developed in collaboration with the Alliance for Excellent Education's and the US Department of Education's Future Ready Schools effort (see figure 3.2). This framework describes seven key elements to be addressed in a digital learning plan. The circle around these elements summarizes the iterative planning process. At the center is student learning, the essential goal of any plan, and around the outside is leadership, which is essential to the plan's success. Disciplinary Literacy for Deeper Learning uses a model for inquiry-based disciplinary learning developed by the MOOC-Ed team (see figure 3.3).[9] Coaching Digital Learning includes instructional frameworks and an approach to coaching to provide structure in the coach's daily work. One participant commented, "I have been a technology integration coach for the past two years, but only now [after the MOOC-Ed] have a strong

FIGURE 3.1 Instructional elements instantiate design principles in the MOOC-Eds

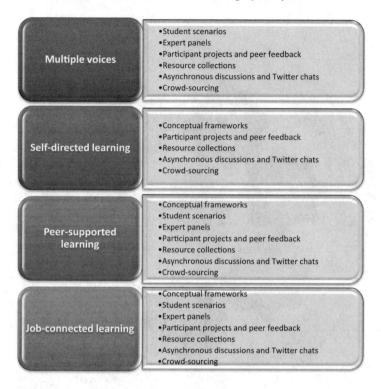

Multiple voices
- Student scenarios
- Expert panels
- Participant projects and peer feedback
- Resource collections
- Asynchronous discussions and Twitter chats
- Crowd-sourcing

Self-directed learning
- Conceptual frameworks
- Participant projects and peer feedback
- Resource collections
- Asynchronous discussions and Twitter chats
- Crowd-sourcing

Peer-supported learning
- Conceptual frameworks
- Student scenarios
- Expert panels
- Participant projects and peer feedback
- Resource collections
- Asynchronous discussions and Twitter chats
- Crowd-sourcing

Job-connected learning
- Conceptual frameworks
- Student scenarios
- Expert panels
- Participant projects and peer feedback
- Resource collections
- Asynchronous discussions and Twitter chats
- Crowd-sourcing

grasp of what that is supposed to mean. I can evolve with this new information. I had heard of most of these topics before, but they hadn't been put into a clear coaching framework for me. I am grateful."

The use of conceptual frameworks with each MOOC-Ed supports three of the four design principles. *Self-directed learning* is achieved by providing an overall picture of the MOOC-Ed content to help participants make decisions about their own path. For *job-connected learning*, they link resources and activities to their professional practices. And with *multiple voices* they provide a structure that shows the value of different perspectives and expertise within the overall goals of the MOOC-Ed.

Student Scenarios

This instructional element combines a video with related resources and discussion. The video shows one or more students working through a chal-

FIGURE 3.2 Conceptual framework for the Digital Learning Transition MOOC-Ed

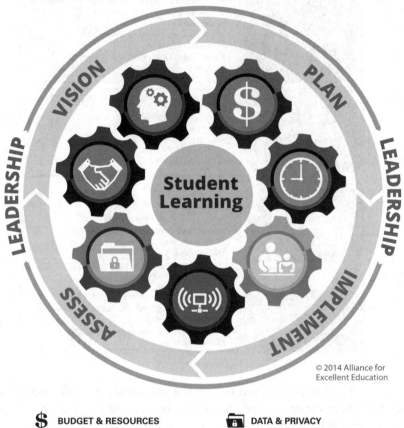

© 2014 Alliance for
Excellent Education

$ BUDGET & RESOURCES

🔒 DATA & PRIVACY

🕐 USE OF TIME

🤝 COMMUNITY PARTNERSHIPS

CURRICULUM, ASSESSMENT & INSTRUCTION

PROFESSIONAL LEARNING

((🖳)) TECHNOLOGY & HARDWARE

FIGURE 3.3   Conceptual framework for the Disciplinary Literacy for Deeper Learning MOOC-Ed

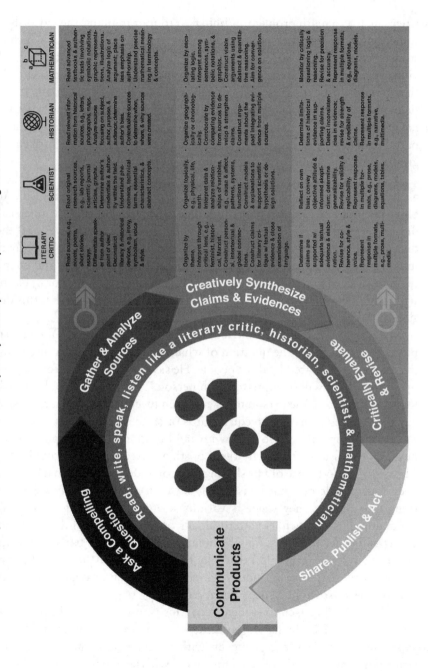

lenge, such as a math problem. Within two to four minutes, the video shows some things the student knows and can do, leading to a point at which the student is puzzled, makes an error, or demonstrates a misconception. The video ends at that *instructional decision* point and participants discuss what they would do next. This leads to rich discussions among groups of participants sharing pedagogical content knowledge in interpreting what they have seen and instructional strategies in recommending next steps. If many participants want to comment during the discussion, they are broken into groups of manageable sizes in order to facilitate conversation.

In Fraction Foundations, Unit 2, for example, a three-minute video shows a third-grade student named Myles working on the following problem: At a party you cut one cake to share fairly among three people. How much cake did each person get? Myles begins dividing the cake into halves and then divides one half into two pieces to get three pieces (figure 3.4). This divide-in-half-repeatedly strategy is common among students his age and enables them to succeed with fractions that have denominators of 2, 4, or 8, but not with other denominators. On examining his work, he realizes that this division of the cake "would not be fair."

Myles then divides the second half into two, so that he has four equal-size pieces. But that raises the question of what to do with the extra piece, since the cake is to be shared by three people. He says, "We cut it [the extra piece] up so that there will be more for each person." He attempts to do so, with the letters marking the person to receive each piece, but he still lacks a strategy for dividing a shape into equal thirds or sixths (figure 3.5).

At that point, the video ends with the question, "What would you do next?" Discussion begins. In their postings, participants recognize that Myles has a good sense of fair sharing and could do the problem if there had been four people but that he is struggling with how to equally split something into thirds. They suggests various strategies, including using physical manipulatives (such as pattern blocks or fraction strips) that can show thirds and other fractions, tangible items such as a candy bar, other shapes (such as circles or rectangles) that may be easier to divide into thirds, paper folding activities, sharing money activities, premade drawings, and other approaches to scaffold Myles's understanding.

A different approach to student scenarios is utilized in the Learning Differences MOOC-Ed by having students who are now in college and beyond share their experiences growing up with learning differences. They share strategies that worked and explain their own views of how teachers sup-

FIGURE 3.4 Myles's first attempt to divide the cake into three equal shares

FIGURE 3.5 Myles's second attempt to divide the cake into three equal shares

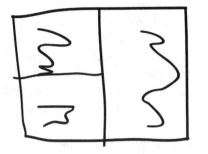

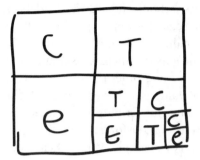

ported them. These videos provide an important context for teachers to consider strategies that can help their own students and also to think about their students who may have learning differences similar to the students in the videos. The discussions about these interviews involve possible strategies and other realizations about how a teacher may support struggling students. One participant shared her reaction to a video about a student named Molly:

> Molly had a great story. I was so glad to see that she had made it—she did what she wanted to do with the support of others. Teachers were a big factor in her success, but they could have been the opposite. It is the caring teachers who offer additional help and who go beyond their ordinary duties that make school a success for students like Molly. Personally, recognizing that working memory deficits are quite common is something I need to work on. I often perceive children that are not focusing, behaving, or completing work as being intentionally off task. I need to work harder on being more attuned to this type of need.

This example encompasses the design principle of *job-connected learning,* in that it is exactly the type of analysis of students' thinking and instructional decision making that teachers need to do in their classrooms every day, and *peer-supported learning* and *multiple voices,* in that the major ideas about scaffolding students' understandings with different types of materials and activities come from the participants themselves, with many different people contributing to the discussion.

Expert Panels

This instructional element brings together the voices of experts—researchers, school and district leaders, teachers, policy makers, and others with specific relevant expertise and experience. In an informal interview setting conducted via Google Hangouts, one of the course facilitators interviews the expert panelists, asking them to share challenges, lessons learned, strategies, and other things they "wish they knew earlier" and believe would be of value to other educators. A carefully edited version in video, audio, and transcript formats is provided with an index of the questions asked with the time marker for each.

For example, Digital Learning Transition has expert panels in each unit comprised of school, district, state, and national leaders who have significant experience in leading digital learning transitions. Over the eight units of the course, more than thirty experts participate in panels. They are encouraged to also participate in the discussions, and some actively do so as guest experts. This instructional element of using experts reflects the *multiple voices* design principle in that there is not a single "guru" for the course or even for a unit, but the panels intentionally have different perspectives represented with interactions among them; it uses educators, students, administrators, or other pertinent individuals to more thoroughly present the information. Another design principle it reflects is *job-connected learning,* in that the panelists are selected based on their significant practical experience in the areas relevant to the topic and are asked to share their personal experience as well as the research and theory that informed their practice. Further, *self-directed learning* is built into the design through a detailed index to the questions and respondents for each panel that enables participants to focus their time on those topics and speakers in which they are most interested.

Participant Projects and Peer Feedback

MOOC-Eds generally incorporate one or more project options for participants that are woven through multiple units. The goal of the projects is for participants to connect what they are learning in the MOOC-Ed with their own professional responsibilities and contexts. The course also incorporates a peer feedback process in which participants are asked to provide constructive feedback to others' projects. This is done in the discussion forum, which enables participant interactions about the projects. Two examples illustrate different ways in which projects are integrated into MOOC-Eds to fit the content and audience of the individual course.

Participants in Coaching Digital Learning are asked to develop an instructional technology coaching action plan for guiding teachers toward effective digital learning. This plan is introduced in the first unit, where templates are provided for both individual and team plans. The template guides additions to be made during each unit of the course, gradually leading to a complete plan that addresses strategies for

- communicating and collaborating
- helping educators expand their online learning networks
- using the Technological Pedagogical Content Knowledge (TPACK) and Substitution Augmentation Modification Redefinition (SAMR) frameworks to guide coaching teachers[10]
- promoting digital-age skills (communication, collaboration, critical thinking, creativity) in the teachers' school
- addressing digital citizenship to develop a safe and responsible digital learning culture
- helping teachers select tools and resources for use in their classrooms.

At each step, participants have the option of sharing their developing plans for feedback from their peers. One participant shared the following feedback after developing the action plan: "Coaching Digital Learning helped me have better conversations with teachers and clarify my own thought process in preparing for those conversations . . . Now I feel very confident in speaking, teaching, and coaching teachers how to effectively reach their idea of an optimal learning environment."

Similarly, Fraction Foundations provides two project options. The first, intended for classroom teachers, asks them to select, in one or more units, a fractions problem to try with their class or a small group of students. They are then asked to conduct interviews with several students to understand their thinking, based on those modeled in the "What would you do next?" activities. Finally, teachers are asked to share their reflections in the discussion forum and provide feedback to their colleagues. Participants who are not current teachers are invited to propose their own project topics that fit their professional roles, such as planning a professional development activity or facilitating a professional learning team.

The project and feedback elements of this type of MOOC-Ed encourage *self-directed learning* by allowing participants to design their own project to meet their own professional needs and *job-connected learning* by specifically relating the projects to the work and context of each participant. *Multiple voices* are also employed through feedback received from multiple peers, not just from one instructor, and *peer-supported learning* is evident in the feedback as well as in the encouragement, when possible, of participants to collaborate with local colleagues on their projects.

Resource Collections

Each MOOC-Ed contains carefully selected and annotated sets of core resources for each unit. Many units also provide additional resources for those who want more information about selected topics. Resource collections typically include:

- *short videos,* including presentations by educators, researchers, policy makers, and organizational leaders; video case studies of classrooms, schools, and districts; summaries of relevant conceptual frameworks and research; first-person accounts by students, teachers, and administrators; and provocative scenarios (e.g., about schools of the future)
- *documents,* which in some cases provide an alternative source of similar content to that found in the videos; other documents may complement a video and provide more in-depth information or provide information that is not available in video form
- *websites* that provide rich resources relevant to the topic of the unit; these may focus on research, practice, or policy, depending on the MOOC-Ed; they may be designed for specific members of the audience (e.g., online communities for literacy teachers or math teachers); or they may address specific topics (e.g., competency-based education, responsible use of technology, learning management systems) of interest to a subset of participants
- *apps* that participants may find useful, including student learning activities and tools that teachers may integrate into the curriculum; tools to help organize a collaborative planning process; communication tools; information collection tools; and tools with many other functions
- *recommended activities* for local professional learning teams related to the MOOC-Ed, which may include a replicable activity, like completing a learner sketch, that an educator could then use with her staff or students.

Far more resources are provided than any one participant would be expected to use. The goal is to provide resources that meet the variety of goals and interests of the participants while providing information that enables them to select those that are most valuable to them. For example, Digital Learning Transition contains case study resources from small and large public schools, charter schools, and independent schools at the elementary, middle, and high school levels, so participants can select those that are most relevant to their own schools. Learning Differences contains personalized pathways with resources for teachers of various age levels and types of learning differences, while Disciplinary Literacy for Deeper Learning contains pathways for teachers of different disciplinary areas.

The MOOC-Ed resource collections offer *multiple voices*, since they contain a range of presenters and authors representing different perspectives and areas of expertise. They also promote *self-directed learning,* since resources are grouped and annotated to support participants in meeting their own goals, and since participants can choose from among the resources those that best fit their learning needs. As well, they represent *job-connected learning* because they are selected to be relevant and useful in participants' contexts.

Asynchronous Discussions and Twitter Chats

Given the number of participants and the time flexibility required to allow 24/7 engagement across worldwide time zones, asynchronous discussions are the primary form of exchange in all the MOOC-Eds. Facilitators pose discussion starter topics, and participants can contribute to those topics, start new ones, comment on prior postings, and rate messages. To keep discussions manageable, participants are typically divided according to the first letter of their city, state, or country, which limits the numbers but keeps a mix of roles and other factors in each discussion. However, in some cases participants have been divided by areas of interest or roles. The Friday Institute staff has used groups ranging from one hundred to five hundred participants and continues to explore optimal ways to form discussion groups.

The MOOC-Eds focused on digital learning have also conducted scheduled synchronous Twitter chats and then provide an archive of the tweets. For example, Coaching Digital Learning provides three opportunities for Twitter chats based on the current unit. Participation has been very high, and the Twitter hashtag used in conjunction with the course has continued to be used with the community long beyond the MOOC-Ed. This provides an opportunity for those who prefer this form of short, informal synchronous messages to share their questions and ideas.

The discussion forum and Twitter chats demonstrate *peer-supported learning*, by encouraging interaction and knowledge creation; *job-connected learning*, through these peer exchanges about their own experiences, challenges, and questions; and *self-directed learning*, with participants choosing which discussions and chats they use, either as contributors or just as viewers.

Crowd-Sourcing

One of the questions for designers of MOOC-Eds is how to take advantage of opportunities afforded by a large number of participants. While MOOC-Eds do not have the registration size of some other MOOCs, the numbers are sufficient to collect valuable information with crowd-sourcing techniques to both inform current participants and improve future versions of the MOOC-Ed.

The most recent MOOC-Eds have used a star rating system for each resource, similar to that used by Netflix, Amazon, and others. Participants can view a summary of these ratings to help them select resources—videos, documents, websites, and apps—to explore further and to share with their local colleagues. These ratings are also used when revising the MOOC-Eds for the next group of participants. In addition, the Friday Institute staff plans to analyze patterns of ratings to inform a simple recommendation system for future MOOC-Eds. For example, if teachers tend to prefer one resource, instructional coaches a second, and administrators a third, that information can be used to provide role-specific information to help participants choose resources they are most likely to find valuable. Also, the staff solicits recommendations for additional resources from participants and provides annotated lists of participant recommended resources.

Another use of crowd-sourcing is in the discussion forum. In the current version, participants can choose one of four tags for a discussion posting: critical issue, great tip, agree, and not convinced. This provides a very quick way for participants to respond to postings without entering their own statements. It also enables other participants to quickly identify postings of interest and allows the course facilitators to elevate highly rated postings to the top of a discussion.

This instructional element supports all four of the design principles for research-based practices for educators' professional learning, providing information from peers to help participants self-direct their experience, with the recommendations adding job-connected resources that provide additional perspectives and voices.

MOOC-EDS WITHIN BLENDED LEARNING PROGRAMS

Based on the existing experience and research of the Friday Institute, MOOC-Eds seem to be valuable additions to the set of professional learning opportunities for educators. However, feedback from participants indicates that MOOC-Eds are most valuable when participants work through them together with local colleagues and discuss how the resources and activities apply to their local context. Many instructional elements of the MOOC-Eds provide tools and connections for blended learning programs. For example, the resource collections can be used in local activities; the projects can directly connect with local contexts and professional roles; and classroom activities such as "What would you do next?" provide opportunities for peer discussions and coaching.

The Friday Institute has been conducting a variety of explorations into different ways of connecting MOOC-Eds to other professional learning activities, among them:

- "wrapped" for-credit graduate courses at NC State around the Digital Learning Transition and Coaching Digital Learning MOOC-Eds in which students engage in initial small-group discussions with the instructors (each participant selecting a project topic), participate in the MOOC-Ed while also working on their projects, and then present their projects to complete the requirements for course credit
- connecting the Digital Learning Transition MOOC-Ed with a yearlong blended program involving six day-and-a-half face-to-face sessions with intervening online activities designed to prepare North Carolina principals to lead digital learning initiatives in their schools (a revised version of this program will be piloted in other states); the MOOC-Ed provided the online activities for the first two sessions
- the Disciplinary Literacy for Deeper Learning MOOC-Ed, which works with a group of teachers in a local school who are using it to structure their face-to-face interactions in their professional learning team; the designers have drafted a guide for facilitating local face-to-face sessions that extend the MOOC-Ed experience

- the Learning Differences MOOC-Ed, which works with Teach For America, New Teacher Center, Teach For All, and Big Brothers Big Sisters, with each organization planning to blend the MOOC-Ed with other professional learning activities for its members, with a particular focus on coaches who are working with the teachers who participated in the MOOC-Ed.

RESEARCH DIRECTIONS

The MOOC-Ed initiative involves a significant research agenda using the abundance of data available.[11] Major areas this research is addressing include questions about *self-directed learning, peer-supported learning*, and the impact of the MOOC-Ed on participants' knowledge and practices.

Questions about *self-directed learning* include:

- Do participants' stated goals for participating in the MOOC-Ed or their occupational roles lead them to take different paths through the course?
- Are there patterns in the use and ratings of resources that differ across participants with different goals and/or roles?
- Did the perceived usefulness of various course instructional elements differ by stated goals or occupational roles in a MOOC?

Exploring these questions involves using in combination the participants' characteristics as determined in the registration survey, participants' ratings of the value of the different elements in the course, and the extensive analytics data. The data allows the researchers to trace which resources participants selected, how long they watched selected videos, how they rated the resources they selected, and how they engaged in discussions, projects, and other activities. The results will help the Friday Institute staff develop more effective ways to guide participants to self-direct their experiences in the MOOC-Ed to meet their own goals and interests, including the use of simple recommendation engines.

Questions about *peer-supported learning* include:

- In what ways, and to what extent, do educators engage in peer interactions in the discussion forum?
- How do educator characteristics—such as roles, goals for taking the course, levels of experience, and comfort with online learning—influence their interactions?

- What is the content and quality of peer interactions, and to what extent do they support learning?

The Friday Institute staff is addressing these questions by conducting social network analyses of the discussion forum postings to describe and categorize the patterns of interactions and the roles different participants play in the discussions, along with network modeling and discourse analyses to assess the content, depth, and educational value of the discussions. These analyses also make use of participant data obtained through a registration survey and examined in light of participants' engagement in other aspects of the MOOC-Ed, through the detailed analytic data that is used to track each individual's participation. The results may help refine how discussions are framed and participants are grouped for discussions.

Questions about impact of the MOOC-Ed on participants' knowledge and practices include:

- Does participation in a MOOC-Ed lead to changes in participants' professional knowledge?
- Does participation in a MOOC-Ed lead to changes in participants' professional practices?
- Does participation in a MOOC-Ed lead to increased performance by students, teachers, or schools (depending on the focus of the MOOC-Ed)?

Each MOOC-Ed uses surveys to ask participants to rate how much they have learned and the likelihood it will impact their professional practices. Several MOOC-Eds also include a pre/post assessment of some of the major content. For example, Fraction Foundations uses pre/post assessments of participants' pedagogical content knowledge. In the Learning Differences MOOC-Ed, there is follow-up with some participants, especially the coaches, to see changes in the work of educators months after the course ends. Evidence of impact of participation is also found in the discussions and submitted projects.

CONCLUSION

The MOOC-Ed initiative, now just two years old, has shown that MOOCs can provide personalized, accessible, effective, scalable professional development for motivated professionals. It has also shown that the design principles of *multiple voices, self-directed learning, peer-supported learning*, and *job-connecting learning* provide a solid foundation for MOOC-Eds. The research is beginning to provide information to inform further improvements in how MOOC-Eds can meet the needs of large number of educators through *self-directed, peer-supported, job-connected learning*. It also confirms that the critical question is not, Do MOOC-Eds work? but, rather, How can the value of MOOC-Eds be optimized? What professional development needs do they best serve? And how can MOOC-Eds be blended effectively with other professional development approaches?

CHAPTER 4

Supporting Deep Change with an Immersive Online Course

RUTH SCHOENBACH, CYNTHIA GREENLEAF,
WILLARD BROWN, AND HEATHER HOWLETT

> As a teacher responsible to work to increase students' science literacy, I now see the importance of modeling my thinking to my students and creating learning experiences in which students must actively think about texts. My role has changed in that I no longer just tell students to read a certain piece of text. I must lead them to become more actively engaged in texts.
> —iRAISE teacher participant, May 2014

> What [my students] looked like in September versus what they look like now, they are totally different. They can take an article and they can start breaking it apart, and they can ask questions. They ask each other questions. They ask clarifying questions of each other. They can start making summaries. They are really good at that. Do they still depend on me somewhat? Definitely, but they are working together toward the same goal of making sense of an article.
> —iRAISE teacher participant, May 2014

As the breadth of examples described in other chapters of this volume show, there is a wide range of purposes, audiences, and designs in online professional learning. Although several studies have successfully traced the link between teachers' online learning and positive student outcomes, online learning designed to achieve direct and measurable student impact is still relatively rare.[1] The work described in this chapter attempts to build teachers' capacities to support students' critical reading and comprehension of science texts. It shows early indications of success. The online professional learning discussed here was developed to test a hypothesis: an online learning environment for teachers can create the kinds of changes in those teachers' classroom practices and positive changes in the engagement and achievement of their students that have been documented in prior studies of similar intensive face-to-face professional learning.[2]

This chapter describes the iRAISE (Internet-based Reading Apprenticeship Improving Science Education) course, a yearlong online course designed for high school science teachers. This course, focused on disciplinary literacy in science, was based on the Reading Apprenticeship instructional framework, a pedagogical approach that has been developed over twenty-plus years of iterative research and development with communities of practitioners.

Before presenting details about the course design, context, and teachers' responses, the chapter discusses the educational problems iRAISE was created to address. It then briefly outlines the Reading Apprenticeship instructional framework and Reading Apprenticeship professional development design principles. Following the description of the instructional framework and professional development model, the chapter addresses the aims and questions that guided the "translation" of a successful ten-day, face-to-face professional development sequence into an all-online, mostly synchronous course. It briefly describes the project evaluation and promising early findings from the pilot year of this course. The chapter closes with reflections on strengths and challenges of this approach, including issues of scalability and access.

BUILDING TEACHERS' CAPACITY TO INTEGRATE COMPREHENSION STRATEGY INSTRUCTION INTO SUBJECT-AREA READING

Approximately two-thirds of high school students in the United States are unable to read and comprehend complex academic materials, think critically about texts, synthesize information from multiple sources, or communicate clearly what they have learned.[3] High school achievement levels in science mirror these statistics. The Common Core, as well as other new standards, calls for students to demonstrate advanced literacy proficiency in English classes and in other academic subjects, such as history, science, and math.[4]

Science education leaders have concluded that shifting science learning from acquiring scientific facts through memorization to building deeper understandings of core science concepts will require a focus on both science content knowledge and science practices.[5] The ability to make meaning of oral, written, and visual language representations is now recognized to be central to the development of robust science knowledge, to participation in scientific inquiry, and to meaningful engagement in public discourse about science.[6] However, in large part, high school science teachers are unprepared to meet this challenge, not knowing how to simultaneously build students' academic literacy skills and engage them in a rigorous curriculum of science study.[7] Many science teachers hold misconceptions or limited conceptions of literacy teaching and learning; they tend to think of reading and writing as basic skills that are developed in elementary or middle school or down the hall in the English department. They do not expect to teach reading and writing for science, yet they are confronted with students who do not comprehend the specialized language of science texts or the many ways scientific ideas are conveyed in words, diagrams, images, models, graphs, and tables.

In response, science teachers typically reduce their expectations when students struggle with the assigned texts.[8] In lieu of helping students develop the proficiencies needed to read, write, and reason with the language, texts, and dispositions of science, typical instructional strategies for struggling readers involve simplifying, slowing the pace, and often abandoning more rigorous coursework, virtually assuring low levels of achievement for students who are already behind.[9] A student's "literacy ceiling" becomes his or her de facto achievement ceiling, undermining academic futures and life chances.[10]

Yet, greater literacy proficiency is essential to students' abilities to gain deep scientific understandings and inquiry skills, and science classrooms can offer significant opportunities for students to acquire such proficiencies. Science inquiry and literacy practices share important properties that make the integration of literacy and science particularly powerful.[11] Participation in investigation-oriented science relies on sophisticated literacy skills such as the ability to access scientific terminology, interpret arrays of data, comprehend scientific texts, engage in interpretive and critical reading, and read and write scientific explanations.[12] Research has shown that when teachers participate in inquiry activities related to disciplinary literacy, they can make profound changes in their teaching practice.[13] These changes in turn make a significant positive difference in student achievement and dispositions for learning for high-needs students.[14] By supporting a wide range of students to "join the conversation" in the sciences—that is, to develop students' confidence in reasoning, reading, and writing—the Reading Apprenticeship instructional framework enables teachers to put academic equity and inclusion at the center of their work.

THE READING APPRENTICESHIP INSTRUCTIONAL FRAMEWORK

Reading Apprenticeship is an approach to reading instruction that helps teachers improve their practice so that students can more easily develop strategies, dispositions, and the knowledge they need to become more powerful readers. It is at heart a partnership of expertise, drawing on what teachers know and do as discipline-based readers and on adolescents' and young adults' unique and often underestimated strengths as learners.[15] Reading Apprenticeship instructional routines and approaches are based on a framework of four interacting dimensions—social, personal, cognitive, and knowledge building—woven into subject-area teaching through metacognitive conversations. These are conversations about the thinking processes students and teachers engage in as they read (see figure 4.1). Extensive reading—that is, increased opportunities for students to practice reading as collaborative problem-solving activities central to learning the content of a discipline—is the surrounding context for this framework.

The *social* dimension draws on learners' interests in peer interaction as well as on their interests in larger social, political, economic, and cultural issues. Reading Apprenticeship creates a safe environment for students to share their confusion and difficulties with texts and to recognize and make use of their diverse perspectives and knowledge.

The *personal* dimension draws on strategic skills students use in out-of-school settings, their interest in exploring new aspects of their own identities and self-awareness as readers, their purposes for reading, and their goals for reading improvement.

The *cognitive* dimension develops readers' mental processes, including their repertoire of specific comprehension and problem-solving strategies. The work of generating cognitive strategies that support reading comprehension is carried out through shared classroom inquiry.

The *knowledge building* dimension includes identifying and expanding the knowledge readers bring to a text and further developing it through personal, social, and cognitive interaction with that text. Students build knowledge about language and word construction, genre and text structure, and the discourse practices specific to a discipline—in addition to the concepts and content embedded in the text.

Adaptability and Scalability

Since 1999, this simple but powerful instructional framework has been used by thousands of teachers, teacher leaders, and administrators from around the United States and in several other countries (Germany, Canada, New Zealand) and has proven to be adaptable, scalable, and impactful beyond what the creators could have imagined. Teachers repeatedly report that being able to refer to a framework that includes the affective as well as cognitive aspects of supporting students in their disciplines helps them move toward student-centered, text-based teaching. Because Reading Apprenticeship focuses on changing the classroom dynamic and conversation, *not* on implementing a packaged program or a simple step-by-step process, once teachers and students get comfortable with the core ideas and routines, they can apply and adapt the framework in myriad ways. From middle school history to organic chemistry, teachers and college faculty have found ways to make Reading Apprenticeship their own. The fact that it is adaptable makes the framework more transportable and scalable.

However, there is a fine line between adapting an approach and implementing it in ways that make it ineffective. By encouraging "flexible fidelity," the developers help educators keep their eyes on the core elements of the framework as they adapt and scale it in ways appropriate to their contexts.

Professional Development

Multiple research studies of classrooms where teachers have been trained in Reading Apprenticeship methods show significant changes in teachers' classroom practice and gains in students' sense of engagement and self-efficacy, reading comprehension, and content learning.[16] Reading Apprenticeship aims to expand teachers' flexible repertoire of instructional practices. The model emphasizes formative assessment through metacognitive conversation about disciplinary texts as a core classroom practice. It is assumed that teachers bring varied subject and pedagogical expertise, beliefs, and identities to the professional development experience. Wherever feasible, teachers are encouraged to make use of peer interaction beyond the core professional development offered by Reading Apprenticeship facilitators—such as school team and cross-district meetings.

FIGURE 4.1 The Reading Apprenticeship framework

At its core, the Reading Apprenticeship approach to professional development is a series of inquiries designed to build teachers' understandings of the myriad internal and invisible processes by which they comprehend complex texts and recognize the specific literacy practices of their disciplines. Recognizing such processes enables teachers to become more aware of the ways in which texts can present challenges to inexperienced readers. Moreover, by understanding and using Reading Apprenticeship's tools and approaches, teachers are able to learn from their students in the very process of teaching—through ongoing formative assessment, inquiry, and reflection.

Clearly, this kind of teaching is a complex endeavor, involving thinking, planning, decision making, and assessment of students in the dynamic flow of classroom instruction.[17] Teachers carry out instructional actions that bring new ideas in education to life, shape students' opportunities to learn, evaluate students' performance and capabilities, and orchestrate students' interactions with one another and class materials, including texts.[18] To orchestrate such complexity moment by moment, teachers require access to well-structured professional training that further develops their professional capacities.

By engaging teachers in a variety of inquiries into their own and their students' reading practices, programs like this can assist teachers in constructing richer and more complex theories of reading, in seeing their students' capacities to read and learn in new and more generous ways, and in drawing on and developing their own resources and knowledge as teachers of reading *within their discipline*. In this process, teachers transform their classrooms into places where students develop new identities as capable academic readers.

Building Teachers' Generative Knowledge of Reading

To help teachers understand the power of the Reading Apprenticeship framework for students, Reading Apprenticeship professional development immerses teachers in the same instructional approaches they are asked to promote in their classrooms. They participate in close reading of complex disciplinary texts and inquire into how they, as expert readers in their discipline, engage with and make meaning of complex text. They participate in close inquiry by examining videos and transcripts of individual students in the process of reading and of classroom interactions where teachers implement the Reading Apprenticeship framework. As they participate in these inquiries, teachers are better able to envision ways to engage students in the core routines of Reading Apprenticeship.

By hearing their colleagues work to construct meaning with texts, they see how many alternate understandings are possible. By having challenging experiences in which they themselves learn from text and build knowledge about words, content, and genres with which they were previously inexperienced, teachers come to reassess the role that active interaction with texts can play in learning. As teachers participate in these explorations, they begin to value the contributions they are uniquely positioned to make to their students' learning. Through these transformative moments in professional development, teachers internalize new understandings that they can then carry into their classrooms. This is not a one-time process but a series of iterative inquires, reflections, and connections to their own classrooms. This is a markedly different process from typical professional development in which teachers hear from experts or practice new strategies without exploring the challenges and processes of reading, writing, and reasoning within their own discipline.

This approach to changing teaching practice parallels the approach to changing the practice of students, particularly in its emphasis on social and personal learning as a necessary foundation for cognitive learning and knowledge development. This emphasis is as important for teachers as it is for students. Reading Apprenticeship provides an immersive experience for teachers to learn to create intellectual engagement and safe learning environments for their students. Facilitators frequently pause after an activity and ask teachers to reflect on how the activity influenced their own adult learning before thinking about transferring these kinds of activities to their own classrooms.

A wide range of teachers have benefited from this intensive intellectually and personally challenging approach to professional learning, even as it challenges some of their assumptions about their students' capacities. Many participants who initially reject some of the core premises of the Reading Apprenticeship framework with statements such as, "My students aren't ready for metacognition," make profound shifts—transforming their classroom practice and beliefs and coming back in subsequent sessions with comments such as, "I never realized my students were capable of asking each other better questions than I could!"

THE iRAISE COURSE

> The iRAISE has been good because, even though the twice a month meetings were a pain in the butt . . . it was good. They were true PLCs [professional learning communities] . . . I've been teaching for a while, and I have had "PLCs" when it first became popular eight years or ten years ago, and this was really the first experience where our get-togethers have truly been PLCs, where we had a format to follow, or a protocol, to follow, and we actually talked and shared lessons and we were all speaking the same language and we were all on task. So that's how it's been different. The support has been very good.
>
> —iRAISE participant, July 2014

The Internet-based Reading Apprenticeship Improving Science Education course (iRAISE) was funded through a 2013–2017 Investing in Innovation (i3) development grant from the US Department of Education.[19] In the winter of 2013, the project staff recruited twenty-five teachers from existing networks of schools in Michigan and Pennsylvania for the 2013–2014 pilot course.[20] Participants received modest stipends for their participation.

iRAISE Course Design

The iRAISE course was based on the Reading Apprenticeship professional development design principles. Project developers carried out multiple refinements of tools and protocols used in several iterations of an intensive sixty-five-hour face-to-face professional development sequence for high school science teachers. These were funded by three prior federal grants.[21] The structure of the face-to-face professional development in two of the three grants was identical: a five-day initial summer institute followed by a two-day winter institute and then a three-day final summer institute.

The iRAISE design team "translated" the knowledge and tools refined in these prior face-to-face sequences into the new online iRAISE course.[22] In addition to drawing on these design elements and lessons, the Reading Apprenticeship online design team collaboratively designed seven online courses and four other online learning environments for a variety of audiences and purposes based on the Reading Apprenticeship instructional framework (see table 4.1).

The team learned a great deal in the process of developing these online learning environments. In addition to fidelity to Reading Apprenticeship professional development design principles, the following broad design goals guided the translation of iRAISE from the face-to-face versions of the sixty-five-hour yearlong science course to a fully online course:

- to replicate the immersive experience of a face-to-face five-day introductory summer institute
- to replicate the vivid real-time experience of investigating one's own and others' reading processes—the core Reading Apprenticeship routine in professional development and in classrooms
- to create a community in which participants feel safe to explore confusion and reveal their mistakes, in order to be able to build that kind of community in their own classrooms

- to help science teachers become personally and intellectually involved in the course and sustain their involvement across the academic year, given all the competing demands on their time
- to make best use of the online medium to improve teachers' confidence and fidelity in implementing new practices.

To achieve the degree of immersion, community, and vivid experience of reading process analysis essential for the deep learning built into the face-to-face work, the iRAISE design team decided to adopt a mostly synchronous model for this online professional development. Initially, the course had been imagined as completely asynchronous, like the highly popular and successful six-week Reading Apprenticeship 101 community college course. However, as the team explored the problem of how to keep high school teachers engaged in the course over an entire year of in-depth work, the importance of peer-to-peer and whole-group accountability emerged as a key issue. The design team explored various platform possibilities and decided to use the course management platform Canvas for asynchronous sessions (also used for prior online courses) and to add Blackboard Collaborate for the synchronous sessions.

The three designer-facilitators for the iRAISE pilot cohort were all experienced facilitators of Reading Apprenticeship in face-to-face professional development.[23] Although they had all participated in online collaboration with peers and some online learning, they essentially learned to facilitate iRAISE as they designed and began to teach the course.

The facilitators launched the iRAISE course with the five-day introductory session in August 2013. The basic architecture for the course included two main parts: an intensive five-day summer introductory institute and a school year cycle from September through May (see table 4.2). The week of summer sessions included all the inquiry routines of face-to-face Reading Apprenticeship professional development: individual reflection, small-group talk and whole-group share-out sessions for viewing and discussing video cases; reading text excerpts; written reflection on one's own learning and connections to classroom context; and assignments for the next online session. For the school year cycle, two different types of online interactions defined the work. One type, called Ignite sessions included the whole group of twenty-five teachers in Blackboard Collaborate, and used many of the same activity structures to circle back to core ideas introduced in the summer institute as well as to introduce new practices. These Ignite sessions were abbreviated versions of the longer summer sessions and followed the same

TABLE 4.1   Reading Apprenticeship online learning environments developed by WestEd's Strategic Literacy Initiative, 2011–2014

	Learning experience, launch	Audience, format, duration
1	Community College Faculty Reading Apprenticeship Introduction, spring 2011	Community college faculty across all subjects interested in supporting students' reading comprehension; all asynchronous, close facilitation with one instructor; 6 weeks, 30 hours
2	Facilitator Intensive Training, February 2011	Facilitators of Reading Apprenticeship professional development learning to facilitate new versions of Reading Apprenticeship professional development; wiki site, self-paced within timeframe before face-to-face meeting
3	Reading Apprenticeship Improving Secondary Education (RAISE), fall 2012	Site-based middle and high school administrators, all asynchronous, then moved to more synch in later versions; intensive facilitation by 1–2 facilitators; originally 10 modules, 30 hours, changed to 8 modules
4	Leadership Community of Practice, fall 2012	Community college faculty community leading professional development and campus literacy change and dissemination
5	iRAISE, summer 2013	Online professional development synchronous and asynchronous; 65 hours: 28 hours in summer, 4 hours each month during school year; high school science teachers
6	Campus Coach, spring 2013	Community college faculty leading colleagues exploring Reading Apprenticeship
7	Reading Apprenticeship: Writing Connections*	Middle school science, history, and English teachers; hybrid face-to-face and online professional development (synchronous and asynchronous); yearlong
8	Reading for Understanding: Literacy for Learning in the 21st Century, February 2013	International, open-to-all MOOC; 12 hours over 4 weeks; 2–3 instructors; light facilitation
9	ThinkingAloud, August 2012	Wiki site for teachers and teacher leaders in 5-state 3-discipline team project
10	Facilitator Central, June 2014	Facilitators of Reading Apprenticeship professional development open-ended space for team planning, practice, communication, and learning
11	STEM Community College Reading Apprenticeship Online, April 2015	Community college STEM faculty from 13 California campus teams; 30 hours over 6 weeks; intensive facilitation; 2 instructors

Note: *Reading Apprenticeship: Writing Connections is a hybrid course with online interaction in Ignite (whole-group online sessions) and a professional learning community (small-group sessions for sharing implementation) and sessions in between three face-to-face professional development sessions (summer, winter, summer). The course is being developed through a Supporting Effective Educator Development (SEED) grant (U367D130023) from the federal Office of Innovation and Improvement.

general learning flow. The other type of session in the school year cycles were professional learning community (PLC) meetings—smaller groups of three to five teachers—each facilitated by one of the iRAISE instructors using a structured protocol to discuss their classroom work. Throughout the summer and school year cycles of the course, teachers read excerpts from the course's main text, *Reading for Understanding: How Reading Apprenticeship Improves Disciplinary Learning in Secondary and College Classrooms*.[24]

Following the first summer's introductory institute, the iRAISE design team held an in-depth meeting in which they closely examined teachers' learning in several of the key protocols (student video case, classroom case, and others). Over the course of the year, facilitators continued to listen to feedback from participants, discussed their own observations, and considered findings from the formative reports by the project's external evaluation team, Empirical Education. Based on these multiple sources of feedback, the facilitation team decided to drop one of the two PLC meetings each month, thereby decreasing synchronous time demands, something many participants had mentioned as a problem. For similar reasons, the team also removed the discussion of texts from these meetings and instead had participants post to an asynchronous discussion forum.

During the pilot year, to prepare for scale-up the next year, the facilitation team also developed a training program for apprentice iRAISE facilitators. Because facilitating Reading Apprenticeship professional development requires significant depth of knowledge of the program's tools, protocols, and social interaction, the team recruited only experienced Reading Apprenticeship facilitators. However, these experienced face-to-face facilitators still needed additional training and ongoing support to be comfortable in the online environment.

Research and Evaluation

Empirical Education conducted a two-year evaluation of iRAISE implementation and outcomes. In the pilot year (2013–2014) it evaluated teachers' implementation of iRAISE in their classrooms.[25] In the study year (2014–2015) it conducted a randomized controlled study of classroom implementation among both treatment and control teachers. In addition to the survey data of implementation by teachers, the study included measures of students' reading comprehension of sets of thematically linked science texts.[26] To measure student impact, the evaluation team used a computer-

TABLE 4.2   iRAISE yearlong course outline

I. iRAISE Summer Introductory Institute: 5 days, 5 hours each day

- *Platform and group size:* 25 teachers and facilitators use Blackboard Collaborate, with breaks for individual and small-group work
- *Opening routine:* Individual reflection and small-group talk on previous learning and a warm-up related to the day's learning goals
- *Small-group practice and discussion:* Held in breakout rooms where participants practice a metacognitive routine while discussing texts and videos
- *Whole-group share-out:* Facilitators capture participant thinking on the whiteboard and probe for deeper connections
- *Individual and paired work time:* For viewing videos, reading text excerpts, and reflective writing within the synchronous session
- *End-of-day reflection and homework*

II. iRAISE School Year Cycles (September–May): 3.5 hours each month, online

Ignite sessions (one 2-hour synchronous session each month)
- *Platform and group size:* 25 teachers and facilitators use Blackboard Collaborate
- *Opening metacognitive routine:* Facilitators present a metacognitive routine tied to the advance reading
- *Small-group practice and discussion* of the modeled routine
- *Whole-group discussions*
- *Individual planning time:* Teachers develop classroom plans to incorporate what they have just seen modeled and have themselves practiced
- *Written reflection and homework:* Includes additional assigned reading and the assignment to implement classroom plans before the synchronous PLC meeting two weeks later

PLC meeting: (one 1.5-hour session each month)
- *Platform and group size:* Groups of 3–5 teachers use Blackboard Collaborate to meet synchronously with facilitator*
- *Routine for sharing classroom practice:* Teachers share classroom practice through the structured Successes and Challenges Consultancy Protocol
- *PLC discussion:* Group discusses assigned text related to the focus of that month's topic
- *Feedback and classroom plan revision:* Teachers provide end-of-session feedback and revise their classroom plans, with a charge to implement the plans before the next PLC meeting

Note: *In year 3 of the iRAISE course, designers switched to using Google Hangout with the PLCs, thus providing the "visual presence" that was missing in the prior platform. Participant response has been very positive.

based reading comprehension assessment instrument developed as part of Education Testing Service's family of new content-area literacy assessments designed to measure higher-level skills associated with reading.[27]

For the evaluation of teachers' implementation of Reading Apprenticeship approaches, Empirical Education created, administered, and analyzed ten surveys each year to provide a series of formative reports and a set of program measures for reports to funders of the iRAISE grant. These program measures were based on three clusters of classroom practices that had been identified in prior research as being associated with high levels of implementation of Reading Apprenticeship. Each of the ten surveys asked teachers if they had implemented certain specific activities in the past week, such as, "Model a Think-Aloud with a graphic scientific text" or "Have students work in pairs to understand challenging text." The responses were clustered into three overall groups: (1) teachers' support for student-to-student interaction regarding the meaning of texts; (2) teachers' modeling and guided practice of metacognitive routines; and (3) teachers' engagement of students to use high-leverage cognitive strategies. The evaluators defined criterion for "successful implementation" as teachers using activities from two of these three clusters. For each activity measure, Empirical Education calculated the percentage of teachers who used at least two of three clusters during all weeks they were surveyed. For the pilot year, the only year for which data are currently available, Empirical Education reported that 84 percent of the twenty-five teachers said they had used activities in at least two of the three clusters for all the weeks they were surveyed.

The final survey of the pilot year asked teachers what they felt were the most beneficial aspects of implementing Reading Apprenticeship. Teachers listed various strategies used in their classroom and ways in which their own practice and that of their students had changed. Teachers highlighted that the students were reading more and that instruction was more student centered:

> More discussion about science!
>
> ...
>
> Implementing Reading Apprenticeship definitely helped my students understand their own reading, and it gave many of them more confidence in their reading and writing.
>
> ...

Students actually read. It's as simple as that. Many of my students . . . don't read very much outside of school, so especially in science, they need the practice.

...

I have gotten to both see and hear what my students are thinking. They can no longer just sit and veg. Reading Apprenticeship has given me strategies to keep students engaged.

...

Getting the students to think metacognitively. Having students work more collaboratively.

The survey also asked teachers what they felt were the most challenging aspects of implementing Reading Apprenticeship. The most frequently cited challenge was time, including time to plan, time to find additional readings, time away from "covering content," and time to implement Reading Apprenticeship routines. These challenges can be seen in comments like the following:

Time, honestly, was my biggest concern . . . I don't want to fall short at the end of the year as far as what I would cover, you know if I am taking away one to two periods a week due to participating in iRAISE type activities, so I think that was my challenge there.

...

The biggest demand on the time was researching and locating selected reading assignments, especially outside of the textbook, let's say from *Discover* magazine, *Scientific American*, an Internet-type article. But well worth it, though. Students enjoy reading a different variety of things.

Others noted challenges the course presented for their own learning, for example:

For me, the most challenging [aspect of implementing Reading Apprenticeship] was getting myself to understand my reading process and make it visible so I could teach my students how to do it for themselves.

It was hard in the beginning to shift my grading and thought process. I also wondered a lot if I was doing it right and exactly what questions to ask . . . to keep the Reading Apprenticeship rolling in my classrooms.

...

It was almost like being a first-year teacher again in terms of rethinking how I structured my lessons.

Many teachers talked about experiencing a major shift in their sense of their role as science teachers:

I now recognize that I have a role in improving my students' ability to read. Who else, but me, is going to teach them to read difficult science text?

I had somewhat thought it was an English or reading teacher's responsibility to teach literacy, period. I had figured it was just my job to make some science reading available. Plus, so many of my kids have learning impairments and could not tackle science texts, so I just worked around them. I do not expect anyone else to teach them how to read science, and I know I need to help them.

CHALLENGES AND LESSONS LEARNED

Pros and Cons of Online Versus Face-to-Face Professional Learning

Overall, the Empirical Education evaluation reports for the pilot year of iRAISE showed that a large majority of participants found the online environment a satisfying professional learning environment. Many saw it as offering a kind of access and/or interaction they would not have in face-to-face professional development:

Without the opportunity to complete this training online, I would have most likely not received it. As a father of three involved in many other things outside of school, I have declined to attend other in-person trainings. The online format enabled me to receive it.

...

I loved the technology—I could see the information provided, I liked talking and interacting with classmates, and I liked the format—not as scary as face to face.

...

Having direct links to the video in the note-taker was very helpful. I really enjoyed the fact that I could pause the video, replay sections that I missed, etc. This was a huge benefit to having an online format.

Others, however, missed being able to read body language and facial expressions as cues to communication with colleagues.

One participant who had also been involved in the face-to-face ten-day training presented an interesting perspective on the pros and cons of face-to-face versus online professional development:

> With the [face-to-face] Reading Apprenticeship experience that we did, it was a weeklong session in the summer. I think that was a pro because we were focused on it, and being able to actually see other people and talk to them is a lot easier to do face-to-face than it is in those little small groups on that Blackboard Collaborate. It's very hard to speak and know when it's your turn to speak, or when someone else is getting ready to speak. You can't see them. It's very difficult. So I feel that you miss something on the Blackboard Collaborate sessions that I got when I was face to face with people.

However, that same participant also mentioned what the course designers hoped would be the biggest benefit of iRAISE, saying, "One of the pros of the iRAISE program now is I can do the stuff that they're talking about in real time. So I can actually do the stuff they're asking me to do in my class right now, instead of waiting six weeks later when I am back in school. So that is a positive to the iRAISE program. I have kids right now, I can do it, and I can try it."

Scalability and Sustainability

Professional development that has the power to transform teachers' ways of teaching is ultimately sustainable only when it supports deep changes in teachers' identities, their understandings about their role, their subject, and their students' capacities. Each teacher's journey of learning, testing, adapting, and change is a personal one. At the same time, without social and institutional support, individual teachers can become isolated and discouraged during the ups and downs of the process of learning to teach in profoundly new ways.

The iRAISE course meets three of the key criteria for building trust and generating knowledge sharing in online learning communities Sherry Booth describes: the online community of peers was committed to common goals; they had skillful moderation by credible and knowledgeable moderators; and the design of the course used structured conversations for teachers' learning.[28] However, although teacher surveys offer indications of positive impact for the iRAISE pilot teachers and their students, the issue of scale for such an intensive online learning experience raises broad systemic issues. To achieve the depth and impact most of the iRAISE teachers reported in the pilot year, they had to commit to a high level of accountability and perseverance. In most US public schools, the time for this kind of in-depth professional learning is not built into teachers' workdays. iRAISE teachers, who took on this yearlong intensive learning commitment for a modest stipend, participated in online synchronous sessions in the evenings and often had to catch up on asynchronous parts of iRAISE on the weekends. Unless time for deeper learning is built into teachers' workdays, most high school teachers—who already spend many out-of-school hours grading papers and planning lessons—will be unwilling or unable to invest this amount of additional time in their own intensive learning. Thus, scaling up this kind of transformative online learning will not be accessible to most teachers, and that limited access means less access to state-of-the-art teaching for their students.

iRAISE teachers' comments about the changes they and their students experienced during the program's pilot year seem to confirm that a fully online and largely synchronous course can—for most of the participants—replicate the kind of immersive, collaborative, and vivid learning experiences which lead to transformative shifts in teacher practice that are similar to those previously documented in Reading Apprenticeship's face-to-face professional development. As the team continues to develop new hybrid courses and explore the potential of shorter Reading Apprenticeship–based online courses for secondary and postsecondary content-area teachers, they hope to learn more about addressing the many challenges and benefits involved in supporting powerful online learning for many different types of participants.

Online Teacher Professional Development from the American Museum of Natural History

ROBERT V. STEINER, ASHTON APPLEWHITE, ADRIANA E. AQUINO,
LISA J. GUGENHEIM, MARIA JANELLI, ROSAMOND KINZLER,
MARITZA MACDONALD, DAVID RANDLE, KAREN TABER,
JAMIE WALLACE, DANIEL WOLFF, AND LAURA STOKES

The American Museum of Natural History (AMNH) centerpiece program Seminars on Science is a series of online professional development courses created by AMNH scientists to share their own knowledge, questions, and investigations with teachers. The massive open online courses (MOOCs) are crafted with the intent to inspire educators to become lifelong learners of science beyond the content they need to teach to their students. Course design is based on a theory of action model of how the course will help strengthen science teaching.[1] The model considers teachers to be adult learners and proposes that contributing to their content knowledge and understanding of science prepares them to guide their own students' knowledge and understanding.

The Museum's commitment to providing access to expert scientists, master teachers, and rich digital resources in a discussion-based asynchronous learning environment has anchored Seminars on Science in an ever-changing and competitive digital world, and the model's strength and endurance emerge as consistent themes throughout the history of the program and its extensions.

SEMINARS ON SCIENCE

Program Genesis

Teachers have always been a core audience for the American Museum of Natural History, located in New York City. As early as 1880, the Museum's first president, Albert Bickmore, developed a set of illustrated lectures designed specifically for New York City schoolteachers, and class visits and teacher courses have been a continuous part of the Museum's practice ever since. In the late 1990s, the AMNH Education Department began to develop digital resources and online courses in earnest. Over the decades since, these efforts have helped contribute to the Museum's national and international reach.

Seminars on Science was created in 1998 as part of the Museum's effort to help address the national crisis in science education and to explore how an informal science institution—and its scientists, educators, professional developers, and educational technologists—might engage in online teacher professional development. The first Seminars on Science courses were piloted in the spring of 2000, at the bleeding edge of such professional development, and since then have successfully adapted to a relentlessly shifting landscape. The program has steadily expanded its course catalog, enrollments, partnerships, and dissemination.

Educational Goals, Strategies, and Tactics

Since its inception, Seminars on Science has sought to increase teachers' understanding of and experience with authentic science and to provide resources for classrooms. As Dede states in this book's predecessor, *Online Professional Development for Teachers*, "Teachers can deepen their understanding of science, as well as of scientific inquiry, when treated as adult learners, through connection to research scientists and scientific and educational resources as they grapple with challenging contemporary scientific research within a networked community of teachers."[2]

The AMNH Seminars on Science model strives to pair deep content knowledge with the ability to use science-rich resources to support active learning in the classroom. Teaching methods are addressed primarily with the final project, which requires learners to develop curricular unit plans related to the course content. Many participants adapt course assignments, essays, and other resources for classroom use. Pedagogy is explicitly explored in the discussion required in the final project, which is designed to motivate learners to discuss their practice. It is also common in the weekly discussions of how course content relates to teaching. In one offering of the Evolution course, for example, of participants' 843 posts, almost a third addressed the application of course materials to classroom practice.[3]

The model reflects best practices in science education by emphasizing active learning, close analysis of texts and media, higher-order questions, and evidence-based discussions. The next phase will align the program with the National Research Council's recently released Framework for K–12 Science Education and the Next Generation Science Standards (NGSS).[4] Given that Seminars on Science is rooted in authentic scientific endeavors and that the Framework was conceived to describe authentic science, this should be a relatively straightforward endeavor, with preliminary analysis indicating that many of the assignments and lessons can be used to help participants' students meet the NGSS performance expectations.

The Professional Development Model

The Seminars on Science course model described in *Online Professional Development for Teachers* remains fundamentally intact.[5] Course offerings have been expanded and now include thirteen courses in the life, earth, and physical sciences. The courses are six-week-long, semester-equivalent, graduate-level courses, with graduate credit available from several higher education partners.

Seminars on Science is a program that aims to deepen teacher understanding of science and to provide additional understandings and digital resources that can be used in the classroom. It is built on a foundation of AMNH expertise and resources that span its scientific, educational, and exhibition divisions; additional outside expertise and resources; higher education, K–12, and other partnerships; and an ongoing commitment to faculty support, learner support, innovation, and evaluation. The course model includes one or more AMNH authoring scientists; use of rich and diverse media (including original essays, images, video, data visualization, and interactive simulations); coteaching of fifteen to thirty participants by an educator and a scientist using asynchronous discussion forums and graded weekly assignments; and a final project that requires synthesis of course material into a set of lesson plans. The instruction in each course is based on essays and media that support a content outline based on essential questions determined by a team of scientists, educators, writers, and digital media producers. For example, essential questions from the Evolution course include: What is the evidence for evolution? How do we reconstruct evolutionary history? How does evolution work? How do new species form? How have humans evolved? How does evolution impact our lives? (See figure 5.1.)

Learners participate in weekly asynchronous discussions prompted by open-ended questions. Using a "guide on the side" instructional model, the program pairs experienced educators with a working scientist who is a specialist in the field; larger classes (with about twenty-two to thirty students) also have a teaching assistant.[6] This team supports discussions that address each question but also encourages wider-ranging discourse about the nature of scientific investigation. Learners are graded on the content of their posts and their level of participation.

Scientists and instructors try to respect the point of view of the learner while addressing misunderstandings. For instance, a learner in the Diversity of Fishes course proposed that fish would adapt to the current climate change in the same way they confronted environmental changes in the past. The scientist posted: "Well . . . I have to jump in here. Yes, it is true fishes as a group have survived the great extinction waves [but only] some lineages were able to adapt . . . What is different about the changes occurring today?" The scientist challenges the learner to apply the knowledge gained from the course to encourage conceptual change grounded in scientific understanding.

In addition to the weekly discussion forum contributions and the final project, learners are also required to submit two to five assignments. These provide an opportunity to use scientific tools, investigate a question from a scientific perspective, and demonstrate understanding of course content. In the Earth: Inside and Out course, for example, learners use cameras, field notes, and geologic maps to establish the history of a local geologic feature and then share their work through digital mapping software and online field journals. Similarly, in order to connect climate modeling to the content of the Climate Change course, learners use a web-based simulation of climate modeling software developed by NASA to manipulate NASA climate data. As another example, The Ocean System course's "Find a Vent" interactive asks learners to use simulated scientific instruments that draw on real-world data in order to locate hydrothermal vents two thousand meters below the sea surface while bearing in mind the limits of real scientific expeditions. Learners are provided and assessed with a detailed rubric that clearly indicates the expectations of each assignment.

A third type of assessment is based on a final project that involves learners creating a five-day curricular unit plan describing how they would trans-

FIGURE 5.1   Samples from the Seminars on Science Evolution course

Clockwise from upper left: part of a scientific essay, an interactive visualization facilitating comparison of anatomical features of different hominids, and an image from the Tree of Life video.

fer course content to their teaching practice. This assignment includes three targets: in the third week, participants are expected to post ideas for their units to a discussion board for input from faculty and fellow learners; in the fifth week, they submit an outline or draft to the instructor, who uses an evaluation rubric and gives them detailed feedback; and in the seventh week, the unit plan is due and is evaluated by the faculty as part of a final assessment.

Faculty support. While courses are in session, instructors are supported by weekly conversations with a course manager who acts as a sounding board and adviser. The course manager also mentors new instructors and provides guidance in areas such as grading and corresponding with students via email, posting announcements in the learning management system (LMS), and facilitating discussions. The program has also created a short online course, Teaching Science Online, for its instructors (who typically serve first as participants and then as teaching assistants before assuming full instructor duties).

Learner support. A course rubric is embedded in the LMS to guide instructors in providing both grades and written feedback to students. Rubric items include discussion content and participation, as well as required components for all assignments and the final project. Instructors also comment on each assignment and provide detailed feedback on discussions. Seminars on Science also makes available a staff member who, in addition to the course faculty, broadly supports learners' needs. This project coordinator fulfills the roles of registrar, bursar, and technical support found at traditional universities and is the first point of contact for both current and potential learners.

The learning management system. Seminars on Science previously used proprietary LMSs (eCollege was used from 2003 to 2013) but has since migrated to Moodle. It has added or improved features that include interactive transcripts for videos, digital mapping, learning interactives, and streamlined support services. Access to the robust LMS database, through both integrated reporting tools and custom SQL queries, has provided new insights into learner and faculty behavior.

Partnerships with higher education. Approximately 70 percent of current participants seek graduate credit through the program's higher education partners. The Seminars on Science courses approved by five institutions carry three graduate credits each, for both matriculated and nonmatriculated students. (One partner, Western Governors University, does not currently provide graduate credit for the courses but utilizes them as "learning resources" within its online competency-based model.) Some aspects of the learner experience, typically the requirements of the final project, are tailored to specific institutional needs. Partnership enrollments are interwoven with other dimensions of the program, including participant characteristics, engagement, and attrition and are vital to its dissemination and sustainability strategies.

Course Development

Course development is a collaborative effort that includes content development (writing/editing, graphic design, media production), technical production (interactive media and web development), and curriculum development (standards alignment and instructional design). The core development team includes a producer, one or more authoring scientists, a writer/editor, a graphic designer, and an instructional designer. Supporting team members include an image researcher, a technical producer, a videographer, a video editor, and a web developer.

It takes about a year to develop a Seminars on Science course from inception to launch. About three months are typically allotted to develop a detailed course outline that reveals the narrative structure of the course: *What is it about? What's the point of view? How should it be structured?* Addressing those questions is a creative process that takes into account a host of factors that include educational goals, expertise among the authoring scientists, existing AMNH and outside content, and science education standards. Overarching priorities include a focus on contemporary scientific research, social relevance, and the process of scientific discovery.

The content outline describes each of the course modules and the course as a whole, includes learning objectives, and identifies core essays. Outline development is iterative; multiple rounds of revision are typically necessary, and early input and support from all team members is critical to avoid major revisions later in the process.

Essay and media production can take up to six months. Drafts are reviewed and edited multiple times. Meanwhile, image acquisition and production begin. Because most images will be available for download, almost all need to be high resolution. Securing image rights is a significant task, because there are sixty to 120 images per course. For images that have to be created, scientific review is necessary to ensure accuracy, so their production is also iterative.

Program Operations

The Seminars on Science staff has been continuously improving its program operations since its inception in 2000. An eight-person team manages approximately one thousand enrollments in the core program. The workflow includes course scheduling, registration, technical support, course communications and implementation oversight, professional development for course instructors, and course evaluations.

The program typically schedules six sessions per year, with sessions beginning in September, October, January, March, June, and July. Each six-week session includes five to ten course offerings, depending on the anticipated demand. Courses are scheduled about a year before the session begins in order to provide higher education partners sufficient time to incorporate the Seminars on Science course schedule into their own academic calendars. In some cases, Seminars on Science courses appear in university course catalogs, which considerably aids in dissemination. Many participants heard about the program from a friend or colleague, but most learned about Seminars on Science courses through the program's website.

Between finishing the coursework and receiving a grade, every student receives a link to a course evaluation survey. The survey asks participants for background information, such as professional role, level of education, what grade(s) they teach, and whether they are receiving graduate credit or continuing education units. It also asks them to evaluate their course experience, using prompts such as: How appropriate was the pace of the course? How accessible was the level of the content given your background in science? The responses, which are used to improve future offerings, are one component of the evaluation process.

Program Evaluation

The formative evaluation of Mark St. John, Laura Stokes, and their colleagues at Inverness Research, Inc., has been critical to the evolution of the course model and the program's success. As external evaluators, they employed a mixed methods approach, providing qualitative and quantitative analysis from design and developmental stages through expansion, refinement, evolution, iteration, and establishing partnerships. Evaluation of the program over time has encompassed formative and summative findings, lessons learned for the field, literature reviews, in-depth interviews with course participants, surveys, focus groups with scientists and guides, and critical reviews of courses by learners, researchers, and independent experts.

Findings show that the majority of learners deepen their scientific knowledge and understanding of the process of scientific inquiry, acquire useful classroom resources and skills, and prefer Seminars on Science to other professional development offerings.[7] Sample findings across the courses are shown in table 5.1.

TABLE 5.1   Sample findings from Seminars on Science course evaluations

Overarching question	Finding	Course with the highest percentage of survey responses in agreement with the finding
What do teachers gain from their own learning from the course?	"A bank of resources for my own learning"	The Ocean System (96%)
	"Additional background knowledge of science"	The Ocean System (93%)
How does the course help strengthen teaching?	"It helped me to learn a new content area that I may teach in the future"	Sharks and Rays (92%)
	"Introduced me to new kinds of materials and media such as simulations and websites that I can use in science class"	The Ocean System (92%)
How do teachers say that this course helps their students?	"Students better connect science in school with the real world"	Water (90%)

Source: Inverness Research, Inc., 2008–2010.

Since 2007, the program has used instruments developed by the evaluators to assess repeated course offerings. Conducted online, the course surveys provide useful feedback, including information about learner engagement, instructional support, and other issues. Findings about Seminars on Science include:

> The Seminars on Science project has created course designs and structures, as well as educational resources of multiple kinds that indeed make it possible to bring the human, intellectual, and material assets of AMNH to teachers across the country in appropriate ways.[8]

> ...

> Seminars on Science courses place AMNH's world-class scientists at the center, sharing their knowledge, questions, and investigations with teachers.[9]

> ...

Courses make use of online learning technologies to bring the scientific resources of the AMNH to teachers across the nation.[10]

...

Seminars on Science courses aim to inspire teachers as adult learners of science.[11]

...

Many teachers state that "the content knowledge they gain enables them to serve their students better because it is more up-to-date and reflects scientists and their work more vividly and authentically."[12]

...

Teachers believe their renewed love of science rubs off on their students.[13]

...

The great majority of teachers apply what they learn directly to courses they are teaching.[14]

...

Students are able to benefit from what the teachers share—content and scientific aptitudes and attitudes.[15]

...

The science that teachers say they encounter in the courses is "rigorous," "uniquely engaging," and "accessible."[16]

In 2012, AMNH piloted a blended—in-person and online—version of the Climate Change course. Evaluators looked at the strengths and limitations of this format and found that learners appreciated both the blended and the purely online versions and expressed no clear preference.[17] Those in the blended class benefited from hands-on experiences and the ability to model instructional techniques, but enrollment was restricted by geographic proximity to the Museum.[18]

In addition to the independent evaluation provided by Inverness Research, Seminars on Science has also benefited from case study research by David Randle.[19]

More specifically, research supports asynchronous discussion as an educationally useful setting that allows learners to consider posts and to reflect before sharing with the online community.[20] To analyze whether this holds true in Seminars on Science discussions, Randle conducted case-study research on one offering of the Evolution course and coded all discussion posts using the community of inquiry framework, which views course inter-actions through *cognitive, social,* and *teaching presences.*[21]

Coding and analyzing discussion posts from the Evolution course, the case study research focused on cognitive presence, the construction of meaning through online collaboration, which can be manifested in discussion posts through a *triggering event* (when students recognized a problem, expressed puzzlement, or asked a question that started a new topic of discussion); through *exploration* posts (including unsubstantiated ideas or opinion); through *integration* posts (including substantive agreement or disagreement with previous messages, tentative hypotheses, or integrated information from authoritative sources to develop an argument or explanation); and through *resolution* (when learners solve problems or defend solutions.)

In comparison to other studies using community of inquiry coding for cognitive presence, this study found a relatively high level of integration. Forty-seven percent of total posts by learners were coded at the integration level, with 7 percent coded as trigger events and 38 percent as at the exploration level. (Since the discussion prompts supplied the initial question for each discussion, it is not surprising that few triggering events were recorded.) The discussion prompts in the course were open-ended questions that did not have specific solutions, so resolution was not observed. However, the percentage of integration level posts was higher than other studies that have presented cognitive presence levels as percentages of total posts and may be related to how the discussion prompts framed the tasks and were also influenced by performance expectations laid out in the course discussion rubric and communicated by the faculty.[22]

PROGRAM EXTENSIONS AND ADAPTABILITY

Integration with Other Educational Programs

Perhaps fueled in part by the situating of Seminars on Science within an informal science institution with scientific expertise and digital resources, AMNH's higher education institution partners not only provide graduate credit for the courses but use these courses within their own programs. The Museum has also made use of Seminars on Science in its other educational programs.

AMNH and the School of Professional Studies at the City University of New York (CUNY) have been partners since 2003.[23] CUNY preservice and in-service teachers, who reflect the ethnically and culturally diverse New York City population, currently comprise more than a quarter of total Seminars on Science enrollments. They have access to all approved Seminars on Science courses, and approximately four hundred students enroll each year. Seminars on Science has worked especially closely with CUNY's Brooklyn College to help "mitigate the chronic shortage of qualified science teachers in New York City by enabling students to receive graduate credit for the courses and teachers to apply those credits toward New York State science teacher certification."[24] Some Seminars on Science courses are required as part of CUNY middle school science education degree programs.[25] Although early attempts to integrate the online courses with physical labs at Brooklyn College were not sustainable, a recent collaboration with CUNY's Lehman College is now in its second year. Preservice or in-service teachers take the Earth: Inside and Out course while completing related laboratory or field trip activities organized by Lehman College faculty, thus earning graduate credit for a faculty-approved lab course. Program and instructional staff from both institutions coordinate these offerings to ensure their effectiveness. Future offerings could include an online instructor who also plays a role in the in-person labs and field trips. Another partner, Western Governors University (WGU), is an accredited nonprofit online university that offers Seminars on Science courses as part of its competency-based model of higher education. WGU students earn undergraduate and graduate degrees by completing batteries of competency-based assessments instead of accumulating traditional seat time. Seminars on Science provides students in the WGU Teachers College science education and other programs with inquiry-based explorations and connections to scientists, which complement other resources available to them. WGU course mentors provide an additional layer of support to their students and are provided with regular updates of student progress in the Seminars on Science courses.

Similarly, Florida's Nova Southeastern University used Seminars on Science courses to help equip elementary and middle school teachers with advanced degrees in science education. The 2008–2010 programs graduated approximately 150 students who used Seminars on Science courses to fulfill their degree requirements.

At the primary and secondary levels, International Baccalaureate (IB), which provides an internationally oriented curriculum for children ages three to nineteen at public and private schools across the United States and around the world through four major educational programs, partners with

AMNH to provide online and blended science professional development to teachers in its Primary Years, Middle Years, and Diploma Programmes. IB participants in Seminars on Science courses receive support from an IB instructor in creating a final project consistent with the requirements of the IB curriculum. Blended offerings include a Primary Years Programme Science Workshop and a Middle Years Programme Interdisciplinary Workshop, including an online component with background material, an orientation to the AMNH, and discussion forums to support communications before, during, and after the in-person portion.

Seminars on Science content is being leveraged in other ways, too. For example, AMNH has licensed course materials to CUNY for the undergraduate online baccalaureate program in its School of Professional Studies. As described further below, AMNH's own Master of Arts in Teaching (MAT) program uses Seminars on Science for one course in its residency-based teacher preparation program. The Museum has also begun to use Seminars on Science content to develop adult education courses.

Blended Teacher Professional Development

Since 2008 Seminars on Science has offered a variety of blended versions of the core online courses, generally through partnerships or grant commitments. These blended offerings draw on AMNH strengths in both online learning and Museum-based professional development. Course formats range from three-week excerpted course adaptations, with one or two days of in-person classes hosted at the Museum, to nine-week offerings of full courses paired with four in-person sessions. Their timing depends on the type of course and nature of the content. This format focuses more on pedagogy. During part of each in-person session, educator participants reflect on teaching practices. Where relevant, they also discuss and reflect on how to use AMNH exhibits and other resources in the classroom.

One unique blended offering was a summer course titled Art, Science and Inquiry. This course was offered in collaboration with the Metropolitan Museum of Art and subsequently expanded to include the de Young Museum and the California Academy of Sciences (both in San Francisco). The course design relied on previous experience conducting online discussions and was AMNH's first serious foray into synchronous online learning.

A blended version of The Solar System was created in 2014 for AMNH's MAT students. It was partly staffed by MAT faculty and restricted to a MAT cohort in order to combine the online course content with faculty expertise, increase the opportunity for in-person discussions, and take advantage of Museum laboratories and exhibitions. This allowed the participants to tailor content from the course to their teaching practice under the mentorship of an experienced educator.

With funding from the Arthur Vining Davis Foundation, AMNH collaborated from 2013 to 2015 with the Denver Museum of Nature and Science and the Exploratorium in San Francisco to create a set of inter-institutional blended teacher professional development courses that draw on the Seminars on Science course The Brain: Structure, Function and Evolution. The idea was to create a common online environment with possible customizations for each institution that would connect learners from New York, San Francisco, and Denver while also allowing for customized in-person sessions at each of the three informal science institutions. If sustainable, such collaborations could help offset the considerable costs of course development and defray the costs of course instruction by linking all participants to a single online session. Such a model could also take advantage of the multiple modalities and the unique resources available to each institution and, in turn, support more locally customized professional learning.

MOOCs

In 2013, AMNH was invited to be an inaugural partner in Coursera's Teacher Professional Development Program. This has allowed it to reach teachers who might not want or need full graduate-level Seminars on Science courses, to extend the work and leverage existing AMNH resources to international audiences, and to test the Museum's capacity to innovate in a rapidly evolving environment.

AMNH initially created three four-week courses for this partnership: Genetics and Society: A Course for Educators; The Dynamic Earth: A Course for Educators; and Evolution: A Course for Educators. Each course is comprised of lectures, supplementary videos, and links to education resources, quizzes, and a peer-reviewed assignment. Each also incorporates weekly essays authored by AMNH scientists and their colleagues—a departure from the typical MOOC model, in which videos are the primary resource. Course designers drew some content from AMNH's extensive resources and used it to create a series of new video lectures by Museum curators and educators. Between September 2013 and December 2014, the partnership offered each course three times. The courses' migration to Coursera's new on-demand platform was recently completed and includes a new AMNH MOOC focusing on climate change.

Although the courses were designed for science teachers, most of the current learners (60 percent) are not educators. The educator participants are divided fairly evenly among novice, intermediate, and veteran teachers. A common MOOC statistic is course enrollment, but given typically high attrition rates (many enrollees never enter the course), its importance is questionable in this case. Consequently, AMNH tracks the engagement of "active students" (those who log in to the course) and "video-active students" (those who watch at least one video). Data such as video views, video downloads, essay views, quiz completion, forum participation, and assignment completion are also monitored and used for both real-time feedback in the forums and to inform how and when content is updated. For example, quiz data is used to identify the questions with which learners are struggling, and quizzes are updated accordingly. This course data is supplemented by three surveys: one pre-course survey, one post-course survey, and one follow-up survey that is administered six to nine months after a course ends. The follow-up survey is particularly illuminating, since it is through these responses that it becomes apparent if and how learners are using the course materials with their own students.

For example, one participant, a high school teacher in Tennessee, took the Evolution MOOC with several colleagues and organized a weekly face-to-face component. He spoke about the Next Generation Science Standards videos that were produced for the course: "It's an interesting and important happening going on in science education, and the instructor was pointing out good connections . . . Even my colleagues that were not in science education perked up. That might have been my biggest takeaway from the course." Another participant teaches middle school biology and geology in Greece and uses material from the courses in several ways, one that required her to translate a video into Greek. She created a worksheet to complement the video and built a classroom activity around those resources. She reported that her students "were fascinated. They feel like they do something scientists do. They are very engaged with the activities and don't feel bored at all. It's like they do science on their own. All the educational objectives were achieved." These are just two examples among many that illustrate the successful integration of AMNH content into the classroom via MOOCs.

The advent of MOOCs challenges course creators to refine notions of the relationship among open educational resources, mass audiences, and quality online education—and what constitutes success. While the course completion rate in the Seminars on Science program (approximately 92 percent) is a key metric, its relevance to MOOCs is less clear. AMNH surveys indicate, in fact, that many Seminars on Science MOOC participants enroll primarily to gain access to course resources. As a result, different assessment metrics may need to be developed.

Typical MOOC enrollments and attrition rates are much higher than in Seminars on Science, while the MOOC discussion forum participation is much lower. (The graded aspect of the Seminars on Science discussion forums is presumably a factor.) The MOOC offerings do, however, provide a potential path to scale and may—with new developments in pedagogy, blended models, and technology—offer a more powerful educational experience that includes opportunities for discussion, collaboration, adaptive learning, and authentic assessment. In addition, by leveraging the marketing and dissemination power of Coursera, the Museum is likely introducing educators around the world to AMNH videos and other media and enriching their classroom practice.

SCALE AND SUSTAINABILITY

AMNH possessed the vision, funding, and infrastructure to explore, expand, and refine the Seminars on Science program for about a decade as online teacher professional development gained more mainstream acceptance. This likely gave the Museum something of a "first mover advantage." Early and ongoing evaluation by Inverness Research shaped an "educational engineering" process of developing and refining courses in a deliberate and thoughtful manner.[26] The program has also been able to leverage the digital resources and tools of a large institution with a scientific, education, and exhibitions base. In addition, the interest in online science education opportunities for educators has vastly expanded since the program's inception.

Approximately one thousand educators from across the United States—and a much smaller number from around the world—currently take a Seminars on Science course each year. This enrollment is a tiny fraction of the 3.5 million teachers teaching in public and private schools in the United States.[27] This fact is consistent with the sprawling and fragmented framework—online, in-person, and blended—of graduate STEM education and

STEM teacher professional development offered by thousands of higher education institutions, school districts, and other providers across the country. However, as part of that framework, Seminars on Science actually constitutes one of the larger online science professional development programs offering semester-equivalent graduate courses.

In terms of the program's impact, it is beyond the scope of this chapter to fully assess its effect on the more than ten thousand enrollments by elementary, middle, and high school teachers since Seminars on Science courses were first offered in 2000. The program evaluation by Inverness Research certainly speaks to transformed scientific understandings, classroom resources, classroom applications, and attitudinal changes. Furthermore, Seminars on Science has played a critical role as a required part of STEM degree programs at Brooklyn College and Nova Southeastern University. And many resources originally created for Seminars on Science courses have since been made freely available and have been utilized by both AMNH and other institutions to the benefit of many thousands of teachers, students, and the general public over the past fifteen years.

Between 2000 and 2008, Seminars on Science enrollment grew rapidly, averaging 25–30 percent growth per year. Since that time, despite an extended recession and the slashing of district professional development funding, program enrollments have been relatively stable. With the brighter economic outlook, the program is now seeking to add new participants, new partnering institutions, and new course opportunities.

From its inception in 1998 until 2006, Seminars on Science received funding from The Atlantic Philanthropies to support its activities, principally course development, partnership development, and evaluation. Since 2006 the program has been largely self-sustaining, typically requiring external funding only for the development of new courses, which is very staff and resource intensive. In addition to grants from both the government and private foundations, program costs are supported through revenues derived from the course fee (currently $495), from graduate credit partnerships, and from some course licensing agreements in which Seminars on Science content is made available and can be customized for use at other institutions using their own instructors, instructional models, policies, practices, and learning management systems.

The program's capacity to leverage the remarkable staff and resources of the scientific, education, and exhibition departments of one of the world's largest natural history museums gives it the ability to infuse all of the demands of online education—including program creation, course design and development, marketing and dissemination, and internal evaluation—with a strength and a quality that would be difficult to achieve in a smaller organization. That same organizational richness is inextricably interwoven with an institutional reputation and a brand that allows Seminars on Science to compete effectively in the increasingly crowded marketplace of STEM professional development. However, while AMNH is familiar to many on a national and even international level, it is most familiar to those in the New York City metropolitan region and the Northeast region of the United States, providing both opportunities and challenges to expanding program penetration in other areas.

Program sustainability faces two additional challenges. One involves course pricing. The course instructional model, utilizing both an educator and a scientist, is more expensive to run than many single-instructor models and nearly all self-guided online experiences. In the absence of other funding, however, it would be difficult to reduce course fees in order to make the program more competitive. Yet, given the competitive landscape (as well as the desire to maximize program reach), it is not clear whether raising prices substantially is either realistic or desirable.

Another challenge to sustainability is in the ongoing evolution of STEM professional development, including the emergence of wholly or largely self-guided experiences, like many current MOOCs. Most of these experiences, however, do not yet offer graduate credit and do not directly compete with Seminars on Science. But for learners not seeking graduate credit—which includes many educators who are simply meeting state or district professional development requirements or are working toward salary increments—the Seminars on Science courses probably cannot compete effectively with less expensive and less challenging professional development options. Interestingly, the AMNH teacher professional development MOOCs may compete more effectively with such offerings in the United States because of the trust that educators have traditionally placed in AMNH offerings. With either a revenue stream or some form of external funding in place, such MOOCs (or variants thereof) might contribute to a sustainable array of AMNH online and blended efforts.

The emergence of globally available professional development opportunities has increased possibilities and also created an increasingly competitive environment that tends to favor brand awareness and economies of scale and to discount the importance of physical location. Given this dynamic environment, the ability to sustain an online professional development program will require continued close attention to educational trends, funding trends, partnership opportunities, and new technologies.

CONCLUSION

For more than fifteen years, the American Museum of Natural History has been involved in the design and development of online and blended education. During this evolution, the need for access to high-quality content design and development has remained constant, while the needs of the policy, education, and school district landscapes have shifted and networked learning technologies have been transformed. The Museum's leadership in online science professional development is due to its deep scientific roots and to its ability to respond to a rapidly changing environment.

Since 2000, Seminars on Science has provided high-quality online professional development to approximately ten thousand teachers through semester-equivalent graduate courses in the life, earth, and physical sciences. The program has gone through distinct phases of course model development and field testing, partnership development, and sustainability. The model has been extended through integration with other educational programs at the Museum, with other partners, and in MOOCs.

The endurance of Seminars on Science as a strong online teacher professional development program is due in large measure to its ability to leverage the scientific, educational, and exhibition strengths of AMNH. In addition, the course model has benefited from years of development, field testing, and iteration and has proved to be durable: utilizing an educator and a scientist as co-instructors, championing the value of rich discussion in a networked community of learners, emphasizing both scientific understandings and classroom applications, treating educators as adult learners, providing strong support to faculty and learners, keeping the technology accessible but effective, and utilizing strong narratives that inspire passion, wonder, and a thirst for more. Finally, the program has benefited from a strong institutional commitment to quality online teaching and learning that has resulted in a correspondingly deep knowledge base for both online education and digital resource development.

Seminars on Science highlights the importance of institutional vision and commitment, the value of collaboration between scientific researchers and educators across course development and instruction, the multiple dimensions of online teacher professional development, and the unique role that informal science institutions can play in STEM professional development.

The lines between formal and informal education, between online and in-person teaching, and between K–12 and higher education continue to blur; the recurring themes of access, innovation, costs, and revenues are likely to continue to make their presence felt; and the opportunities, challenges and issues that abound in this area are likely to have a profound effect on the future professional development of educators, the opportunities afforded their students, and the economic vitality of nations.

The future may not be easy, but it will surely be interesting.

CURRICULUM SUPPORT

Part II focuses on online professional development created to support teachers as they implement a specific curriculum, highlighting three such programs: the Active Physics Teacher Community, a unique model of just-in-time professional development designed to serve the needs of Active Physics teachers nationwide; the Electronic Teacher Guide, developed to determine whether a print guide for an inquiry-based, educative curriculum could be redesigned as a cybertool; and the Project-Based Inquiry Science Cyberlearning Professional Development System, which demonstrates adaptability along a variety of features. Since many teachers are wedded to a specific curriculum, these models have the potential to change the way in which teachers get assistance in their instruction. All of these models attempt to use some of the unique attributes of online platforms to improve on the print teacher support materials that currently exist for textbooks.

CHAPTER 6

Just-in-Time Professional Development
The Active Physics Teacher Community

ABIGAIL JURIST LEVY, ARTHUR EISENKRAFT, AND ERICA FIELDS

Online communities take care and feeding so that they can evolve as participants' needs change and can adapt to varying contexts and environments. This chapter describes a unique model of online, just-in-time professional development and its evolutionary path from a community designed to serve distinct groups of teachers and a particular research study to a platform serving the needs of Active Physics teachers nationwide. The Active Physics curriculum was created by a large group of physicists and physics educators (led by Arthur Eisenkraft) under the auspices of the American Association of Physics Teachers and the American Institute of Physics with funding from the National Science Foundation. Some of this team then went on to structure the Active Physics Teacher Community (APTC) with the specific intention of helping teachers *prepare* for their classes each day by providing them with formal instruction that is directly related to the lessons they are teaching; *share* their knowledge, experiences, successes, and challenges with other teachers who are using the same lesson plans and curriculum; and *compare* the effectiveness of their teaching with the effectiveness of others' teaching, thereby allowing them to use data to inform their instruction and modify their strategies appropriately. The ability to prepare, share, and compare are the enduring pillars of the APTC experience, around which the unique needs and constraints of teachers, coupled with the constraints of the study itself, contribute to the way the model and the community have changed over time.

THE ACTIVE PHYSICS AND ACTIVE CHEMISTRY MODELS

The Active Physics Teacher Community (APTC) model was developed to provide support to teachers of the Active Physics curriculum. Researchers at Education Development Center, Inc., studied its development, implementation, and impact as part of a study also funded by the National Science Foundation, the goals of which were: (1) to document the nature and extent of teachers' engagement with the APTC; (2) to determine the model's effect on teachers' content knowledge, pedagogy, lesson pacing, approach to presenting new topics, assessment procedures, and expectations for what students will know, understand, or have difficulty learning; and (3) to understand teachers' views regarding the factors that influenced their engagement and the outcomes observed. To determine whether and to what extent teachers' experiences were consistent across science domains, the developers adapted the APTC model for teachers using the Active Chemistry curriculum, becoming the Active Chemistry Teachers Community (ACTC) and enabling these teachers to be included in the study as well.

Active Physics is for use with all high school students and is organized into themes that are relevant to students' lives, such as sports, transportation, and home. Each chapter is intended to be taught over a five-to-six-week period and is independent of the others. Chapters are comprised of between eight and ten sections, including a scenario, which introduces students to the general concepts being covered; a chapter challenge, which requires students to apply what they've learned to solve a real-world problem; chapter activities; and a chapter assessment. Active Chemistry also uses thematic challenges to teach chemistry in the context of students' everyday lives.

Both curricula adhere to the 7E instructional model: elicit, engage, explore, explain, elaborate, evaluate, and extend.[1] Both also meet the criteria for exemplary project-based learning curriculum, in that each chapter defines a new problem that the students must solve using physics and engineering design, and all science concepts presented are used to complete the required project.[2] Similarly, both curricula merge science and engineering practices with disciplinary core ideas in each section and link the content to crosscutting concepts as recommended by the Framework for K–12 Science Education and the Next Generation Science Standards.[3]

The APTC and ACTC platforms are just-in-time online professional development programs for teachers implementing either the Active Physics or Active Chemistry project-based curriculum in their classrooms. The initial APTC platform used materials that pertained to two specific chapters in the text *Active Physics*—"Physics in Action," which covers forces, momentum, and energy, and "Let Us Entertain You," which covers waves, sound, and light. The ACTC platform was initially designed for the first chapter in *Active Chemistry,* "Fun with the Periodic Table," which focuses on the properties of materials, ionization, and atomic structure. Both platforms rely on teachers moving through the chapters at a relatively synchronized pace in order to maintain a critical mass of teachers working on a given lesson at a given time. This common pacing gives teachers the opportunity to share and compare their students' work as they teach the selected chapters and to think together about how they can teach topics more effectively, thus allowing them to try out new ideas almost in real time. Teachers can access helpful information from people in the community who are presently teaching the same chapter and section or from those who have taught it in the past.

On most e-lists a teacher can post a question on any topic at any time, but most e-lists do not have indexing functions. However, in the APTC and ACTC platforms, all comments are organized by chapter and by section. For example, as teachers teach section 5 of chapter 3, they can go directly to section 5 on the platform and see all past comments related to that section. Comments that clarify the science content, or those that give suggestions for pedagogy in general or pedagogical content knowledge, are also contained in the relevant sections.

Blackboard, an online education platform, was used to make the contents of the online professional development available to teachers. As teachers from each of the five sites logged on to the homepage, they were taken directly to their district's folder so that they were communicating only with their peers in the same district. Once participants logged on, they saw a screen similar to the one shown in figure 6.1.

The folder for each chapter contained links to the various sections within the chapter. For example:

- In "Introduce Yourself" teachers posted brief profiles of themselves and learned more about the other teachers using the site.
- "Introduction and Chapter Challenge" provided a series of videos and background materials to familiarize teachers with the chapter, a video explaining the 7E instructional model, a description of the chapter challenge that students had to complete, video introductions to Active Physics concepts and helpful tips for managing the course, frequently asked questions, and tutorial videos on using the course.

FIGURE 6.1   Sample APTC chapter

Chapter 1: Sports in Action

Introduce Yourself
Introduce youself and learn a bit about everyone else. Let's get started!

Introduction and Chapter Challenge
Maximize your success with these introductory videos and references, and be sure to check out the Chapter Challenge

Activity 1: Newton's 1st Law — A Running Start

Activity 2: Push or Pull — Adding Vectors

Activity 3: Center of Mass

Activity 4: Defy Gravity

Activity 5: Run and Jump

Activity 6: The Mu of the Shoe — Frictional Forces

Activity 7: Concentrating on Collisions

Activity 8: Conservation of Momentum

Activity 9: Circulation Motion

Submit Teacher Log

- "Activities" linked to the chapter's activities, each of which included Prepare, Share, and Compare windows.
- Teachers participating in the research were asked to fill out a log at prescribed intervals as they taught the chapter and to submit the log when the chapter was finished. This log was designed to be both a research and a professional development tool, with teachers using the information to discuss their pacing (e.g., How long did it take to complete Activity 3? How were you able to get through it so quickly? Why did you spend so much more time than I did on this activity?) and a researcher tool to document any changes in teachers' pacing of their instruction.

Each activity folder contained a pre-quiz, which, during the study phase, teachers were required to take. The other content was "conditional," or not available until the teacher completed the pre-quiz. The conditional status of the content was a constraint demanded by the ongoing research. Researchers used the pre-quiz to identify changes in teachers' content knowledge, but it also alerted teachers to the most important concepts in the activity and helped them identify content that they wanted or needed to understand better in order to teach it more effectively. In addition, teachers could administer some or all of the pre-quiz to their students if they desired and in any manner they chose—as a pre-assessment for the class as a whole, as a tool just for particular students, or as a means of checking for understanding as students completed the activity.

The activity folder also held the following:

- a section for each of the three main components of the online teacher professional development—the Prepare, Share, and Compare windows
- a multiple choice post-quiz that teachers were required to take as well as administer to their students; in addition to answering the quiz's content questions, teachers were asked (a) to predict the percentage of students that would select each of the four possible answer options to the fifth question on the quiz and (b) what they could learn about the thinking of students who chose each answer option; student responses provided the data for discussions in the Compare window
- a resources section, including lesson plans, quizzes, answer keys, and handouts that could be downloaded and edited
- a link for teachers to submit their logs.

UNIQUE FEATURES OF THE MODEL

In his edited book *Online Professional Development for Teachers: Emerging Models and Methods*, Chris Dede describes ten effective online teacher professional development models that vary in many ways—including audience, content, pedagogy, and media—and have their own key characteristics.[4] For example, some models feature one-to-one support, such as the WIDE World program, which offers personalized support from an expert online coach to every participant, and the eMentoring for Student Success project, which pairs new teachers with mentor teachers in the same state. Another effective online teacher professional development program, the EdTech Leaders Online model, takes a train-the-trainer approach; school districts choose a six-person leadership team that is trained to deliver the professional development and then participates in an online teaching practicum prior to facilitating any online workshops. The professional development course for Quest Atlantis, a 3-D multiuser environment, is a model that is somewhat similar to the APTC and ACTC platforms in that it is embedded in teachers' classroom experiences by focusing on a single curriculum.

While the APTC and ACTC platforms share some features with other high-quality online learning communities, the platforms also include some components that distinguish them—namely, the Prepare, Share, and Compare windows, the platforms' defining characteristic, which are presented for each of the eight to ten activities in a chapter and give participants the opportunity to be consumers of information, producers of information, or both (see table 6.1).[5]

Prepare

The Prepare window, essentially an enhanced electronic teacher edition to accompany the textbook, supports the lesson preparation that teachers generally do in isolation. This is the component with which teachers are most familiar, as it is most like what they find in other teacher support materials. In the Prepare window, teachers are only consumers of the materials. Since all teachers on the website are using the Active Physics curriculum, the Prepare window is designed to help them plan for their daily classes; it is integrated into the content of their instruction as they progress through the chapters. There is no discussion at this stage and therefore no need for a moderator.

The Prepare window contains the following content for teachers:

- "Crucial Physics" provides an overview of the big ideas that students should understand and the crucial physics that students will learn about in the activity, and it includes a video of a master teacher demonstrating the activity, showing the equipment to use, and sharing helpful hints for teaching the activity. In addition, teachers can try the experiment themselves with their own equipment by following the directions in the student text.
- "Misconceptions" provides a list of common misconceptions that students have regarding the physics content specific to the activity. Presented in a two-column table format, one column listing "What Students May Say" and the other suggesting "What a Physicist May Say" (i.e., how teachers might respond). In addition, for each misconception there are

TABLE 6.1 Overview of the Prepare, Share, and Compare windows

	Materials are presented by the site creators	Teachers have the opportunity to be consumers	Teachers have the opportunity to contribute and be producers
Prepare: Teachers can access videos, lesson plans, common misconceptions, science content, etc.	Yes	Yes	No
Share: Teachers can share experiences, ask questions, and receive responses on content knowledge, pedagogical knowledge, and pedagogical specialized content knowledge	No	Yes	Yes
Compare: Teachers can use student data from quizzes to inform their future instruction	Yes	Yes	Yes

examples of identifiers, formative assessment questions, and interventions to help students see things differently. Teachers reported this format as helpful because it clearly portrayed the accurate expression of a concept along with students' related misconceptions.

- Lesson plans are provided for each day devoted to a particular activity. Each lesson plan relies on the 7E model and includes internal pacing guides (i.e., how many minutes are required for each part of the activity) and suggestions for the activity. The full lesson plans can be downloaded in Word and edited.

Some of the Prepare windows also include "Additional Details" and/ or "Teaching Notes," which offer fuller explanations of physics concepts; helpful diagrams, animations, and illustrations; further tips on conducting the activities; and additional instructional tips for the teacher.

Share

The Share window is intended to foster teachers' reflections on their work. Each activity in each chapter has its own Share window. This window is distinct from the Prepare window in that no postings are originated by the creators of the site, whereas everything in the Prepare window—lesson plans, videos, content—is posted by the site's creators. All the posts in the Share window come from the teachers or a moderator, whose main role is to engage teachers in discussion. It is an opportunity for teachers to relate their classroom experiences to others while they are teaching the material. They can share successes or challenges; they can ask questions of the group or comment on struggles that their students are having; they can ask how other teachers have solved issues concerning laboratory investigations, for example; or they can upload helpful diagrams or worksheets they used with their students.

Some examples of threaded discussions created by teachers include:

> I had trouble in class today creating exact standing waves with the Slinkies. Does anyone have suggestions? I finally used a simulation to show standing waves.
>
> ...
>
> My students had trouble seeing the acceleration last year with the balls. I am going to try and use carts (by themselves and with boxes of clay on them) to see if they will see the acceleration better. I will let you know how it works on Monday.
>
> ...
>
> My kids do not appear, on the whole, to be "getting it" regarding the various transformations and calculations of energy transfer . . . The math (and equations) appears to be the stumbling block. Is anyone else having this challenge with their students? If so, what are you doing to help student comprehension?

The moderator, an experienced physics teacher and moderator of online forums in physics and chemistry, also initiates discussions in the Share window discussion forum. She often introduces questions to get teachers to think more deeply about the content or about assessing student understanding, or simply to encourage them to share with one another. Some examples of moderator-initiated discussion prompts include:

- How are the students doing on interpreting and doing this first activity? Are they grasping the physics concepts? How do you know? What are the students saying that helps you to know?
- Often as we listen to the "language"/"vocabulary" of the students, it tells us something about their understanding. Let us know how students describe Galileo's Principal of Inertia and what you discover from their descriptions. Do you think this could relate to any of the questions found on the pre-quiz?

• What did your students have to say about conservation of momentum and action-reaction forces while they were studying the content for this activity and after they did the activity?

The forums are intended to provide just-in-time support for teachers. For example, a teacher with questions about teaching Activity 3 in the "Let Us Entertain You" chapter could go to the Activity 3 portion of the website to find all the materials for and discussions on that activity. These could include teaching strategies, useful questions that other teachers asked their students, and reports of unexpected occurrences. All of this information can be gathered and used as they teach the activity.

As teachers post and/or read other teachers' posts, they reflect on their own instruction. By posting to the Share forum and relating stories of what went well in their classrooms (or what didn't, and how they handled it), teachers provide invaluable just-in-time support that can help other teachers tackle their lesson plans for each week. In addition to sharing their experiences, teachers can use the forum to share ideas about assessment, materials, student work, questions, solutions, quizzes, and modifications and augmentations introduced to assist students with special needs or English language learners.

Compare

Similar to the Share forum, the Compare window has no postings originated by the creators of the site. It enables teachers to compare their students' quiz scores and overall progress to the scores and progress of other teachers' students and to discuss what might explain their differential outcomes. For example, teachers with different class averages on the quiz have an opportunity to compare and contrast the two classes: Did one teacher summarize the activity differently? Did one teacher ask students to write something during the week? As teachers reflect on their teaching in this way, more effective strategies may emerge, which can be implemented in subsequent classes. Teachers trying new approaches can observe and report back about whether and how their students' understanding improved.

On a more detailed level, teachers can discuss the incorrect answer options that students found most appealing and use student data to inform their instruction. For example, if a distractor is not chosen by the majority of students in one class but is chosen by the majority in another class, the teachers can deconstruct the classroom dynamics of the past three days to try to determine if something was done to limit the appeal of the distractor. It is then possible for all teachers to adopt this strategy for the next section and see if it works for their students as well. This just-in-time analysis of student results and memory of what transpired in classes is a unique feature of the Compare forum, which cannot be duplicated in traditional, face-to-face professional development because of the time delay and the tendency to forget some of the details of the classroom environment.

Enabling teachers to compare their classrooms using data generated during instruction is an adaptation of lesson study, a Japanese form of professional development in which teachers collaboratively plan and examine actual lessons.[6] The consistent discussion, dissection, and sharing of lessons and classroom performance data on a regular basis is intended to hold some of the same promise as the traditional lesson study approach, while opening it up to greater numbers of teachers via an online, real-time, just-in-time context.

Connection to Curriculum

Another distinctive feature of the APTC model is that it is directly connected to a published curriculum. Research shows that professional development is most effective when the content is linked directly to the curriculum a teacher is using.[7] And while a wide variety of online teacher professional development models and online learning communities focus on different content areas, pedagogies, and other features, it is much more difficult to find any that link directly to a published curriculum. The one exception mentioned in Dede's book, Quest Atlantis, is linked to more of a supplementary curriculum rather than a full curriculum program like Active Physics.

Moderator

A moderator who directs the conversation and may vet comments before they are posted is a fairly common feature of online learning communities. The APTC moderator poses questions as a means of engaging teachers in the discussions in the Share and Compare windows and of generating attachment to the community. The moderator provides various content-related resources, assists with navigation for those new to APTC, and responds to queries to clarify content or to problem solve if other teachers do not step up as mentors within the community. The moderator also lays out the rules of participation so that discussions remain thoughtful, respectful, and constructive and so that teachers feel comfortable sharing their questions and ideas with others. Occasionally the moderator recognizes gaps in teachers' content knowledge, in which case closed communication with the teacher through the forum's email allows for one-on-one discussions that clarify questions and deepen the teacher's understanding.

When teachers' questions highlight their own misconceptions, the moderator uses a variety of strategies to provide clarification. For example, the moderator might ask the teacher to open a discussion thread around that topic or, if the teacher seems reluctant to do this, might request permission to rephrase privately discussed questions and re-post them under the moderator's identification on the open forum. The intent is to encourage the discussion of content in general, particularly regarding specific test questions, as well as appropriate wording and language for students. When the opportunity arises, the moderator works with teachers to support their understanding of the content in an effort to keep them engaged.

Although teachers teach the same curriculum, they usually do not teach the same activities in the same way. To foster conversations and encourage social networking among the community, the moderator poses a variety of questions and prompts to the whole group, ranging from concrete and specific to more open-ended queries, all of which encourage reflection and/or data analysis. For example, one simple prompt by the moderator is: How do you deal with Slinkies in class? How many got tangled? This results in teachers discussing how they prepare students to work with the Slinkies; some even provide links to YouTube videos of how to untangle a Slinky. Prompts that encourage greater reflection include: What questions are your students asking about projectile motion? Do they believe there is an upward force on a projectile once it leaves the hand or the launching mechanism?

One such prompt—Do your students make connections with the earlier section on inertia, motion, and forces?—led to an especially rich discussion. First, one teacher wrote:

> As a way to check that they understood the nature of projectiles, I showed them a clip from the movie *Pearl Harbor* in which the USS *Arizona* was bombed. In the clip, the bomb is released directly above the ship and has no horizontal component. I wanted to see if the students would pick up on the "bad" physics. To my surprise no one picked up on it. After a little discussion as to what should have happened, I showed the clip again and they acted amazed that they didn't notice it the first time. If you can access YouTube, I recommend trying it as a class intro, it seemed to hit home with my class.

Another teacher in the community picked up on this comment and requested the URL for the clip the teacher used. And another teacher was prompted by the comment to reflect on his own students' understanding of constant vertical acceleration and their understanding that the horizontal and vertical components are separate. However, just as with teacher-generated topics, while some moderator-posed questions elicit responses, others do not.

ONLINE LEARNING COMMUNITIES

A great deal of research has already been done on online teacher professional development and online learning communities, showing their positive impact and meaningfulness to teachers.[8] Traditional, face-to-face professional development, while providing teachers with skills and instructional strategies, often includes a mix of theoretical foundations and practical applications. Online communities, however, because they are typically more teacher driven, tend to be more relevant and applicable to teachers' practice.[9] And just-in-time online professional development models, such as the one offered by APTC and ACTC, are often the best fit for teachers' needs because they link theory directly to teachers' daily practice and allow teachers to self-pace.[10] In addition, unlike a traditional professional development workshop, teachers in an online environment can communicate with one another immediately and indefinitely, right when they need strategies, feedback, or encouragement.

The notion of critical mass is essential when assessing the health of an online learning community. Online communities necessarily have both producers (those who post content) and consumers (those who only read posts or lurk). Developing critical mass—the minimum number of active participants needed to be self-sustaining, where new members engage at the same or greater rate as older members depart—is not only an important indicator of the future success of a community, it is also essential if both consumers and producers are to find the community beneficial.[11] Unlike an online course, where teachers and students may be required to post (and can be graded on the frequency, variety, and complexity of their posts), the APTC and ACTC are voluntary online teacher professional development opportunities, similar to Wikipedia in that no one is required to post. The vast majority of Wikipedia users are lurkers and are more likely to consume a great deal from the site while producing very little. However, just as Wikipedia would be far less valuable and engaging to consumers if a critical mass of producers hadn't already posted a wealth of information, the APTC and ACTC platforms require a certain amount of teacher input in order to maintain a healthy community.

THE APTC AND ACTC STUDY

The APTC and ACTC study took place between 2008 and 2013. During that time, the APTC model was implemented in five large, urban districts— one in the Northeast, two in the South, and two in the West. Investigators selected these sites because they used the Active Physics curriculum, and district science leaders were eager to make this online teacher professional development available to their physics teachers. In the fourth year of the study, the principal investigator expanded the availability of APTC and the parallel ACTC to teachers nationwide via open websites available to all Active Physics and Active Chemistry teachers.

It is important to note that the research was an integral component of the development of the APTC and ACTC platforms. The authors of the study explicitly wove the demands of the research into the design of the platforms and the interactions with them that teachers would experience. A variety of data collection tasks, rewards, and incentives accompanied teachers' participation in the research. These tasks aimed to serve the needs of the study as well as provide the participants with intrinsic professional development value. For example, the research team hypothesized that the support provided by the APTC and ACTC platforms would enable teachers to teach more effectively *and* efficiently, and so it asked teachers to track their pacing over the course of several chapter activities using a log created for this purpose. In addition to providing pacing data for the study, this work also intended to give teachers a view of their pacing that would invite individual reflection as well as conversations with others within the community.

RESEARCH FOUNDATION FOR THE APTC MODEL

What makes professional development effective has been explored by researchers for well over thirty years. In order to consider the APTC/ACTC model as an example of high-quality online teacher professional development, it is imperative to ground the features of the model in a research-based definition of successful professional development. Synthesizing the research on this topic, Desimone arrives at a set of five characteristics of professional development that the literature has consistently found to be associated with changes in instruction and student learning.[12] Her findings are consistent with other such syntheses.[13] According to Desimone, effective professional development includes five components:

- The *content focus* of teacher learning may be the most influential feature of professional development. A compilation of evidence in the past decade points to the link between activities that focus on subject matter content and how students learn that content and increases in teacher knowledge and skills, improvements in practice, and (to a more limited extent) increases in student achievement.
- Opportunities for teachers to engage in *active learning* can take a number of forms, including (but not limited to) observing expert teachers or being observed, followed by an opportunity for interactive feedback and discussion; reviewing student work in the topic areas being covered; and leading discussions.
- Important aspects of *coherence* include the extent to which teacher learning is consistent with teachers' knowledge and beliefs and the consistency of school, district, and state reforms and policies with what is taught in professional development.
- The *duration* of professional development, including both the span of time over which the activity is spread (e.g., one day or one semester) and the number of hours spent on the activity, has been the subject of much investigation. Research shows that intellectual and pedagogical change requires professional development activities to be of sufficient duration, although there is no exact "tipping point." Still, studies show support for activities that are spread over a semester (or intense summer institutes with follow-up during the semester) and include twenty hours or more of contact time.
- *Collective participation* can be accomplished through participation of teachers from the same school, grade, or department. Such arrangements set up potential interaction and discourse, which can be a powerful form of teacher learning.

The APTC model was conceived with these components in mind. The three pillars of the APTC platform—Prepare, Share, and Compare—embody the five characteristics of effective professional development.

Both the Prepare and Share windows have a content focus. The content in the discussion forum of the Share window is primarily chosen by the teachers (though it can also be influenced by a moderator). Whether the questions or topics that are introduced get no responses or a flood of responses, an examination of the posts can provide insights into what teachers find important to share, what they are struggling with, and what topics they find least interesting. And since the content is driven by the teachers' interests, it may better meet the content focus component that Desimone describes than the content in the Prepare forum, which is provided by the developers.

Active learning is present in both the Share and Compare forums, allowing for interactive feedback and discussion and a chance to share and review student work related to the content being taught. Teachers drive the discussions based on their interests and need for support, and they have the opportunity to share and reflect on the products of their instruction. Coherence plays a role in the Share forum by providing a place for teachers to discuss the value of (and debate the need for) different components of the curriculum and to discuss the impact of each component on their teaching, their professional knowledge, and their beliefs about instruction. With regard to duration, the goal of APTC was to create a site where teachers were engaged throughout their teaching of the curriculum as they interacted with colleagues in the Share and Compare forums.

Finally, the Share window provides a forum for collective participation, a place where all teachers can participate, and offers an opportunity for deep interaction and discourse if they so choose.

EVOLUTION OF THE MODEL

Throughout the study, investigators collected data to document and understand the nature and extent of teachers' engagement with the APTC and ACTC platforms, as well as the challenges and opportunities that affected their use. One of the main challenges was the pacing of the professional development. The model, as it was used during the study, relied on teachers moving through the curriculum chapters at a relatively synchronized pace so they could share and compare their students' work and think together about how to teach topics more effectively. This common pacing led to the just-in-time nature of the online teacher professional development, allowing teachers to implement new ideas or strategies in real time. However, variations in school schedules (trimester versus block scheduling), unique conditions for schools and teachers (special programs or absences), or teachers' own lesson pacing were some of the ways that the synchronicity was thrown off course and that the dynamic, on-demand nature of the forum discussions waned. As one teacher commented, "I did not like the asynchronous discussion format. Many had completed the lessons before I had even started them." It was not that the teachers found the discussion forums unhelpful but, rather, that there were not enough teachers teaching the same activity at the same time to make the discussions as valuable as they could have been.

Presenting a second challenge was the small number of teachers posting new content; at any given time the total number of teachers using APTC/ACTC was never more than 100, and often not more than 10 or 20. As noted earlier, this is a perpetual challenge with online communities that do not require participants to do anything other than lurk. For the APTC and ACTC sites to be sustained, however, they need a critical mass of people contributing substantive content and comments in the Share and Compare forums. As one teacher noted, "The population seemed so small. Even though we introduced ourselves, we never made connections. It would have been nice to have the same relationship with the community as I do with science teachers in my school. I wanted to write more, but I didn't want to overwhelm the conversation."

At the same time, the Prepare windows, the most frequently visited and used of both the APTC and ACTC platforms, offered teachers easy access to materials and resources that they valued. A common view among novice teachers or teachers newly assigned to teach physics was that the platforms provided access to the supports they needed to teach a subject for which they felt underprepared.

> I would say it was awesome to have the extra resources. I used these resources frequently when planning my lessons. It was also nice having additional background info considering I am a bio major and have forgotten most of my college physics.
>
> ...
>
> It was good to see what others are doing with the material and seeing that it wasn't just me when things didn't go right or seeing that students all over were struggling with concepts and not just my students.

The APTC and ACTC platforms also offered an opportunity to teachers who were isolated in their buildings because they were the only physics or chemistry teachers in their schools, connecting them to others who were using the same curricula, and providing an opportunity to interact that might not otherwise exist.

Part of the model's evolution can be linked to these findings. With only a few chapters included on the website (which is all that the initial funding could support), it is no surprise that pacing and critical mass have become an issue. The intent was always to provide all the components for each chapter of the curricula, and, in fact, the publisher of Active Physics and Active Chemistry has launched a national site that is now available to teachers around the country who use these curricula. The platforms now contain the Prepare, Share, and Compare windows for every chapter in the curricula. As for the second concern, without a critical mass of participants, the discussion forums would likely remain underutilized. Both the complete curricula and the larger pool of teachers should make a significant difference in the use of the Share and Compare discussion forums and provide a community of users to teachers working in rural or otherwise isolated conditions.

CONCLUSION

The APTC and ACTC platforms have evolved since their creation. The initial model developed for the study was launched on a small scale, with only specific districts having access to the platforms and only a few chapters of content available. Findings from an analysis of teacher data indicate that teachers find the Prepare window to be the most useful. This speaks to the issue of critical mass and the lack of participation in the Share and Compare forums. The question remains as to what the minimum number of participants and the ideal ratio of producers to consumers are for this particular online environment to be considered a healthy, living entity. Other important questions for future research stem from this study, for example:

- How does one measure the success of an online community? Is it the number of posts? The number of producers? The number of consumers?
- For which teachers is the APTC/ACTC site most valuable—novice or experienced?
- Should a district, when first implementing a new curriculum, require professional development and make participation in the online teacher community for that curriculum a requirement?
- How can teachers be encouraged to participate, share, and contribute to the vitality of the community?

Finally, the issues of scalability and sustainability are entwined, and, in this case, scaling the APTC and ACTC platforms will be done without the additional tools that were driven by the research. There are no moderators to facilitate discussion, nor are the logs in use. The pre-quizzes are still available on the site for teachers to use as they wish; however, there is no requirement that they be used or shared with others. Examining the model's use on the publisher's website will therefore produce new insights about the conditions necessary for the success of online communities.

CHAPTER 7

Taking Print to Digital
An Electronic Teacher Guide

JACQUELINE S. MILLER AND KATHERINE F. PAGET

A great deal of educational research has focused on investigating the resources and conditions that lead to an effective, rigorous science education that can meet the needs of all students. Based on this research, curriculum developers have designed many instructional materials that promote student engagement, motivation, and deep learning, and researchers have identified instructional strategies that optimize student learning. Most recently, multi-disciplinary teams have explored new educational technologies that provide learning and teaching opportunities not possible in print formats.[1]

This work in science education reform, while very wide ranging, shares a common commitment to four elements of effective science instruction that also inform the project described in this chapter: coherent instructional materials, student exploration, appropriate assessments, and teacher practice.

- *Coherent instructional materials* present concepts in a logical progression that build on prior understandings and connect to big ideas of the discipline. A coherent curriculum will also provide teachers with opportunities to customize and modify the instructional materials for a wide range of student learning styles and needs.[2]
- *Student exploration* ensures that students learn as scientists learn: by exploring real-world questions, engaging in guided investigations and design challenges, participating in discourse, and forming evidence-based conclusions. Student exploration also provides opportunities to develop

skills such as collaboration, critical and creative thinking, effective communication, and information and media literacy—skills students will need throughout their lifetimes.[3]

- *Appropriate assessments* reflect the pedagogical approach of instruction and provide both formative and summative analyses of student achievement of the learning goals. Frequent formative assessments can give insight into students' understanding of the materials, helping teachers make midcourse adjustments to their teaching.[4]

- *Teacher practice* is important. Teacher materials should include tools that enable the teacher to implement the curriculum in keeping with the intentions of the developers while also allowing them to modify the materials to reflect the needs of their students. The materials should also be educative; that is, they should provide opportunities for enhancing teachers' pedagogical content knowledge and moving them toward a more ambitious practice.[5]

Over the last two decades, educational technologies have had an impact in all of these areas. Students now read their textbooks as e-books on computers, tablets, and even cell phones. They augment their reading with simulations and visuals and communicate electronically about assignments from a distance. Digital tools help teachers manage their classrooms; communicate with students and parents; enhance learning with videos, simulations, and other multimedia accoutrements; and assess student learning. Unfortunately, despite the vast array of digital resources available, the full potential of these tools is not being realized in instructional materials, assessment, or teacher support materials.[6]

In its 2008 report on cyberlearning, a task force commissioned by the National Science Foundation (NSF) called for proof-of-concept studies to strengthen proven methods of learning and improve learning by creating new learning environments.[7] Two recommended areas of research were (a) the identification of tools that could facilitate the adaptation of materials to different learning settings and (b) support for teachers seeking to make a transition to cyberlearning in the classroom.

In 2009 the team began work on the Electronic Teacher Guide (eTG) Project with the goal of determining whether a print guide for an inquiry-based, educative biology curriculum could be effectively redesigned as a cybertool. The project was funded by a grant from NSF to the Education Development Center, Inc., under the direction of Jacqueline S. Miller and William J. Tally, co–principal investigators. This chapter reports the results of that project, including a description of the developed Electronic Teacher Guide, some findings from field tests in two public high schools, and a report on feedback from a teacher review panel.

THE ELECTRONIC TEACHER GUIDE PROJECT

The goal of developing digital version of a print teacher guide was prompted by the recognition that even the best of guides are of no use if the teachers do not use them. Unfortunately, research shows that the use of teacher guides is often random and occasional; many end up buried, still in their shrink wrap, at the bottom of the teacher's desk drawer. While the reasons teachers fail to avail themselves of this resource are not totally clear, they may involve the fact that teacher guides, especially those developed for educative curricula, tend to be large, dense, and separate from the student materials, making them unwieldy, difficult to navigate, and time consuming to use. Most teachers have neither the time nor inclination to read extensive collateral materials no matter how potentially useful or well written.[8] Teachers also need different levels of support depending on their backgrounds and teaching experience, but the linearity and equal weighting of the support materials in print formats provide little choice or guidance in their appropriate use. The eTG Project wondered whether a digital version of a teacher guide would be of greater use to teachers.

The work on the eTG Project was guided by the belief that successful student learning outcomes depend on the use of inquiry-based educative curricula and on teachers who use these curricula as intended. Educative curricula support both student learning and teacher learning. As they implement these curricula, teachers develop more general pedagogical knowledge that can be applied to any teaching situation.[9] Educative curricula, when used as intended, can effect deep-seated change in instructional practice. Unfortunately, the educative component of many inquiry-based curricula has typically been supported by exactly the kind of hefty print teacher guides that teachers tend not to use.

But these teacher guides are powerful resources, carefully designed and exhaustively resourced to facilitate implementation of the curricula, deepen student understanding, build scientific skills, support teacher learning, encourage new instructional strategies, and accommodate curriculum modifications while remaining faithful to the conceptual structure and pedagogy of the developers. Because it was clear that the print format was the obstacle to teachers in using these guides, the eTG Project wanted to know whether a digital format would encourage greater use. Digital affordances can overcome many of the difficulties inherent in a print teacher guide by making the support materials and educative resources easier to use and readily accessible at the point of use, whether during planning or teaching. Digital features can enable mindful modification of the student materials while ensuring that the enacted curriculum reflects the intended curriculum. A digital format can put less text on a page by using different interfaces and modes, allowing teachers to choose how much they want to read, when they want to read, and how deeply they want to delve. Digitized materials can also increase options for content presentation by using different media, such as videos, charts, animations, and graphics, which can help reduce the cognitive load that text often presents and can appeal to different learning styles.

Based on this thinking, and with funding from NSF, the eTG Project undertook to redesign the print guide for the genetics unit of Foundation Science: Biology, an inquiry-based high school science curriculum, to serve as an exemplar of a cybertool that could help transform science teaching and learning. The tasks of the project included developing an interactive, web-based electronic teacher guide; testing the guide for usability in classroom implementation; providing access to rich multimedia science content and best teaching practice support; and determining which features teachers found most useful for curriculum planning, teaching, and reflection.

The project sparked many collaborative interactions among curriculum developers, technology designers, software developers, researchers, teachers, students, and evaluators. It is hoped that the eTG prototype will now serve as a model for science curriculum developers and publishers in supporting teachers' move into the digital classroom.

DESIGN APPROACHES

The primary goal of the eTG, as with any print teacher guide, is to support the implementation of the curriculum with fidelity to the author's intentions. To transform the existing print materials into a useful digital resource, the project team identified the components of a robust teacher guide that could be enhanced through interactivity. These components included an overview of the scope and sequence of instruction, explicit pedagogical guidance, teacher planning tools, supports for content knowledge, and tools for reflecting on teacher practice.

To support the educative aspects of the curriculum, the team focused on three areas of teacher learning: conducting productive discussions in the classroom, using formative assessments to monitor student understanding, and understanding the content structure of the curriculum. The team then specified the characteristics and features of an electronic guide that could address the challenges presented by print guides while optimizing a digital environment to support implementation and enhance teacher practice.

Characteristics of the eTG

The team determined that an effective electronic teacher guide would have three characteristics.

First, the eTG would integrate digital tools that make optimal use of digital technology. For example, instead of recapitulating print design by posting PDFs that require sustained, linear reading, the eTG would accommodate the way users actually read on screens, by searching, scanning, and following hyperlinks. The eTG would be dynamic, not static, using selected affordances of the digital environment such as hyperlinks, multimedia resources, responsive interfaces, editable materials, and personalized accounts. The eTG would also manage cognitive load by replacing a clutter of margin notes, boxes, and callouts—a print legacy—with more screen-friendly user-controlled displays.

Second, the eTG would reflect different modes of a teachers' work life, such as planning, teaching, and reflection. For example, respecting the temporal rhythms of teachers' professional lives, the eTG would provide materials teachers could use for just-in-time support and over an extended period of time. It would provide simple visual overviews of the instructional arc of key segments of the curriculum and also provide editing tools to help teachers customize curriculum as they desire. Because the chosen curriculum is both inquiry based and educative, the eTG would also include tools to help teachers make mindful modifications to their teaching practice and reflect on the outcomes of the resulting teaching.

Third, the eTG would accommodate different levels of interaction with the materials by differentiating support along several dimensions, including domain, grade level, pedagogical approach, and instructional model. It would also take into consideration three types of usability: software usability (human/computer interaction), classroom usability (instructional utility), and professional usability (teacher experience).

Features of the eTG

With these characteristics in mind, the project team built the eTG around six major features (see table 7.1).

The main menu and the navigation bar. These provide navigation that reinforces the instructional sequence while helping the teacher find student content and teaching supports in the learning experience (chapter equivalent) and in the planning, teaching, and reflecting tools. A persistent menu facilitates navigation through the curriculum by recapitulating the structure of the learning experience and providing concise information about the teaching and learning tasks through rollover "tool tips."

The eBook. This is an integrated, HTML version of the print versions of the teacher guide and student book. This feature was developed to mitigate the cognitive load presented by combining two print texts in a wraparound format (student book surrounded by teacher material); it also mitigates the inconvenience of using two separate texts. Users can toggle between views of the eBook as the integrated document or as the student book only.

My Lesson Planner. This tool is built around an editable slide presentation called the Basic Slide Deck, which presents the intended flow of ideas and activities for each learning experience; as such, the Basic Slide Deck is an instantiation of content coherency. Each slide contains materials for the student, such as questions or instructions for an activity, as well as materials visible only to the teacher, such as science background, teaching strategies, and other supports.

The teacher can modify the slides in the Basic Slide Deck to change the wording or image in the student view or add a new slide containing additional materials from the eBook or Web Resources (see page following). Once the slide deck has been modified, the teacher can save it and export it to PowerPoint.

My Lesson Planner serves two purposes. In the *planning process,* the tool helps teachers think about prominence and sequence of concepts to be presented to ensure coherence from one idea to the next; it also helps them think about the kind of information they would like to keep in front of students as students read, investigate, and discuss. In the *teaching process,* the material on each slide serves as an instructional prompt for students and the teacher, providing, for example, a visual schematic to interpret, a question to discuss, a reminder of emphasis, or a checkpoint to assess.

Web Resources. This collection of vetted images, videos, simulations, and interactives relates to the concepts in each learning experience. Each learning experience includes a hyperlinked concept map that provides an overview of the concepts covered in the learning experience; by clicking on a term, the teacher can obtain resources related to that concept. The teacher can import materials from the Web Resources to the Basic Slide Deck and then export it to PowerPoint for class presentation.

Essential Supports. This collection of multimedia resources supports teachers' learning of such professional skills as facilitating productive classroom discussions, using formative assessments, understanding the content structure of the curriculum, and making mindful modifications to the instructional materials. Links to these resources are placed in the eBook at the point of use, or when the teacher is preparing to teach or reflect on a lesson. Resource links are also collected in the Essential Supports section of the eTG, where they can be used as teacher learning resources over time on an individual basis.

The resources for supporting teachers in conducting productive discussions in the classroom include text describing productive talk in the classroom; a chart of productive talk moves; a video modeling how brainstorming can be used to determine students' prior knowledge, introduce new content, and establish a safe classroom culture for sharing ideas; and a sequence of six videos showing the progression of a productive discussion related to genetically modified foods. A short text and an animation discuss the importance of content sequencing and coherence in student learning. Another short text and three examples demonstrate the use of formative assessments to determine student achievement of learning objectives as they proceed through the learning experience. A third short text describes why a teacher might want to modify the instructional materials and provides examples of mindful modifications, including changing a story; simplifying, augmenting, or substituting an activity; modifying a reading; and adjusting the pathway of a unit.

Taking Stock. This interactive reflection tool helps teachers consider the effectiveness of various components of their teaching and use those reflections to revise and tailor their teaching to meet students' needs. Three instruments, one for each of three learning experiences, are designed to help teachers reflect on their teaching by providing opportunities to assess student progress and engagement.

TABLE 7.1   Features of the eTG

Feature	Components	Function	Supports
Main menu	Unit map Table of contents Index of Essential Supports Taking Stock index	Provides access to learning experiences, Essential Supports, and Taking Stock reflection tools for each learning experience	Implementation
Navigation bar	Learning experience preview Sections of learning experience	Allows navigation through the stages of the learning experience. The bar synchronizes with the eBook and My Lesson Planner as stages of the learning experience load; related slides appear in the slide deck	Implementation
Teaching sequence preview	Graphic timeline of learning experience	Provides an overview of the learning experience with a brief descriptions of each	Implementation
eBook	Teacher guide Student book	Provides an integrated version of the student book and teacher guide; materials from the eBook can be exported to the slide deck	Implementation
My Lesson Planner (Deck Maker)	Slide viewer that is synchronized with the eBook content and navigation Slide presentation for each learning experience with student-facing materials and teacher notes Slide editor that allows for teacher modification of basic presentations and creation of new presentations Preview and export to PowerPoint	Provides a Basic Slide Deck that can be modified and augmented from the eBook and Web Resources	Implementation

Feature	Components	Function	Supports
Web Resources	Clickable concept map of each learning experience Vetted web resources	Allows access to reliable websites related to concepts in each learning experience Web Resources function sorts and sifts vetted resources	Implementation
Essential Supports: Discussion	Brainstorming video Six "Holding a Productive Discussion" videos Productive talk chart Productive talk primer Short text on productive talk	Provides explanations, guidance, and modeling for using discussion in the classroom	Practice
Essential Supports: Formative Assessment	Short text with exemplars for each learning experience	Provides rationale for using formative assessments and examples	Practice
Essential Supports: Curriculum Structure	Short text on content sequencing Animation on content coherence Short text on modifying the curriculum	Provides a rationale and discussion for content sequencing along with a rationale, discussion, and examples of modifications to the curriculum	Practice
Taking Stock tool	Interactive reflection protocol for each learning experience Reflections saved to the user's account	Supports reflection on classroom implementation and progress toward instructional success	Implementation/ Practice

After teaching a lesson or a set of lessons, teachers can use the Taking Stock tool to consider what went well, what didn't go well, whether students are making progress toward meeting the learning objectives, and whether they will make adjustments for teaching the next class or the same curriculum unit the next year. This feature serves as a planning tool, helping teachers modify and customize the curriculum. It also serves as a pedagogical support, helping teachers change their practice through reflection, which can lead to more effective teaching strategies.

USE OF ETG FEATURES IN THE CLASSROOM

To determine how teachers would use the different features of the eTG, the research team piloted the prototype tool in six biology classrooms, studying it in depth in two of those six classrooms. For the pilot tests and case studies, teachers focused primarily on Learning Experience 3, "Of Traits and Proteins: Exploring the Molecular Basis of Traits," from the Foundation Science Biology curriculum. In this learning experience, students consider transgenic plants as an approach to understanding the biochemical basis of traits. Students first brainstorm about what they think they know about genes, traits, and genetically modified organisms (GMOs). They read about potatoes that have been genetically modified to increase their nutritive value and potatoes that have been modified to be pest resistant. Students are then challenged to decide whether the school cafeteria should offer genetically modified French fries and, if so, which kind.

To gain enough information about how organisms are modified so that they can make an informed decision, students carry out an investigation in which they insert a new gene into bacteria and observe a new trait. Following the investigation with bacteria, they read about how plants are genetically modified to obtain desirable traits and about the pros and cons of GMOs. Armed with this information, they decide whether GMO potatoes should be used in the cafeteria and state their position using evidence to defend their decision.

Findings from the two in-depth classroom implementations of the eTG follow. (Since the other four classrooms in which the eTG was piloted yielded primarily formative findings, observations from those sites are not included here.) The research team observed a total of thirteen class sessions and conducted pre/post interviews with both teachers in the classrooms chosen for the in-depth case studies, exploring two questions in particular:

- In what ways and to what extent do features of the eTG prove useful as tools for dynamic curriculum planning and teaching?
- In what ways and to what extent does the eTG show promise as a professional learning environment that can help teachers deepen their practice over time?

The eTG research team addressed the first question in both biology classroom implementations. Since one of the biology teachers taught the same learning experience using the eTG tool in two consecutive academic years, the research team could address the second question in this classroom as well.

Case 1: Ms. J

Ms. J, a ten-year veteran, teaches in a Massachusetts suburban high school. Her students were primarily Caucasian and Asian seniors enrolled in a Biology 2 class. The study of molecular genetics was a prominent aspect of the curriculum; therefore, the unit's bacterial transformation lab served as the focal point for Ms. J's curriculum enactment. The features of the eTG explored were the Basic Slide Deck, Web Resources, and the Essential Supports for productive discussion and for formative assessment. The following data were obtained during observations of six class sessions by a senior researcher and from pre/post teaching interviews.

To emphasize the molecular and cellular bases of developing transgenic organisms, Ms. J added to the Basic Slide Deck of about thirty slides, creating a sixty-item slide presentation replete with information about the lab procedures, the bacteria used to transform plant cells, the concept of totipotency, and processes of bioengineering. Although Ms. J engaged students in various practices of science (e.g., developing questions, arguing from evidence, and obtaining, evaluating, and communicating information), the core science content and the analysis and interpretation of findings took precedence.

Findings. Ms. J created a set of slides from the Basic Slide Deck that reflected her own teaching goals and her goals for the students. These modifications included (1) augmentation of the science content and elaboration of the lab procedures; (2) inclusion of strategies from the Essential Supports (returning to prior understandings and using summative assessment questions for discussion) into her practice; and (3) planning for whole-class, group, and individual work. The resulting slide deck served as an organizer for her students and for herself. Use of the brainstorming session to elucidate prior knowledge and a return to students' initial ideas at the end of the unit were new practices for Ms. J, indicating she had incorporated teaching strategies gleaned from the brainstorming video into her practice. She watched the five videos on productive talk in the classroom but did not have enough class time to use any of the productive talk strategies. If Ms. J were to teach this learning experience again, she might allow more time for discussion.

Case 2: Mr. H

Mr. H is a fourteen-year veteran educator teaching biology in a medium-sized alternative high school in New York City. Most of the students enrolled in his tenth-grade biology class were from minority and immigrant backgrounds; many seemed underprepared for high school science. Two senior researchers observed seven of Mr. H's class sessions and conducted pre/post teaching interviews.

Mr. H viewed the brainstorming video but reported that conducting discussions was something he was skilled at, so he did not spend time looking at the other discussion videos. He found the Taking Stock tool (in hardcopy form during this implementation) very useful and, after going through it activity by activity, he became aware that he may have omitted some important sections of the learning experience and changed others in ways that might have altered the learning outcomes for the students.

Because Mr. H agreed to teach the learning experience for a second time—this time with his ninth-grade biology class, the research team could address the second question, about the ability of the eTG to help teachers deepen their practice over time. A senior researcher gathered data on changes in Mr. H's planning and instruction practices, along with information about improvements in the quality of students' educational experience that may have resulted from Mr. H's use of features of the eTG.

As part of his planning for the second year, Mr. H consulted his eTG Taking Stock reflection notes from the year before. He decided that student confusions about the transformation lab experiment were rooted in three things: (1) his own lack of understanding of the structure of the experiment; (2) the insufficient class time he had devoted to the experiment and to teaching students about it; and (3) students' need for more careful scaffolding—especially through visuals—of the experimental conditions.

To remedy his lack of science content knowledge, Mr. H spent a summer in a genetics lab at Columbia University doing research to help clarify his understanding of the process of inserting a gene into bacteria. He also carefully read the eTG eBook's explanation of the lab and its underlying concepts. Armed with this knowledge, he planned a longer, two-week approach to the learning experience. Instructionally, in year 2, Mr. H devoted more time to the learning experience overall and provided more scaffolding and more opportunities for students to learn the key concepts in the unit. The class spent ten days of classroom time, instead of seven, on the entire learning experience and five days, instead of two and a half, on the experiment itself. Mr. H developed twice as many teaching slides to aid students in understanding the experimental procedure. He had students draw each of the conditions and submit annotations of the drawings for feedback before researching and preparing their final debate on GMOs.

In terms of student outcomes, researchers found improvement in student understanding both in in-class comments and in final work products. In year 1, no students were able to explain the experiment and its structure coherently, but in year 2 students could explain the experiment using their detailed annotated drawings of the conditions. While not always totally accurate, the drawings showed a solid grasp of the structure of the experiment. In addition, final student write-ups in year 2 showed greater integration of the molecular biology of GMOs, as opposed to the focus on social and environmental debates about GMOs that predominated in year 1. In year 1, only 2 of 23 (9%) student posters integrated visual and textual descriptions of the processes by which organisms are modified; in year 2, 13 of 26 (50%) posters or presentations did so.

Findings. The eTG, with its opportunities to reflect on instructional practice and student learning, particularly using the Taking Stock reflection tool, served as a wake-up call for Mr. H, who realized that his practice, already strong in promoting argumentation and debate, fell short on understanding the science content of molecular genetics. His enrollment in a summer course to learn more about the science is high praise for the eTG as a professional learning environment.

EVALUATION OF FEATURES BY THE ONLINE TEACHER REVIEW PANEL

To probe the value of specific eTG features, the lead project researcher designed and moderated an online review panel where, outside of the fray of daily classroom life, teachers could explore and think reflectively about the many features contained in the eTG. The research team investigated three questions:

- To what extent do teachers value the Essential Supports? Did teachers incorporate any of the Essential Supports as modification strategies into their planning? If so, which ones and in what ways?
- To what extent do teachers value the Basic Slide Deck? In what ways do they modify it? Do suburban and urban teachers modify the Basic Slide Deck differently?
- How do teachers value the Web Resources tool?

The review panel met virtually over a four-week period and paid particular attention to the Essential Supports, the Web Resources, and the Preview function as they considered modifying the Basic Slide Deck for teaching the unit on genetically modified organisms in their classrooms.

The twelve high school biology teachers who formed the panel were recruited from a group of thirty who applied from New Jersey and Pennsylvania. The panel included an equal distribution of teachers in urban and suburban districts. In all the urban districts, over 80 percent of students qualified for free or reduced-price lunch. Teachers had between two and eleven years of experience teaching biology in general and molecular genetics in particular. All twelve teachers reported using digital tools in planning their instruction and having a high level of comfort with technology.

The teacher review panel produced four major findings:

- The Essential Supports for productive discussion, formative assessment, and reflection is a useful and highly valuable professional learning tool.
- The Basic Slide Deck, with its pathway through the curriculum and because of the ease with which they could modify it, is a compelling feature.
- Suburban and urban teachers access and evaluate the features in the Basic Slide Deck with similar frequency and in similar fashions but modify their teaching slide decks differently.
- Providing a place where teachers can share the Web Resources they find instructionally valuable is a good "notion" but requires someone to manage it.

The Use of the Essential Supports

Essential Supports were developed to help teachers meet some of the challenges of teaching inquiry-oriented science, and teachers appreciated them.

As one teacher from New Jersey commented, "I would find these resources very helpful in modifying a lesson. It is like having an expert teacher readily at hand without reading the literature. As a relatively young teacher like myself, I can see learning a lot of best practices. I also love that the videos are embedded in the teacher notes on the slide deck. It's great having that resource right there. Overall, I see great potential in the eTG being a resource for teachers interested in reflective teaching."

There was special regard among the panelists for the productive discussion materials, both the set of six videos and the supporting texts. One experienced teacher wrote, "These materials show how to brainstorm; how to get students to expand on their ideas; I have been to workshops where that was the goal but they never showed us how to do it; I thought those little movies were just great." Though most teachers reported that they use discussion routinely in their teaching, many felt they had not yet mastered truly productive discussion in the classroom.

All the teachers also highly valued the formative assessment materials. Several thought formative assessment strategies would be useful beyond the realm of science teaching. One teacher commented, "Any teacher worth their salt can take something in another discipline and modify it for their own."

Teachers commented most extensively on the Taking Stock reflection tool, enthusiastically evaluating it as a useful tool for keeping track of instructional successes and challenges to inform their teaching. Nine of the twelve teachers reported that it would be helpful for planning changes to subsequent implementations and/or could be shared with administrators to anchor teacher evaluation. One teacher noted, "Reflecting on a lesson or unit is key and one of the ways to grow as a teacher. This tool puts the reflection process in a nice neat package that any teacher will find comfortable and easy to use." Another wrote, "I like that you have tried to quantify each aspect of the unit, and you still left space for open-ended responses. I would also like to see my previous years' reflection when I am re-teaching the concept the following year. It would be a friendly reminder of what I would have changed when I was already mentally involved in the unit, right when I need it."

The Use of the Basic Slide Deck

Teachers found the Basic Slide Deck, which laid out a pathway through the curriculum and was easy to modify, a compelling feature of the eTG.

Teachers were enthusiastic about the way that the ordering of the slide deck helped them keep track of the learning sequence, think through their instructional choices, and make modifications geared to their students' needs while staying on track to the end goal. They especially appreciated having digital access to the teacher notes, which they felt made making modifications to the slide deck fast and easy. Many panelists viewed the possibilities for customizing the instructional sequence as the eTG's greatest strength, valuable not only for the novice teacher but for the experienced teacher as well.

One panelist valued the slide deck for "how flexible it is," saying, "You can use it as a PowerPoint, you can add and take things away from it. Of all the teacher tools I have had, this is the most flexible, maybe you can make it higher order, or you can add some things or shift it to a lower-level group." Another summed up the value of the Basic Slide Deck: "It provides a roadmap where the teacher creates a unique learning experience based on the abilities of their students."

Modification of the Basic Slide Deck by Suburban and Urban Teachers

Suburban and urban teachers accessed and evaluated the features in the eTG Basic Slide Deck with similar frequency and in similar fashion, but they modified their teaching slide decks differently.

The teachers in urban schools substituted virtual labs for wet labs, added extensive vocabulary/word banks, and considered appropriateness of lessons for honors or higher-level students. These changes were accompanied by comments about the need for vocabulary building, the difficulties anticipated for students trying to follow the laboratory procedures, and the need for ways to evaluate degrees of excellence.

The teachers in suburban schools tended to modify the real-world challenge presented in the learning experience, elaborate on the focus on genes and traits and human values, add information about isolation and restriction to the transformation lab, and make the experimental controls more explicit. Their modified slide decks included comments about refocusing the challenge and removing it from the school arena, questions about human values in decision making, explicit descriptions of the experimental design, and ideas about how some of the performance tasks could be used as assessment opportunities.

The Use of Web Resources

Teachers were intrigued by the Web Resources feature but had concerns about its usefulness and sustainability, and they wanted ways to share the resources with colleagues.

Teachers appreciated the web search tool as a resource for augmenting their instructional plans, but they were concerned about keeping the resources current and accessible over time. Teachers also suggested that the ability to share resources would be useful. Although there was much enthusiasm for this idea (over half the teachers endorsed it), several of them realized that a site for pooled resources would require someone to maintain it.

CONCLUSION

The Electronic Teacher Guide was designed as a proof-of-concept digital tool to support implementation of a core curriculum and provide accessible, user-friendly, and effective resources for teacher learning. From the studies described here, it is clear that teachers find certain eTG features extremely useful in planning and teaching their lessons, reflecting on their practice, modifying and customizing the core curriculum, and accessing resources to augment the instructional materials for short-term, just-in-time, and long-term teacher professional learning.

The eTG addresses problems that plague science teaching as it moves further into the era of digital teaching and learning. As the role of textbooks has declined, teachers who are reaching to meet higher curriculum standards are often left to assemble lessons on their own using the wide variety of resources on the Internet. Unfortunately, while many engaging resources can be found online, cobbled-together lessons often result in a loss of conceptual coherence. Teachers may be engaging students' interest and imparting lesson-level knowledge, but they may be doing little to build cumulative conceptual connections that result in deeper learning.

To foster true conceptual understanding, teachers need to guide students through carefully structured and tested sequences of concepts that are connected to each other and to the big ideas of a discipline, which are most often provided in inquiry-based educative curricula. Because no one curriculum is appropriate or effective for every classroom, teachers need tools to help them adapt and modify their curricula to the needs of their students. As professionals, teachers also need opportunities to continually grow and enhance their practice over time. It would be of great interest to follow up on the findings of the case study of Mr. H with other teachers to determine how use of the eTG over time can impact teacher practice.

The eTG is not an authoring system, which means it probably cannot be applied directly to other curricula because most teachers would not have the programming skills required to create the necessary software. Given the demonstrated value of the proof-of-concept, an important next step would be to identify another platform that could incorporate the most effective and useful features of the eTG while functioning as an authoring system for other instructional materials.

CHAPTER 8

The Project-Based Inquiry Science Cyberlearning Professional Development System

BARBARA ZAHM AND RUTA DEMERY

> After too many experiences with educational innovations emerging from NSF becoming unusable after a few years, when the original developers have lost funding or moved on to other projects, teachers have become reluctant to implement these innovations . . . Practical sustainability requires not only making materials available to all, but also paying attention to continued training and development, promotion, and business models.
>
> —C. L. Borgman et al., *A 21st Century Agenda for the National Science Foundation* (2008)

For more than forty years, the National Science Foundation (NSF) has funded the development of innovative, research-based, K–12 curricula that provide students with access to fundamental and emerging concepts and processes in the science, technology, engineering, and mathematics (STEM) disciplines. Despite these significant financial investments, few of the materials developed have achieved widespread use in K–12 classrooms.[1] As the preeminent publisher of NSF-funded curricula, It's About Time (IAT) has eighteen-plus years' experience in publishing, disseminating, and supporting the implementation of research-based STEM curricula in school districts across the country. These curricula reflect the latest research in learning and cognitive science and often incorporate instructional models that require teachers to examine, rethink, and change many of their classroom practices. IAT has observed that one of the greatest obstacles to successful and sustainable implementations is providing the comprehensive, timely, and ongoing professional development that teachers need in order to change instructional practices to align with the pedagogical and learning theories associated with innovative research-based curricula. Consequently, when considering whether to adopt research-based curricula, a key factor in school or district decision making is an assessment of its ability or capacity to provide teachers with the necessary professional development and ongoing support. Districts are concerned about the "practical sustainability" of the curricula within their context.[2] If innovative instructional materials are to be used on a national scale, then new scalable, affordable, flexible, and effective models for ongoing teacher professional development are needed.

For the past eighteen years, IAT, working in conjunction with curricula developers, has been supporting district adoptions with workshop-based, face-to-face, comprehensive professional development for each curriculum it publishes and disseminates. Through this wide-ranging implementation support experience, IAT has come to understand that the significant logistical and organizational barriers within traditional professional development models fall into the following three categories: scalability, affordability, and flexibility.

When an innovative research-based curriculum program is adopted in multiple districts and schools, each needing support and professional development at the same time, the logistics for providing the professional development become complex. There is usually a short supply of experienced workshop leaders with the expertise in both a specific program and the pedagogy being adopted. Therefore staffing and delivery of effective workshops at scale becomes difficult.

Also, the workshop-based, face-to-face professional development needed to launch and then sustain an implementation is expensive. Many school budgets cannot afford to support that level of professional development over the several years necessary for a successful and sustainable implementation. Similarly, often workshop-based professional development is offered only during the first year of adoption and not throughout the five-to-seven-year implementation cycle. This means that teachers hired or transferred after the initial implementation phases are neglected. Just-in-time, demand-driven models are needed that provide teachers flexible access to professional learning resources when they need them through a variety of media-rich experiences. Additionally, teachers need varying types of professional development, depending on their knowledge and teaching experience in new classroom management skills, content knowledge, and understanding of new instructional models with new pedagogical methodologies.

THE PROJECT-BASED INQUIRY SCIENCE CYBERLEARNING PROFESSIONAL DEVELOPMENT SYSTEM

In 2011, NSF funded the project Overcoming Barriers to Implementing, Scaling, and Sustaining Innovative Curricula Using a Cyberlearning Professional Development Model. The project's goals were to design, develop, and test a cyberlearning professional development model that could be readily and inexpensively distributed to districts implementing the NSF-funded Project-Based Inquiry Science (PBIS), a middle school science curriculum, in multiple districts simultaneously, thus creating the conditions for large-scale national distribution. The IAT development team proposed that such a cyberlearning professional development system would help to overcome residual teacher resistance to adopting and using reform-based curriculum programs, as well as supporting and sustaining districts' implementation efforts. The team also anticipated that the models, technologies, and know-how developed through this design/development project would be applicable to a broad spectrum of innovative, reform-based curricula.

The IAT team decided to use Project-Based Inquiry Science as the exemplary curriculum in the development of the CyberPD model. This curriculum was chosen in part because of the educative nature of the teacher materials that had already been developed in print form. Educative materials help to promote teacher learning and increase teacher knowledge of instructional decision making. Such a focus distinguishes educative curriculum materials from typical teacher guides that include supports for teaching strategies but not for teacher learning.[3] Also, the student books were written in a way that embedded teacher prompts into the instructional events for the student. The team determined that the CyberPD system could be used to further highlight this design feature.

PBIS is a comprehensive, three-year middle school (grades 6–8) science curriculum comprised of thirteen units, which, in combination, reflect the science content standards identified as the "Disciplinary Core Ideas" in *A Framework for K–12 Science Education* as well as the standards of individual states and districts.[4] In PBIS, these content standards are coherently integrated with the "Science and Engineering Practices" outlined in the Framework, along with its "Crosscutting Concepts," identified as connections that bridge disciplinary boundaries and unite core ideas throughout the fields of science and engineering.[5]

The units originated from three separate research teams, supported by the NSF, at three institutions: Georgia Technical University, headed by Janet L. Kolodner; Northwestern University, headed by Daniel Edelson and Brian Reiser; and the University of Michigan, headed by Joseph Krajcik and Ron Marx. The integration and merging of these projects into a cohesive and comprehensive three-year curriculum was also supported by NSF funding; and in 2005 the developers began working with IAT to bring the curriculum to publication. It became available to school districts during the 2009–2010 academic year, with approximately fifty schools from around the country adopting it; since then, several hundred other schools and districts have come on board.

The four crucial key pedagogical elements used to design the PBIS curriculum are grounded in the cognitive sciences and are consistent with what is known about how students learn science.[6] These pedagogical elements include driving questions, learning by design, sustained inquiry, and engaging in scientific reasoning and practices. These are not separate but are synergistic and common across all thirteen units and facilitate science learning.

In PBIS, students take part in project-based, scientific inquiry framed around *driving questions* (called "big questions" in the curriculum) or big challenges provided at the beginning of each unit. These guide instruction and serve to organize student investigations. As students pursue answers to the big questions or address the big challenges, they conduct investigations, collect data, weigh evidence, write explanations, and discuss and present findings. An average unit takes approximately six weeks to complete. An example of a driving question from the unit "Living Together" is, "How does water quality affect the ecology of a community?" and an example of a big challenge from the unit "Vehicles in Motion" is to "design and build a vehicle that will go straight, far, and fast, and carry a load."

Learning by design engages students in the practices that approximate what engineers and scientists do. By incorporating iteration into the learning cycle, learners have multiple opportunities to revise their thinking and try out new designs. This process leads learners to greater facility with transferring concepts to new situations, a key goal for science learning and an indicator of deep, rather than superficial, understanding.[7] For example, in the unit "Digging Deeper," students construct several iterations using a stream table and soil as a model for an erosion-control solution for a basketball court.

Sustained inquiry, pursued over time, enables students to experience a range of phenomena as they acquire and deepen understanding by integrating new information with prior knowledge and by applying their new knowledge as they engage in different investigations.[8] In PBIS, each inquiry is framed around a specific topic that involves multiple, conceptually rich investigations. For example, in the unit "Weather Watch," students consider the question "Where does rain come from?" by first adding labels to a diagram to describe what they think they know about the water cycle and then observing a physical model of the water cycle using a plastic container and a lamp. Next, they consider the role of solar energy in the water cycle by discussing what happens to a puddle on a sunny day, and then they read about what scientists know about the water cycle. They complete this series of explorations by writing an explanation of how the sun's energy causes precipitation. After sharing their explanations with their classmates, they have an opportunity to revise their explanations.

Engaging in scientific reasoning and practices, particularly the ability to formulate a scientific explanation of a phenomenon, is fundamental to science learning.[9] In PBIS, students design experiments, collect and analyze data, and report their results. They learn to construct arguments and explanations through weighing evidence, interpreting results, and evaluating claims.[10] The Project Board feature helps students generate their own questions and track their progress by answering questions such as: What do we think we know? What do we need to investigate? What are we learning? What is our evidence? What does this mean for the big question or challenge?

PROFESSIONAL DEVELOPMENT FOUNDATIONS

Inquiry models can improve student learning and lower achievement gaps.[11] However, for these learning gains to be realized, inquiry models must be implemented with "medium to high" fidelity.[12] Teachers must understand and reliably implement the critical elements of the instructional model, which often requires them to make fundamental changes in the way they facilitate student learning in the classroom.[13] Implementing student-centered learning models, such as the one embodied in PBIS, requires skills and resources that are very different from those required by more traditional, teacher-centered approaches. Teachers encounter difficulties in all aspects of instruction—planning, implementing, and assessing—and have difficulty transitioning students into the more active roles of the learning process and struggle with formative and authentic methods of assessing student learning.[14]

Therefore, professional development and other forms of teacher support are critical for teachers in their successful implementation of research-based inquiry curricula such as PBIS. Understanding this, the development team created CyberPD support for the PBIS curriculum using, as its base, the existing print educative teacher's resource materials and face-to-face professional development workshops.

Educative Teacher's Resource Materials

Initially to help teachers implement the program with integrity, the PBIS authors wrote the teacher planning guides (TPGs) as an educative resource designed to support teacher learning as teachers use the materials to support student learning.[15] The educative materials developed for PBIS were not just exclusive to the TPGs but were also included in the student edition. In fact, they surround and are embedded within the instructional events designed for students. For example, an important aspect of the PBIS classroom culture is collaborative learning. Students engage in small-group (Conference) and whole-class (Communicate) discussions on an ongoing basis. The student edition provides prompts for when such discussions should take place, what needs to be discussed, what issues need to be resolved, what data need to be shared, and how to productively engage in these discussions.

The amount of content provided in the TPGs is extensive, and in the print format this material often encompasses three to five pages of teacher text for one student page. The print copy of the TPG for a unit is large, heavy, and cumbersome to use in the classroom. Although teachers found the information available to them to be informative and useful, they found the content difficult to locate, and the book itself was hard to manage in the context of the classroom. The feedback was that teachers preferred to use a compact teacher edition in which teacher materials are wrapped around a smaller scale version of the student page, a "wraparound" teacher edition. However, the amount of content that can be provided in a wraparound teacher edition is very restricted, and, as a result, this format is not conducive to the type of educative teacher materials that transitioning to project-based learning requires.

Face-to-Face Professional Development Workshops

Throughout the development and field-testing of PBIS, the developers recognized that extensive professional development would be necessary in order for traditional teachers to shift from a teacher-centered to the student-centered classroom environment needed to successfully implement the program. Working with the curricula research teams, It's About Time developed a face-to-face, workshop-based professional development model to support districts in adopting and implementing project-based, inquiry-oriented curricula. This program reflected prior research recommendations on effective professional development: it was extensive in duration, often up to six to eight days during the school year; it engaged teachers in active learning and hands-on practice in the context of the curriculum materials; it focused on teachers' understanding of the underlying research design and key pedagogical elements of the curriculum; and it helped strengthen working relationships among teachers.[16] The primary goal was for teachers to be able to make independent instructional decisions as they implement the curriculum with fidelity.

However, through IAT's extensive implementation support experience, it became apparent that there were significant logistical and organizational barriers with only face-to-face, workshop-oriented professional development models that inhibited the practical sustainability and scaling up of research-based curricular implementations. Too often, this model was not sustained and was employed only during the first year or two of adoption. With adequate professional development and coaching, a leadership team within the district adopting an innovative curriculum could be developed; however, most often even this did not result in long-term sustainability and scale-up. District leadership and teacher turnover create a constantly changing dynamic within school districts that frequently makes these long-term adoption efforts unsustainable.

THE PBIS CYBERPD SYSTEM: A CYBERLEARNING TOOL SUITE

Face-to-face professional development remains critical and should not be discarded. However, to help promote scalability, affordability, and sustainability, the PBIS CyberPD system can respond to teachers' needs in a just-in-time electronic mode as districts implement the program. Thus far, IAT has found that a blended approach with limited face-to-face time in conjunction with the comprehensive CyberPD system can best provide teachers with the appropriate, scalable, and sustainable learning opportunities needed to be successful over several years. This blended approach might include a one-day face-to-face meeting that takes the teachers through a progression similar to the Getting Started course (described later), introducing them to the CyberPD resources and the curriculum. The teachers then have the comfort level required to effectively begin using the CyberPD resources throughout the school year. It also puts a human face to the professional development supports offered online and encourages their use.

The PBIS CyberPD system has its foundations in the previously developed face-to-face workshop model and the educative teacher's materials developed for the curriculum. It is web based and can be accessed by computers, tablets, and smartphones. The comprehensive system has numerous and varied categories of support assets to accomplish its goals. It is designed to support teachers' professional development needs in four domains: preparation, just-in-time, reflection, and learning-community support.

Preparation Support: The Online Getting Started Course

There are several pedagogical, content, and planning assets available in the CyberPD system to help teachers prepare to teach the curriculum including, the Online Getting Started course. The asynchronous online course takes about ten to fifteen hours to complete and is designed in part to simulate the face-to-face Getting Started workshop held for teachers before they begin teaching the curriculum. It introduces teachers to the instructional model and pedagogy of PBIS and the components of the CyberPD website and prepares them to teach the first unit in the year, the Launcher Unit. It includes several assignments and reflection questions that teachers submit to a facilitator.

During the NSF grant-funded development stage of the CyberPD system, the facilitator of the Getting Started course was a member of the IAT development team. However, it is anticipated that when the product is distributed commercially, IAT will compensate a master teacher or a member of its staff to facilitate the course as needed. The facilitator must be expert in providing professional development to teachers and understand the curriculum pedagogy and content in depth. He or she must be able to respond to teachers' concerns and issues and be able to make appropriate, useful comments to their responses as they answer the probing questions in the course.

Working in conjunction with district incentives, regulations, and personnel, the course can be offered to teachers for professional development or graduate credits. The development team has created additional courses relating to specific units and can offer them throughout the school year for additional associated professional development credits.

The course design encourages the development of online professional learning communities (PLC) for each district implementing the curriculum. At the beginning of the course, all the teachers participating are asked to introduce themselves to others in the course. They are also required to post their responses to several assignments and are encouraged by the facilitator to comment on others' posts.

On the Welcome page of the CyberPD website there are Getting Started materials that are generic to all PBIS units, including: introductory material designed to help teachers begin to understand the instructional model of the program; professional development videos that introduce teachers to the structure and pedagogy of the program; and research papers on the research behind the development of the program and its impact on student learning in studies of classroom use of this project-based learning approach (see figure 8.1).

From the Welcome page teachers can select the unit that they will be teaching, which takes them to the unit's home page, where they can find several links and drop-down menus with documents to help them plan (see figure 8.2). For example, there is the Unit Overview with the Storyline and Science Content, the Pacing and Purpose Guide, and Targeted Concepts, Skills, and Science Practices; materials from the educative TPG; and correlations to the Common Core State Standards and the Framework for K–12 Science Education.

Each unit's Walkthrough and Equipment Set-Up videos are important support materials to help teachers prepare for teaching the unit. In Walkthrough videos, an experienced master PBIS teacher describes in detail the learning experiences and classroom activities that will unfold during each "learning set" (equivalent to a chapter) and section, thus giving new teachers concrete and direct support as they prepare to teach the unit. An average walkthrough for each section is five minutes long. From the analytics, the Walkthrough is the most frequently viewed asset, and the videos have received very positive feedback about their usefulness. Each unit's Equip-

FIGURE 8.1   CyberPD Welcome page

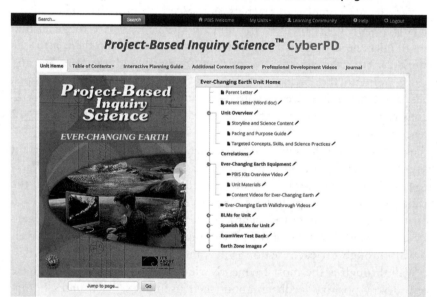

FIGURE 8.2   Preparation materials available on the unit home pages

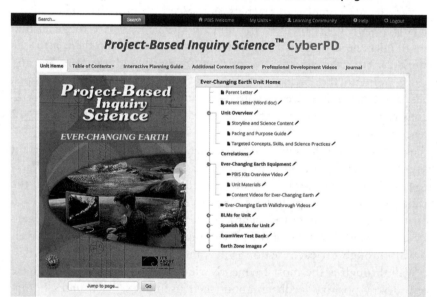

ment Set-Up video averages three minutes in length and illustrates and explains the equipment to be used and what the students are expected to do for each hands-on activity.

The development team members, with assistance from the team at the University Corporation for Atmospheric Research (UCAR), also gathered open educational resources to support the teachers' instruction of the PBIS units. They selected these resources to focus on teacher science content and pedagogical content knowledge and to target concepts students struggle to learn and teachers are challenged to teach. The strategy used to gather these resources was to search existing vetted repositories (DLESE and NSDL) and then search beyond these as needed, following the resource quality guidelines of these digital libraries, emphasizing open source materials. These resources are accessed by clicking on the "Additional Content Support" button.

User feedback identified early on a need to help teachers navigate the assets on the CyberPD site and pace their use of the PBIS units. The development team created an Interactive Planning Guide for each unit, which teachers can download and personalize for their own use and for each class they teach, adjusting dates and times to suit their timetable. The resources mentioned in the Interactive Planning Guides are also hyperlinked, so that teachers have yet another way to access assets such as a video or a blackline master directly from the guide. In this way, in addition to preparation support, the Interactive Planning Guides also provide just-in-time support.

Just-in-Time Support

Electronic just-in-time support provides student-page support assets that teachers can access anytime and anywhere as needed before or during their actual teaching experience. Unlike traditional print materials, the electronic format permits teachers instant access to multimedia assets, such as videos, URLs for additional teacher resources, extensive correlations, and the professional learning community on any electronic device, including smartphones, tablets, and computers. For example, a teacher may wish to listen to the audio portion of a Walkthrough video in the car on the way to school in the morning.

The CyberPD system enhances and extends the technique of a traditional wraparound teacher edition page to a digital format. In print, the amount of content that can be provided is severely restricted by the limited space that is available around the student page. In the digital format, all the educative material needed can be placed directly beside the corresponding student page without any space restrictions. Whether on a computer, a tablet, or a smartphone, teachers have all the material they need to prepare for or teach a lesson at their fingertips. They do not need to rely on flipping through a bulky TPG that needs to be transported by the teacher.

Reflection

An important and powerful professional development tool in the CyberPD system is the journaling feature. This private, electronic journal provides teachers with an opportunity to take and save notes on their successes and struggles in the classroom and gives them a place to keep teaching ideas so they can apply their new understandings to future lesson plans. A shadowed pencil icon indicates that they may add a journal entry at a given point. They can access their journal entry from the actual page or from the "Journal" button at the top of the screen. Teachers also have the ability to save their journal notes as a Word document so that they can print their entries or save them in a location that is convenient for them.

In conjunction with the journal feature, at the end of each section are Teacher Reflection questions. Teachers are asked probing questions that encourage them to reflect on the section they just completed through a process of self-observation and self-evaluation of their practices, which may lead to changes and improvements in their future teaching. All journal notes are private.

Using feedback from the Teacher Advisory Board, the development team created an additional self-assessment and reflection component as a rubric that teachers as well as administrators can use to evaluate the effectiveness of the CyberPD on the fidelity of their implementation of PBIS. The rubric takes into account not only pedagogical components but also student engagement and behaviors. It has seven components, each with a four-point scale (see table 8.1):

- use of the Project Board
- small-group work and discussion
- whole-class presentations and discussions
- creating explanations and arguing from evidence
- teacher as facilitator
- pacing of classroom experiences and units
- accuracy of content

TABLE 8.1   Implementation rubric for small-group work and discussion

Highly proficient (Ideal)	Proficient	Emerging/Beginning	Needs improvement
Component 2: Small-group work and discussion			
1	2	3	4
• Students work in small groups during hands-on activities. All students have clearly defined roles and participate in the activity. • Students participate in small-group discussions for each group discussion suggested in the student edition. They plan investigations, design solutions, analyze data, reflect, synthesize information, and create explanations. • Groups remain on task with or without the teacher present, and all group members participate to the best of their abilities.	• Students work in small groups during most hands-on actvities. Some investigations are presented as teacher demonstrations when time or equipment is limited. • Students participate in small-group discussions for most of the group discussions suggested in the student edition. They plan investigations, design solutons, analyze data, reflect, synthesize information, and create explanations in small groups. Some small-group discussions are omitted due to time restraints. • Groups generally remain on task with or without the teacher present, and all group members participate to the best of their abilities.	• Students seldom work in small groups. Students may occasionally participate in a small-group, teacher-directed hands-on activity. • Some small-group discussions take place, but most discussions are teacher led. • Students have difficulty staying on task and working cooperatively without teacher supervision when asked to work in small groups.	• Students have little or no opportunity to engage in small-group activities. No hands-on activities are observed. • No small-group discussions take place, and classroom discussions are teacher led. • Students show no evidence (or have no opportunity to show evidence) of the skills required to engage in cooperative small-group work.

Professional Learning Community

A professional learning community site is set up for each district (averaging twenty teachers per district) in its adoption and implementation of PBIS. The learning community is presently housed on Edmodo.com, a free online social media forum for educators. This PLC allows teachers to communicate and share with each other and with the project team on an ongoing basis. Although their journal entries are private to them, teachers are encouraged to share their reflections and other journal entries with their fellow teachers. A PLC in which teachers share their practices in an ongoing, reflective, collaborative, inclusive, learning-oriented, growth-promoting way is important to successfully implementing and sustaining change.[17]

DEVELOPMENT OF THE PBIS CYBERPD SYSTEM AND RESEARCH DESIGN

The project team developed the PBIS CyberPD system using an iterative participatory design and evaluation strategy. This strategy involved two parallel threads of research feedback to inform the development process: (1) systematically engaging experienced PBIS teacher advisers in the design and formative evaluation of the cyberlearning assets and tools as they were being developed; and (2) pilot- and field-testing with teachers and administrators in districts implementing PBIS.

In order to ascertain if the CyberPD system offers the support needed for teachers to implement the PBIS curriculum with fidelity, thus creating the conditions for large-scale and sustainable implementation, research focused on three areas: formative evaluation to provide feedback to the development team on its processes and outcomes; CyberPD usability, feasibility, and fidelity of implementation; and CyberPD teacher-learning impact that would ultimately affect student impact. The following research questions informed and focused the work:

- *Formative feedback.* Is the project creating and following a well-specified plan to achieve desired outcomes? How are project staff utilizing feedback and making course corrections as necessary to achieve project aims?
- *Feasibility of intervention.* What is the nature and use of the CyberPD system by teachers?
- *Fidelity of implementation.* Is the implemented professional development faithful to developers' intentions and achieving target professional development goals among teachers?

- *Impact on teachers*. Is teacher use of the CyberPD ideas evidenced in the classroom? In particular, what indicators are there of PBIS-aligned classroom practices?

Phase 1 (August 2011–July 2012): Digital Environment and Assets

The print teachers planning guides, written to be an educative resource for teachers, and the face-to-face professional development workshops both reflected prior research recommendations on effective professional development and therefore informed the initial ideas on the development of the PBIS CyberPD system. The development team envisioned that in the planned system, the professional development resources and activities would surround and be embedded within the instructional events designed for students and therefore situate teachers' learning in the classroom, where it is the most effective. The heart of the design would therefore be digital student pages with teacher resources, which opened up from drop-down menus, wrapped around each individual student page. The design would imitate the traditional print wraparound teacher edition but allow for inclusion of all the educative materials and additional resources to support the teachers' learning needs. Also, building on prior research and experience in a professional development video model, Walkthrough videos would feature an experienced master PBIS teacher describing the learning experiences and classroom activities that unfold in the unit, intercut with footage of students enacting each activity in the classroom.

The project team visited numerous websites, both professional development and commercial in nature, to determine the innovative and useful features that could be incorporated into the PBIS CyberPD system. A variety of applications were also examined. Technology options for structures to support the online professional development site were explored and a series of product mockups were designed and shared for consideration.

The IAT development team then developed an alpha prototype of the CyberPD system using formative and iterative development methodology and significant teacher participation. A group of fifteen PBIS users, both teachers and administrators, from eight states comprised the Teacher Advisory Board and informed the development team on teacher learning needs and provided input and feedback on the system, assets, and services being developed. The University of Colorado and UCAR research team organized and conducted response activities with this group, including a series of tasks and whole-group webinars involving feedback on the system, curriculum components, and video-based professional development supports. Edmodo. com was used to support the dissemination of content to be reviewed and for asynchronous discussions.

Phase 2 (August 2012–July 2013): CyberPD v1.0 Populated

WestEd researchers used a formative and iterative development methodology involving significant teacher participation from two research sources to gather feedback on the system and components. They conducted an implementation pilot study in Beaverton, Oregon, with eleven first-time PBIS users, and incorporated the continued feedback from the Teacher Advisory Board. Additional units on the site were populated with additional professional development components. Also, based on feedback from the teachers and the Teacher Advisory Board, the development team created an online Getting Started course to be used by teachers prior to teaching the curriculum. The project changed from providing solely a cyberlearning website to providing a cyberlearning *system* that integrated the use of online courses with the cyberlearning website.

Phase 3 (August 2013–July 2014): CyberPD v2.0 Populated

During this period, more assets and professional development components continued to be developed, as did a formative and iterative development methodology involving significant teacher participation from the two research sources. The WestEd team gathered feedback and data from the four implementation pilot studies (with nineteen first-time PBIS users) in Beaverton, Oregon; Milwaukee, Wisconsin; Franklin, Wisconsin; and New York City, New York. This included surveys, teacher logs, and interviews with teachers and administrators about the system and components, impact on teacher learning and change, and fidelity of the implementation of the PBIS curriculum. They also gathered ongoing feedback on the system from the Teacher Advisory Board.

Phase 4 (August 2014–July 2015): CyberPD v3.0 Populated

A formative and iterative development methodology involving significant teacher participation from the two research sources continued during the project's final year of research. The WestEd team gathered feedback on the system and components from two implementation field test sites in Beaverton, Oregon, and Howard County, Maryland, with forty first-time PBIS users in all three middle school grades. The team also collected data from surveys, teacher logs, and teacher and administrator interviews on the impact the CyberPD system has on teacher learning, teacher change in practice, and fidelity of implementation of the PBIS program. The research team from the University of Colorado and UCAR gathered feedback from the Teacher Advisory Board on the additional components developed during this final year of research. Working with district regulations and personnel, the IAT development team offered the online Getting Started course in both field test sites for teacher professional development credits. This four-phase process using the unique strategy of two parallel threads of formative evaluation is illustrated in figure 8.3.

THE EFFECTIVENESS AND IMPACT OF THE CYBERPD SYSTEM

Did the CyberPD system offer the support needed for teachers to implement the PBIS curriculum with fidelity? Fidelity is rooted in the question, In what ways does the program-in-operation have to match the program-as-designed in order to be considered successful? The research team at WestEd

Figure 8.3   Parallel threads of formative evaluation

Iterative Project Design

	Stage 1	Stage 2	Stage 3	Stage 4
Cyberlearning Tool Suite	Assets	Assets Site v1.0	Assets Site v2.0 Getting Started Course v1.0 Planning Guide v1.0	Assets Site v3.0 Getting Started Course v2.0 Planning Guide v2.0
Teacher Participants	Design Advisors (11)	Design Advisors (10) One Pilot Site (11)	Design Advisors (10) Three Pilot Sites (19)	Design Advisors (10) Two Field Sites (30)
Research Methods	Needs surveys	Scenario-guided design evaluation Implementation study	Scenario-guided design evaluation Implementation studies	Scenario-guided design evaluation Implementation studies

A unique strategy of two parallel threads of formative evaluation was used in the development of the PBIS CyberPD.

collected data through surveys, teacher logs, and interviews with teachers on the degree to which the PBIS practices were used in the classroom as well as on the quality and fidelity of their implementation. In addition, the IAT development team identified seven components in a rubric that can be used to assist in the assessment, or self-assessment, of a teacher's implementation fidelity of the program-as-designed. Additional research is required to evaluate the effectiveness of the rubric in assessing and promoting the fidelity of implementation.

The research teams will continue to analyze data, disseminate study results, and develop recommendations for both the practitioner and research communities on how cyberlearning professional development systems might be used to support and sustain the adoptions of research-based curricula. These analyses and recommendations will contribute to the collective understanding of the conditions for sustaining implementations and for scaling-up. Analysis to date has been very promising and indicates that a cyberlearning professional development system can be used to overcome some of the obstacles to scaling-up.

The project goals were to design and study scalable, affordable, flexible, educative, and effective cyberlearning tools supporting teachers' adoption and implementation of research-based curricula. Demonstrating its utility, the model, technologies, and know-how developed through this design/development project are now also being applied to other innovative, reform-based curricula. It is being used as the platform for the NSF-funded, problem-based Interactive Mathematics Program's cyberlearning professional development system, which, since it's curriculum based, will be part of any offering to districts adopting PBIS.

CONCLUSION

The PBIS CyberPD system is a curriculum-centric, professional development model designed to help teachers implement the research-based Project-Based Inquiry Science program. Project-based learning has the potential to help maintain students' interest in science and engineering by engaging them in experiences that show the relevance of those disciplines to their lives and to the real world. However, project-based learning requires fundamental changes in the way teachers facilitate student learning in the classroom. Ongoing professional development is critical for implementing and sustaining these programs. Teachers must understand and reliably implement the curricula for any learning gains to be realized.

Therefore, it is crucial to determine if these online approaches are meeting the needs of teachers. The evaluation process for the PBIS CyberPD project involved two research teams, working in parallel, to conduct fine- and coarse-grained formative evaluations of the CyberPD system. One research team conducted targeted teacher adviser focus groups while another research team studied pilot- and field-testing of the CyberPD system. The teacher focus groups provided expert advice in a very timely fashion about assets that could be used to populate the system. Suggestions for the improvement to these assets came even before the materials were piloted and then field-tested on a larger scale, thus resulting in the ability to test very refined resources. The development team found this parallel formative evaluation process an innovative and extremely valuable approach.

Results of the field test indicate that the CyberPD system does address necessary levels of change and implementation support while providing additional feedback for improvements. Ongoing analytics of the system are being, and will continue to be, examined to determine further improvements.

PART III

RESOURCES AND STRATEGIES

In the third section of this volume, we consider several different sets of resources, strategies, and considerations that are important for online teacher professional development as the field continues to evolve. It begins with an example of a completely different online professional development model that provides as-needed resources for a wider variety of science teachers: the National Science Teachers Association Learning Center. This section also highlights two of the many factors that designers of online teacher professional development must consider when creating programs: the role of the moderator in online professional learning communities and the issue of accessibility.

These three chapters share insights that are broadly applicable. The first chapter provides examples of strategies for storing and disseminating large volumes of valuable materials. The second chapter provides guidance for moderators on all sites where learning communities are being nurtured. And the third chapter reminds us of the need to create online professional development that is accessible to wide audiences, including preservice and in-service teachers with disabilities.

CHAPTER 9

Blended Professional Learning for Science Educators

The NSTA Learning Center

AL BYERS AND FLAVIO MENDEZ

Blended learning solutions for teachers that effectively integrate online learning with on-site efforts provide access to convenient, immediate, and self-directed learning resources, tools, and discourse opportunities that may not be locally available. When blended learning systems are closely tied to the local curriculum or instructor course outcomes, as well as made part of an ongoing, coherent, and integrated learning design, online learning extends and enhances local face-to-face professional learning efforts and achieves scale at a cost that is affordable and sustainable.

The National Science Teachers Association (NSTA) maintains an online learning center that has more than 170,000 teachers spending many hours completing self-directed on-demand web modules, taking formal online courses with partners, participating in web seminars and virtual conferences, and sharing online digital resource collections and professional insights through moderated discussion forums. The NSTA Learning Center currently has over 90,000 personally uploaded resources, 14,000 teacher-generated public collections, and 60,000 user-generated posts on 5,800-plus topics across our public and private forums. NSTA has formally collaborated with dozens of school districts and more than seventy universities that use its Learning Center as part of their blended learning solution.

Using case studies, this chapter shares challenges, successes, and insights into how NSTA's platform may be configured for the local needs of individuals as well as for entire school districts and institutions of higher education.

STRATEGY FOR EDUCATIONAL IMPROVEMENT

Strengthening teachers' science content knowledge and teaching abilities has been a national priority for decades. Many researchers agree that teachers' effectiveness in the classroom is linked significantly to their knowledge of subject matter and pedagogical content knowledge. A weak command of science subject matter leads teachers to (a) avoid teaching certain topics; (b) select inappropriate instructional strategies that reduce student understanding or conceptualization; (c) pass on erroneous content knowledge and misconceptions to students; and/or (d) focus on isolated facts rather than facilitate a deeper conceptual understanding of the concept or phenomenon.[1]

With two million science teachers in the United States, it is a challenge to increase teacher subject matter knowledge and pedagogical knowledge at a sustainable scale.[2] One effective, scalable way to address this challenge is by using online systems to extend and enhance face-to-face professional learning within a school district. Indeed, the US Department of Education's National Education Technology Plan recommends online learning for teachers, as it affords them immediate access to resources, experts, and colleagues that would otherwise not be available.[3]

Research also demonstrates that multidimensional learning experiences delivered in an integrated fashion improve teacher engagement and learning and show stronger learning outcomes than unidimensional face-to-face learning experiences.[4] Professional learning is most powerful when it is embedded and sustained through the work of communities of practice. Teacher participation in online communities of practice can foster communication, collaboration, and support among teachers and reduce feelings of disconnectedness or isolation.[5] Educators working and learning together in teams—in efforts aligned with and in support of their local curriculum efforts—can build a culture of success that improves school performance and student achievement.

One way that online resources can enhance teacher professional learning is through an infrastructure for blended professional learning programs. Blended professional learning combines on-site, face-to-face experiences with online opportunities that extend and enhance the face-to-face offerings. Recent research has extolled the virtue of such programs over a "one-shot" or one-size-fits-all approach. Blended professional learning should integrate the best of on-site learning with online opportunities that provide immediacy, convenience, self-direction, and collaboration with other colleagues and experts via professional learning communities.[6]

Many institutions, with the best of intentions, provide blended professional learning experiences by purchasing bulk subscriptions that grant access to a digital repository of lesson plans, teacher practice videos, and/or online short courses. Unfortunately, without integrating the on-site and online components, these blended professional learning options are more akin to a bolt-on approach that fails to inculcate a coherent, integrated, and yearlong learning experience. Further, to be effective, learning communities must have skilled facilitators, a variety of collaborative online tools, and stable, user-friendly platforms.[7] Because of such issues, in order for teachers, administrators, and university instructors to effectively facilitate blended professional learning in their environments, they must experience blended professional learning firsthand as part of their own professional growth.

Since 2010, the National Science Teachers Association has created and refined a professional learning platform, the NSTA Learning Center (LC). The NSTA LC is designed to extend and enhance local face-to-face efforts in a blended fashion that is driven both by emerging technological affordances and by the end-user needs of teachers, schools, districts, and universities. Face-to-face professional learning experiences continue online in a blended fashion where moderated discussion can continue as teachers go back to their classrooms and implement what they experienced in the workshop. Samples of student work can also be shared online and discussed. Online learning experiences such as web seminars or virtual conferences that are thematically aligned to the context of local efforts can extend coherence and learning beyond the original face-to-face experience. The goal of the NSTA LC is to enhance the personal learning of educators by providing a suite of tools, resources, and opportunities within a collaborative learning community that supports their long-term growth based on their unique learning needs and preferences.

The initial NSTA LC took the form of a directory of formal, online science courses. NSTA then envisioned a need for just-in-time learning offered at a smaller scale, not making educators wait until the next formal course was offered. This is especially useful when teachers only need a refresher in a particular subject matter area or pedagogical strategy. As a result,

NSTA developed a series of interactive, self-directed teacher web modules called SciPacks, which are bundles of separate Science Objects. For example, the SciPack called "Force and Motion" contains the Science Objects Position and Motion, Newton's 1st Law, Newton's 2nd Law, and Newton's 3rd Law and a Pedagogical Content Knowledge object.[8] The development team created SciPacks using development principles from Wiggins and McTighe's *Understanding by Design* as well as Dick and Carey's instructional systems design models.[9] Design templates based on the 5Es inquiry model were developed to help ensure both consistency across the modules and deeper teacher engagement beyond simply a "click-next" approach. The developers also incorporated varied interactive media and high-touch experiences for the teacher, such as embedded simulations, multiple choice questions, animations, slideshows, hands-on activities, and drag-n-drop interactives.

Initial SciPack development involved collaboration among three higher education institutions as well as initial funding from both the US Department of Education and the Hewlett Foundation. As time progressed, and with funding from the National Science Foundation (NSF), NSTA applied the principle of convergence by creating a single online destination where educators might access and consume all NSTA digital content and learning opportunities.

Similarly, with the adoption of the Framework for K–12 Science Education and the Next Generation Science Standards (NGSS), there is a real need to identify resource exemplars where educators can see, discuss, and share effective lessons and units that weave together the scientific and engineering practices, disciplinary core ideas, and cross-cutting concepts of the NGSS. An online platform that facilitates the creation, sharing, and rating of instructional units against a common set of metrics is needed in the field. NSTA is working toward these ends with the integration of its NGSS@ NSTA Hub, where a cadre of trained curators is evaluating instructional materials that support the NGSS.[10] The NSTA.org hub will integrate the NSTA LC moderated discussion forums and personal library tools, allowing users to create, share, and rate NSTA's entire collection of digital resources, as well as those from across the open network.

AUDIENCE

The NSTA LC has tens of thousands of K–12 teachers, science coaches, professors, and district science teachers engaging in or facilitating a myriad of asynchronous and synchronous learning experiences (see figure 9.1). One does not need to be a member of NSTA to access the 4,200-plus free digital resources, personal diagnostic tools, and the integrated community forums, and a user is considered to an individual who has at least one resource in their personal library.

According to Google Analytics, in 2014 there were between 35,000 and 40,000 unique visitors each month coming to the learning portal. The average number of top-level pages viewed per visit is six, and the average time spent on these pages is over five minutes, with 58 percent of users being returning visitors. Beyond Google Analytics, NSTA's own internal analytics reveal over the same 2014 annual period that:

- 4,583 new collections were added to the 14,868 public collections created and shared by users
- 76,086 users downloaded 13,478 SciPacks and Science Objects to their personal libraries, and to date 1,800 teachers completed SciPacks and Science Objects last year representing approximately 52,650 hours of learning
- 87 ninety-minute web seminars were offered, with 5,125 participants spending 7,689 synchronous hours in attendance
- the NSTA Learning Center hosted three eight-hour virtual conferences with nearly 1,300 participants investing 10,280 contact hours.

These data exclude the additional time users spend in creating and rating collections and in reviewing and contributing posts to the integrated community forums (see figure 9.1).

The audiences that leverage the NSTA LC's digital resources vary based on the goals of the participants. There are two primary user groups. The first group consists of individual K–12 educators, who are further subdivided into NSTA members or nonmembers. The second group consists of in-service teachers who are part of a school district cohort group or preservice or graduate school educators who are part of a university cohort. The district cohorts are managed by the science district administrators, and the university cohorts are managed by science education methods professors.

Individual teachers using the NSTA LC receive a needs-based, on-demand, and self-directed learning experience. Teachers can select digital resources and learning opportunities from a plethora of alternatives, including NSTA Press e-book chapters, NSTA Press e-journal articles, interactive web modules, synchronous or archived web seminars, virtual conferences, podcasts,

FIGURE 9.1 The NSTA Learning Center's breakdown of users and trend lines in growth, 2011–2015

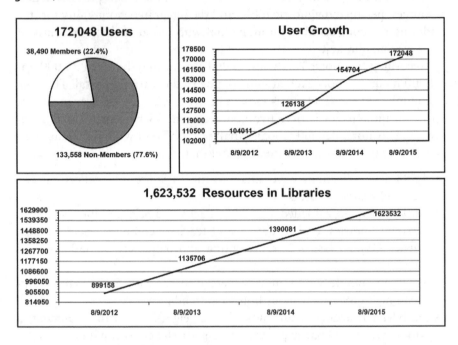

and formal, third-party online courses.[11] These individual resources are also assembled into thematic and grade-banded collections.

A suite of free tools scaffolds the self-directed learner's long-term growth. The Professional Development (PD) Indexer tool helps teachers diagnose, or index, their professional learning needs by formatively assessing their understanding of disciplinary core ideas in science. The formative assessment takes the form of a bank of multiple choice questions (see figure 9.2). These assessments undergo a rigorous development process to ensure validity and reliability.[12] The PD Indexer then recommends free and fee-based digital resources and online learning experiences that teachers may then add to their library or long-term growth plans by using the free Professional Development Plan and Portfolio tool.

Redesigns of the NSTA Learning Center offer NSTA-generated Teacher Learning Journeys (TLJ) that couple aligned resources and experiences into a sequenced package along specific themes with the ability to earn micro-credentials as journeys are completed. Users may also traverse, rate, and share

FIGURE 9.2   Sample assessment item within the PD Indexer and sample
assessment report from the PD Indexer

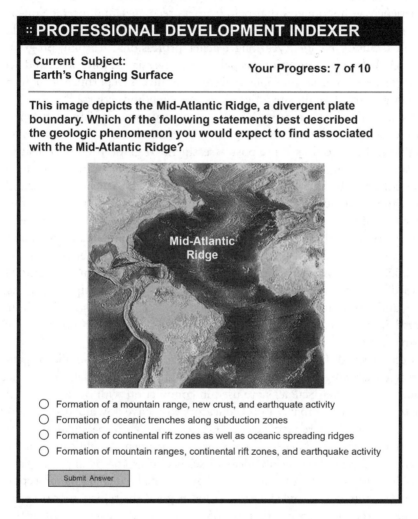

TLJs received by others users or create and share their own personal TLJs
as desired.[13] A pilot study conducted in cooperation with NSTA, NASA,
and Pennsylvania State University found that teachers were highly engaged
when allowed to create learning plans based on their own needs and preferences coupled with badges to validate their completion.[14]

Cohort groups may deploy a fully blended approach. Both online and on-site experiences should be seamlessly integrated for the most coherent experience with strategies that help learners recognize and leverage on-site experiences when online, and vice versa.[15] Many institutions of higher education facilitate blended yearlong teacher professional learning programs through district collaborations as part of a University Mathematics and Science Partnership program sponsored through the US Department of Education or as part of an on-site university science methods course.[16]

Each institution using the NSTA Learning Center configures the platform depending on its needs and goals. For example, many universities use the PD Indexer tool as a pre/post assessment to guide preservice teacher SciPack selection and lesson unit planning and implementation. The initial data collected by the indexer provides a baseline of teacher understanding within a particular science content area. The PD Indexer data can then be reviewed after blended professional learning experiences to help determine learning and growth. SciPacks award a certificate and virtual badge if teachers complete all of the embedded and end-of-chapter quizzes in a module, as well as pass a final assessment. Districts often offer additional rewards and incentives as teachers pass SciPacks, such as stipends, release time, and/or continuing education credits. And some universities have integrated SciPacks as part of the requisites for overall course completion and graduate credit.

Research and third-party evaluations have documented significant gains in teacher learning and self-efficacy across multiple grade levels and science content areas when SciPacks are used in conjunction with on-site efforts.[17] There are now more than 74,000 educators who have downloaded 720,000 SciPacks and their related Science Objects into their personal libraries. In our own studies, NSTA also frequently documents significant gains in teacher understanding of key ideas in science after completing a SciPack. This does not imply that the teacher is now certified to teach this subject but instead documents knowledge acquisition beyond the typical seat time and teacher perception surveys that are often the sole determinants of professional development effectiveness.[18]

NSTA supports preservice teachers leveraging the NSTA Learning Center and its tools and digital resources as an e-textbook. In the fall semester of 2014, more than fifty universities registered to use the NSTA LC to educate their preservice teachers via blended learning solutions.[19] In these instances, science method professors select e-book chapters, e-journal articles, SciPacks, and archived web seminars to create their own e-textbook. They then further customize their e-textbooks by appending their own digital resources as part of the collections. All preservice e-textbook subscriptions include a full NSTA student membership for each student, which also provides each student with his or her own one-year subscription to a NSTA print journal.

During courses, professors often let students self-assess their understanding of particular science concepts via the PD Indexer tool, then assign readings from their NSTA LC collection, and then have students complete selected SciPacks. Many times they incorporate authentic hands-on learning experiences that leverage lesson plan activities from the NSTA LC. Professors also frequently have students create their own digital resource collections to be discussed and shared via an integrated private online community forum as well as in a worldwide public discussion forum network that is linked directly from the course's landing page.

Assignments or other coursework generated by preservice teachers can also be shared among peers in the course (such as samples of K–12 student work during their classroom practicums) using NSTA's digital Professional Development Plan and Portfolio tool. In these instances, preservice student participation is not voluntary, but autonomy is provided (they can choose to make choices within boundaries) in order to qualify for graduate credit as prescribed by their professor.

The mini–case studies that follow provide tangible examples of how the blended models for professional learning are implemented by some science methods professors using the NSTA LC for preservice teachers.

CASE 1: INDIANA UNIVERSITY–PURDUE UNIVERSITY COLUMBUS

Kate Baird is a clinical assistant professor in science education and uses the NSTA Learning Center as part of a course titled Methods of Teaching Natural and Social Science (MTNSS). This experience takes place at Indiana University–Purdue University Columbus, a small, rural, midwestern undergraduate regional campus; the education degree offered is a BS in elementary education. Students enter in cohorts (ten to twenty students) after they have passed PRAXIS I and completed all their general education work. The MTNSS course is focused on supporting inquiry as a way to help K–3 students and teachers make sense of the world around them. *Designing Effective Science Instruction* and the NSTA Learning Center serve as resources.[20]

The big idea for the course is that teachers should make learning about the natural and social sciences inquiry driven, where opportunities for sense making are based on standards linked to child-generated questions. To achieve this outcome, the course must (1) draw from many resources for lesson design with the flexibility necessary to build a student-driven inquiry curriculum; (2) facilitate a deep and readily accessible understanding of content knowledge; (3) enable a clear understanding of preconceptions of children, and (4) empower and inspire teachers to demonstrate life-long professional growth.

Learners engage in three assignments to reach these course goals. First, they pre-assess content knowledge though PD Indexers and then demonstrate growth via a SciPack post-test. Next they demonstrate understanding of known preconceptions through creation of a short instructional movie and field-based interactions. And finally they document professional growth through the NSTA LC teacher portfolio tool. Regarding the PD Indexers, one teacher candidate commented, "The Indexers were very challenging and somewhat aggravating at times due to I couldn't remember any of the answers from high school or didn't know them in general. Taking the Indexers had shown me what things I remembered and what things I need to work on."

After completing this course, teacher candidates express an increase in self-esteem as a result of this set of assignments and referenced growth in useable science content knowledge (table 9.1). They comment on the importance of their growth in both science content and use of technology to support learning. They appreciate not only the opportunity to address specific student needs through creation of instructional videos but what they learn from viewing the videos of their peers. The knowledge that they can "use the NSTA SciPacks within their future lessons to support their instruction" is important to them as well.

Learners who have completed the first two blocks then use the NSTA LC to support their student teaching. They use the hands-on experiences from class in connection with science simulations; the NSTA LC allows the student teachers to customize the existing classroom materials and resources. Comments from many of the teacher candidates mirror the following:

> The information that I learned during the Plate Tectonics SciPack has been truly valuable. It took me 10 hours to complete the SciPack, and I had to pass the final test to earn the certificate. As an educator, gaining this

TABLE 9.1   Examples of preservice teacher growth in science content knowledge

Term	Pretest range	Post-test range	Average % change
Spring 2013	10–54	60–80	22
Fall 2013	10–50	45–90	30
Fall 2014	30–70	58–90	29

deeper understanding about plate tectonics will help me to teach it in a way that is meaningful to my students. It was necessary for me to gain a deeper understanding to allow me to teach this subject with confidence. I look forward to sharing this new knowledge with my students.

...

I plan on using activities that were mentioned in the SciPack as well as some that were discussed in the web seminar so my students have a better understanding of the topics and have fun while learning.

...

I now feel more comfortable teaching students about rocks. Also, taking the SciPack made me realize some of the preconceptions students may have about rocks. Students come into our classrooms not with empty heads, but full of ideas of their own.

Finally, during an end-of-semester whole-class Plus/Delta (a term used by the local school district to indicate positive aspects as a plus and those that should be changed as a delta) for the e-text from NSTA, teacher candidates note that the NSTA LC digital Professional Development Plan and Portfolio tool has helped them begin to conceptualize themselves as professionals who will need to be life-long, self-directed learners. Professional portfolios are now required as part of the local school district's teacher quality process. The teacher candidates say that they will need to review content to prepare for newly added science content on the Indiana Elementary licensure exam (which they will take no sooner than a year after this course) and that the NSTA LC will be a resource to identify areas of weakness and then provide remediation. Additionally, the teacher candidates are looking for content sources for future lessons. The current course focuses on general methods of science instruction with limited sample lessons. The LC will serve as a continuing resource for the candidates during their senior student teaching placements. The teacher candidates are aware of the rate of change in education and value tools from NSTA that help them find, excel at, and retain their jobs. This is especially important as the state moves to adopt new science standards in 2016.

CASE 2: FLORIDA INTERNATIONAL UNIVERSITY

Kathleen Sparrow, George E. O'Brien, and Jennifer Morales from Florida International University use the NSTA Learning Center as an e-text in their elementary science methods course for preservice teacher learning. This learning experience uses a blended approach that includes active learning, online interactive content learning, student-to-student interaction, and application and practice in the field. The content driver for the sixteen-week course is sustainability, which is framed and guided by the nine themes of sustainability literacy.[21] Their overall strategy engages preservice teachers in an integrated environmental and science education approach.[22] Their curriculum and instruction encourages active participation in real-world contexts that provide issues from which concepts and skills can be learned.[23]

Four SciPacks (i.e., Coral Reef Ecosystems, Interdependence of Life, Flow of Matter and Energy in Ecosystems, and Resources and Human Impact) are used for the environmental content in the course. Students choose and complete one of these targeted SciPacks as a central feature of their content resources. They then engage in a study group twice during the semester on their particular SciPack using guided questions from the professor. One focus in each of these SciPacks is the concept of system and a systems approach.[24] As a result, using the PD Indexer tool as a pre/post assessment for the SciPack content, the faculty found that teachers who use the Coral Reef Ecosystems, Interdependence of Life, or Resources and Human Impact SciPacks show highly significant gains in content knowledge over time (<0.001). Effectiveness of the Flow of Matter and Energy in Ecosystems SciPack approaches significance with a $p=.058$ using a paired sample t-test.[25]

According to the research meta-analyses in *How People Learn*, understanding science is more than "knowing."[26] Understanding science means having a deep foundation of factual knowledge, an understanding of facts and ideas in the context of a conceptual framework, an organization of knowledge that allows for retrieval and application, inquiry procedures that help solve new problems, and the ability to transfer knowledge from one context to another.

Following these research findings, one of the projects that the professors have designed is an ongoing study focusing on the concept that ecosystems strive to maintain a balance. Initially, students in the class watch a video of Dr. Seuss's *The Lorax* and are instructed to pay attention to the characters and their relationships with each other.[27] Students take notes in their science journals. After watching the video, they discuss in small groups the characters and the role each plays in the story. The preservice teachers, within their small groups, are then given the challenge to create a concept map depicting the relationships among the characters in the story. The concept cards (pictures of all the characters) are drawn from the NSTA *Science Scope* journal article "Teaching Science Through a Systems Approach," which the students read and can be accessed digitally from the NSTA LC.[28] The posters are displayed, and classmates move from table to table describing the relationships their posters portray.

After this, students watch a video titled "How Wolves Can Alter Rivers" and identify and apply to the science content what they learned about systems.[29] In the subsequent weeks of the semester, many preservice teachers (PSTs) use this concept of balance in an ecosystem to develop preassessment interview questions to ask their field school students to gauge their grade-level knowledge. Based on the interview data analysis, they design a 5E inquiry lesson that they teach to a small group of students and subsequently re-interview to analyze student learning and their own teaching. The design of this teaching, learning, and assessment project responds to the students' alternate conceptions in ways that help them overcome their learning gaps.

The major achievements for the preservice teachers are learning content from an NSTA LC SciPack, subsequently exemplified by a children's story to relate the concepts of balance in a system; designing a 5E lesson to accommodate the students' learning level; and teaching their lesson with an analysis of student learning and their own instruction. In addition to the results from the data analysis of SciPack usage and learning, the PSTs provide the professors with reflection and commentary captured via the NSTA digital Professional Development Plan and Portfolio tool, which documents the impact on PSTs' motivation, interest, science content, and pedagogical content-knowledge learning.

BALANCE OF SCIENCE CONTENT AND PEDAGOGICAL SKILLS

As demonstrated, the NSTA Learning Center is not a professional development model in and of itself but a platform with digital teacher resources, synchronous learning experiences, an integrated community network and recognition system, and a suite of personal diagnostic tools that may be configured for various methods of deployment. Uses include individual just-in-time, just-enough, just-for-me self-directed learning as well as collaborative learning when integrated within a blended model of professional development through a group cohort. The Learning Center makes available NSTA's digital repository of 11,800-plus digital assets and learning opportunities, which grows each month as more e-book chapters, web seminars, lesson plans, and e-journal articles are added.

Professional development is most effective when it not only addresses teachers' beliefs and subject matter knowledge but also increases pedagogical knowledge—that is, knowledge of how students learn and how to conduct instruction.[30] In an effort to provide this balance of content and skills, each SciPack also includes a pedagogical object dedicated to the science content focus of that SciPack. NSTA reviews the literature and identifies for the teacher what science concepts are appropriate to teach by grade level, what the known preconceptions are related to the science concepts addressed, and what promising instructional practices from the literature may facilitate deeper student learning.

NSTA continually develops new digital press titles and online interactive, on-demand learning. Examples include the NSTA e-book on *Hard-to-Teach Biology Concepts*.[31] Another popular NSTA series, *Uncovering Student Ideas in Science*, focuses exclusively on formative assessment and making students think visually in science.[32] In addition, the *Picture-Perfect Science Lessons* series is one that facilitates deeper student learning by coupling picture books and literacy with elementary science lessons and hands-on kits.[33]

WAYS OF ENSURING HIGH QUALITY

NSTA takes a consultative approach when working with a district or university cohort and, prior to deployment, first engages professors and administrators in a series of discussions. The goal of these discussions is to identify the needs and desires of the organization and how professional learning experiences and other resources can be structured to meet those needs. NSTA discusses integration strategies that are drawn from literature recommendations for achieving higher levels of learner engagement across a wide range of learners, enhancing understanding of subject matter knowledge and pedagogical content knowledge, and empowering teachers through school-based, or university collaborative learning.[34] The intent of these strategies is to structure a blended learning environment with the greatest chance of end-user engagement, motivation, and applied learning.

Once a plan is forged and the appropriate resources, tools, and opportunities are identified, NSTA schedules a one-day, on-site face-to-face orientation kickoff. This orientation provides an overview of the NSTA Learning Center platform and can accommodate dozens of teachers, science department chairs, instructional coaches, principals, and science specialists. For smaller cohorts, the orientation can be attended via an interactive web seminar. After orientation, NSTA follows up with additional personalized web seminars, a help desk, and periodic performance reviews with the administrators and professors participating in a given district's locally delivered professional learning experiences.

Learners and administrators can also judge professional learning success using a wide array of tools that provide quantitative and qualitative reports (figure 9.3). These reports are designed to assess professional learning efforts relative to teacher subject matter knowledge acquisition, changes in classroom practice, and teacher contributions back to the district and/or university cohort. Professors and administrators can also track a wealth of information through web-accessible reports displayed on the administrator dashboard. These reports track both individual and group learning using pre/post assessments aligned with the SciPacks. The dashboard displays SciPack final assessment scores and digital reports, the type and number of resources the cohort is uploading and sharing, and their community activity across the entire group, as well as teacher reflections and samples of student work from newly implemented changes in classroom practice.

RESEARCH AND EVALUATION OF NSTA PRODUCTS

Over the last several years, multiple research studies on the effectiveness of SciPacks have been funded by NSF, NASA, the GE Foundation, and the US Department of Education. Past and ongoing research questions include: What components of NSTA self-directed SciPack web modules are most effective? Do SciPacks facilitate teacher knowledge acquisition? How effective is the NSTA platform as part of a blended teacher knowledge acquisition

FIGURE 9.3   Examples of NSTA data reports accessible to administrators and university professors

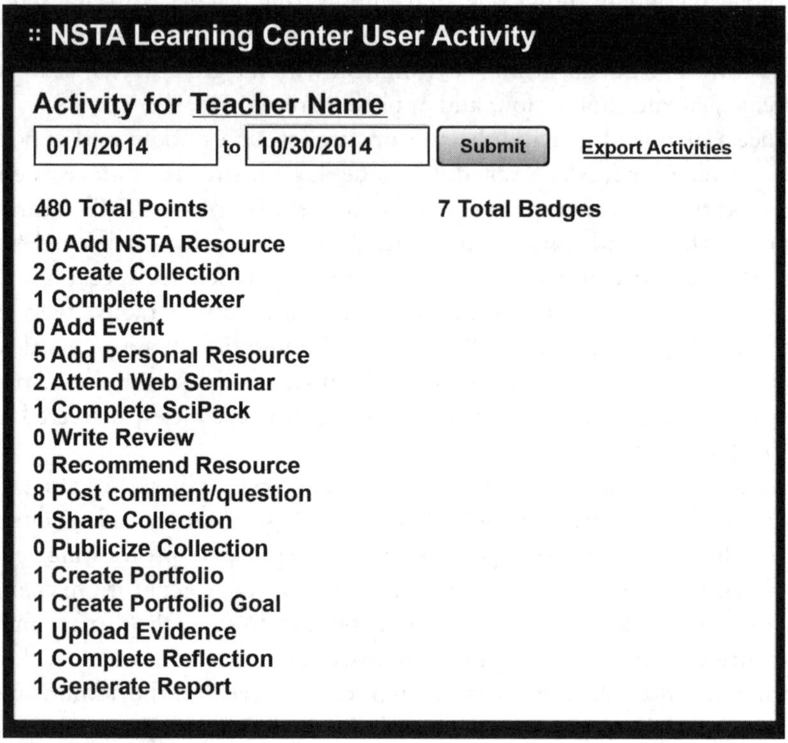

```
:: NSTA Learning Center User Activity

Activity for Teacher Name
┌──────────────┐    ┌──────────────┐      ┌──────────┐
│  01/1/2014   │ to │  10/30/2014  │      │  Submit  │   Export Activities
└──────────────┘    └──────────────┘      └──────────┘

480 Total Points                           7 Total Badges

10 Add NSTA Resource
2 Create Collection
1 Complete Indexer
0 Add Event
5 Add Personal Resource
2 Attend Web Seminar
1 Complete SciPack
0 Write Review
0 Recommend Resource
8 Post comment/question
1 Share Collection
0 Publicize Collection
1 Create Portfolio
1 Create Portfolio Goal
1 Upload Evidence
1 Complete Reflection
1 Generate Report
```

model? What platform affordances facilitate effective online professional learning communities?[35] In studies that evaluated the impact of SciPacks, teachers demonstrated significant gains in subject matter knowledge and self-efficacy across multiple grade levels and subject matter areas.[36]

NSTA diligently works to develop highly interactive content that embeds many levels of engagement and feedback for the teacher learner. This is coupled with the varied levels of social discourse previously described (e.g., discussion forums, live chat, email support, web seminars). To extend on-site experiences, NSTA facilitates both science subject matter and pedagogical content knowledge in online affordances. The findings, which are based on pre/post assessments, independent studies, testimonials, and growth trends, lend credence to this approach.[37]

THE INTENDED MODEL VERSUS THE ENACTED MODEL

NSTA enacted its current blended learning model to (1) increase teachers' autonomy in their own learning; (2) allow time for practice, observation, reflection, and collegial discourse; (3) increase administrator/instructor support, instructional guidance, and recognition of teachers' effort; and (4) provide access to the necessary materials and technology to enact new teaching practices. To achieve these goals and fully enact an integrated blended learning model, NSTA needs to structure its professional learning opportunities after what is espoused in the Framework for K–12 Science Education and the NGSS, as well as to leverage strategies that recognize individuals' valuable investments in their own learning. NSTA needs to develop experiences that help teachers engage students in authentic challenges through hands-on scientific and engineering practices, and to recognize cross-cutting concepts in order to more deeply understand the disciplinary core ideas of science.

Working closely with district administrators and university professors in discussing how the NSTA Learning Center tools, resources, and opportunities may be seamlessly melded into an ongoing, integrated approach to blended learning is critical to the effectiveness of NSTA's model and platform. Its resources need to be organized and structured in such a way that they reflect these strategies of personalized growth and connectedness with others. If these components and a coherent strategy to integrate the online and on-site components do not work toward this end, ultimately, NSTA is doing a disservice to those it is charged with serving.

NSTA is making significant headway in this regard. By employing various "freemium" business models, the NSTA LC can maintain, sustain, and enhance the platform beyond any single finite funding source. Individuals may freely access the portal with over 4,200 resources and do not need to be a member of NSTA. If one is a member, more free content is made available in the portal and member discounts apply for purchases for supports such as books or on-site and virtual conferences.

If the NSTA LC is being deployed via a subscription model to districts, teachers access a large volume of content including the SciPacks at no cost to them, as administrators pay for the subscription. The districts also have secure access to the administrator dashboards to document teacher growth. Similarly, if a university cohort is using the NSTA LC as their e-textbook, a subscription model is also used, where preservice teachers make the purchase for a specific course and the professors gain access to the administrator dashboards to track teacher learning and community activity.

In September 2015, a new NSTA Learning Center was deployed that is responsive to different hardware accessing the portal (e.g., tablets and smartphones) and offers improved connections between those in the open network that have like-minded interests and learning goals. In addition, NSTA has added a recognition system that incorporates micro-credentials and local leaderboards to affirm teachers' investment of their most precious nonrenewable resource—their time. Much of teacher professional development impact is measured by seat time and with little documentation of knowledge gain beyond teacher perception surveys at the end of the experience. NSTA helps teachers diagnose and track their learning through pre- and post-assessments and capture changes in classroom practice through a teacher-generated digital portfolio report sharing reflections of newly acquired pedagogical techniques, samples of student work, and images of classroom enactment. With back-end web dashboards presenting this data in aggregate for a district or university cohort, NSTA also helps administrators and professors advance toward level four of Guskey's five levels of evaluation for professional development.[38]

Other researchers and institutions such as the US Department of Education and NSF are conducting and sponsoring research in this space, seeking the power of various strategies that involve peer-review and promotion, self-reflection, self-direction, collaborative learning, and how these strategies might work in large-scale learning systems and courses.[39] The question about the power of micro-credentials (or badges) is not whether they work to improve formal learning outcomes, but, rather, when they are part of a larger suite of strategies, serving in part as a form of feedback, how might they enhance motivation to learn? As feedback, badges might denote or flag learning, but something else in the system is responsible for the learning. There is a need for more research. One professor from the University of Texas shared:

> I have to admit that I was skeptical about the points/badges system working with my preservice science methods students, but I was *so-o-o-o* wrong! I simply put an announcement on Blackboard praising the top folks to date over the weekend. I didn't even think about the fact that the only man in one class had the overall top points. Several young women announced, "We can't let Terry get away with that!" And so it began . . . The conversation went on for a while. I haven't met with my other class yet, but they too have upped the ante. I don't know what their rea-

son is. I just know that a small group has infected the larger group. They know about their profile page, the leader boards, and the different types of Learning Center activities in a way that will stick with them much better than my overview did.

NSTA's badges cover a wide array of experiences where teachers may earn recognition for, for example, serving on a national committee or advisory board, making contributions to community forums, publishing articles in NSTA journals or book chapters, aggregating and sharing digital resource collections via forums, passing SciPack web modules, or completing learning goals in their personalized professional development plans. While certain badges are intentionally designed to recognize and increase community activity—and research is emerging that supports how this may be employed across various networks and courses—there is also research emerging that examines how technology-enabled badging systems may support and enhance professional learning for teachers.[40] Within NSTA's efforts, we see the potential of the platform and strategies to empower teachers' personal learning goals through a micro-credentialing badge system that seeks to affirm teachers' gains in knowledge, participation in professional learning communities, and change in classroom practice.[41]

The NSTA Learning Center provides a system that begins to address the scale needed on a national level to reach the existing two million in-service teachers of science in the United States and the 50,000 preservice teachers that enter the profession each year. To accomplish this goal, NSTA has developed a platform that enables both personalized just-in-time individual learning and blended models with cohorts across both districts and universities.

CHAPTER 10

The Importance of Moderators

KIM FRUMIN AND CHRIS DEDE

Interest in the important role of moderators in online professional learning communities has emerged from research on the College Board's online Advanced Placement Teacher Community (APTC), as part of the larger National Science Foundation (NSF)–funded longitudinal study of Professional Development for the Redesigned Advanced Placement (PD-RAP) curricula in biology, chemistry, and physics. Advanced Placement (AP) Biology, Chemistry, and Physics curricula and exams were extensively redesigned in 2013, 2014, and 2015, respectively, and these courses now emphasize scientific inquiry and reasoning as well as depth of understanding of big ideas in science, not simply broad content coverage of facts.[1] These are sweeping changes to a long-standing instructional program. In stark contrast to past expectations, hundreds of thousands of AP science students—and more than sixteen thousand teachers—are now expected to succeed on a high-stakes test about the inquiry process, real-world applications of scientific principles, and synthesis of complex content knowledge.

Previously successful teachers will need to make transformational changes in their instructional practice if their students are to continue doing well on the AP tests. Of the many forms of professional development to aid this transformation that the NSF-funded research group has examined thus far, participation in the online APTC has the most positive, direct, and statistically significant association with both teacher practice and student outcomes.[2] Within the PD-RAP study, the specific focus of the team at Harvard aims to understand *how* the online APTC is useful to teachers in responding to the curricular revisions, as compared to more top-down, structured, and instructionally scripted forms of professional development provided by the College Board, and how these APTCs might be made more effective.[3]

The value of an online community lies in its ability to enable the rich and open exchange of ideas, experiences, and resources among its members. Given that getting assistance from other teachers seems to produce positive gains for teachers and for students, understanding what works for teachers supporting each other in an online learning community to help them improve student outcomes is a critical area for research. In particular, successful strategies for online professional support can aid teachers in many fields responding to other impending national large-scale changes in curricula, as well as designers, moderators, and researchers seeking to increase the effectiveness and participation in online professional learning communities.

A review of the scholarly literature highlights the importance of moderators in the effective functioning of online professional learning communities, in part because of the critical role that moderators play as facilitators of community discussions and champions of member engagement. For example, Booth states, "Without the social artistry and guidance of a single leader or a team of leaders, online communities will unlikely reach their full knowledge sharing potential."[4] Therefore, research is under way to investigate the importance of moderators within both the online AP science teacher communities and in other teacher communities related to science learning (e.g., those of the National Science Teachers Association [NSTA]). As part of this focus on the role of moderators, the Harvard research team developed the Moderator Guide to support the APTC moderators in their facilitation.[5]

This chapter shares a literature summary of online teacher learning communities, a brief overview of the Moderator Guide, and empirical data from STEM professional learning communities that support the themes in the Moderator Guide about how moderators are effective. Case study interviews were also used to examine the initial impact of these resources on the participating APTC moderators.

LITERATURE SUMMARY

Wenger, McDermott, and Snyder define an online community as a "group of people who interact, learn together, build relationships, and in the process, develop a sense of belonging and mutual commitment."[6] Barab, MaKinster, and Scheckler further define an online community as "a persistent, sustained social network of individuals who share and develop an overlapping knowledge base, set of beliefs, values, history, and experiences focused on a common practice or mutual enterprise."[7] Specifically, online teacher communities potentially allow educators to learn while they are actively applying new ideas in their own work settings, to provide and receive sustained coaching and feedback, and to cultivate a reflective collaborative professional community.[8]

Web 2.0 tools are proving to be valuable for ongoing teacher professional development and for engagement in professional communities.[9] Researchers have long stressed the importance of participation in a professional community or in communities of practice as a key component in ongoing professional growth.[10] Building connections to other teachers was also a feature in the 2010 National Education Technology Plan, seen as a core part of being a "connected teacher."[11] And in the twenty-first century, a core part of being "connected" means belonging to both a real-world community and a virtual community, one often facilitated by such Web 2.0 tools as Facebook, Twitter, blogs, and wikis.

A common complaint about teaching as a profession is isolation, and a virtual community is one way to overcome physical isolation.[12] Many studies explore the development of teacher collaboration and even team teaching at a distance as a way to help teachers overcome loneliness and isolation or as a means for sharing materials, perspectives, and practices.[13] Teachers who participate in social networks such as Facebook can use them to identify distributed professional communities and help them assimilate into networks of practice.[14]

Recent research on online tools to support teacher learning finds, overall, no difference between online and face-to-face approaches.[15] Rather, the issue, as with much research on technology and learning, is with the questions being asked. The question should not be, "Does technology help teachers learn," but instead a design-oriented question focused on *how* online media can best be utilized to help teachers learn.[16] One important issue is the role of the moderator in online professional learning communities.

OVERVIEW OF THE MODERATOR GUIDE

In an initial analysis of the AP Teacher Community, it was found that while these professional learning environments had strengths, in many ways they did not follow models and strategies widely discussed in the literature as being important for enhancing the effectiveness of professional learning. In particular, it was noted that there were ways in which the moderator's role could be enhanced and extended.

In response, a Moderator Guide was developed with seven research-based tips for supporting and encouraging online communities:

- facilitate organization
- welcome newcomers
- encourage contributions
- support top contributors
- foster commitment
- address problems
- model good behavior.

Facilitate Organization

It is critical that members of an online community be able to easily discover where to add their voices to the discussion and what contributions need to be made. A well-organized community will lead to increased contributions by lowering the barrier to participation. To achieve these results, moderators should encourage the use of informative and specific thread titles and ensure that threads are correctly categorized, including moving contributions and recategorizing when needed. Also, when conversations digress from the original thread topic, threads should be split. The reasoning behind these organizational decisions should be made explicit to members so that new norms are shared and upheld and so that participants understand where to post. In addition, it is useful to curate a list of threads that need responses. The curated list could be its own thread, tagged with a high priority, so that it will always remain at the top of the "recent" list for easy access and visibility.

An empirical perspective supporting these points comes from Flavio Mendez, senior director of the NSTA Learning Center: "As the moderators for the community, the online advisers curate the threads (we call them topics) that need responses. We believe a short but prompt response to a post is more important than a delayed but longer response; that immediacy of a response is important for both the experienced and the new poster (like the 'welcoming' of a new community participant)." An example of categorization in the APTC is shown in figure 10.1.

FIGURE 10.1 Categorization in the APTC Biology

▾ Categories

Category	Threads	Posts	
"Help!" Requests for course-related help Subcategories: I Have Questions, I'm looking for something, New Teacher Advice & Assistance	1381	7714	Actions
Content Biology content for AP Biology Teachers Subcategories: Big Idea 1, Big Idea 2, Big Idea 3, Big Idea 4, Science In The News, More »	1141	2516	Actions
Instruction and Assessment For topics dealing with instruction (pedagogy, structures, etc.) and assessment. Subcategories: Assessments, Inquiry, Instruction, New Curriculum, Projects	980	7612	Actions
Laboratories Everything you every wanted to know about AP-level labs Subcategories: Cool Labs, New Curriculum Labs, Organism/Equipment/Reagent Issues, The Dirty Dozen	624	3801	Actions
Professional Development Events College Board (and non-College Board) announcements about professional development opportunities. Subcategories: College Board PD, Other PD, Summer Institute Questions	146	688	Actions
Technology in the Classroom Share thoughts and opinions on tools and applications being used in your AP classroom Subcategories: Hardware & Software, internetl, Techno-Pedagogy	134	457	Actions
Using the Teacher Community Category for all comments, questions, concerns, and complaints about using the AP Biology Teacher Community. Here to help you. Don't be shy. Subcategories: From the Moderator, Helpful Hints, Suggestions	88	493	Actions
Water Cooler For things that may not be specific to AP Biology. Subcategories: Digressions, Employment Opportunities, Free Stuff	399	1562	Actions

This type of organization is important because approximately 10 percent of the unique APTC Biology and Chemistry users are posters and approximately 90 percent are lurkers. Members who are observing but not actively participating can maximize their benefit from the community if they find the right threads. As noted in a report on the NSTA Learning Center:

> Even though members don't always post in the discussion forums, they still find value in "lurking," checking in on hot-topic conversations, and just reading about what other people are doing.

> One of the things that has been valuable to me is going into the discussion board, even if all I'm doing is lurking and scanning to see what people have said about a subject . . . I've found a lot of things that I can connect to and bring into class. (Eve)

. . .

I just enjoy looking at what other people are saying, what questions they are asking. For example, as part of being the department chair, I'm in charge of planning our science fair every year and science fairs can be a drag. I like looking at some of the new ideas that other people have for science fairs, other ways that students can participate in something like a science fair in a way that's more meaningful. So I may not necessarily put a question up or a comment, but being part of those discussions by just reading what other people are doing and getting ideas is valuable. Also, a lot of people will then link their discussion posts to articles that they've read on the NSTA website or to other journals, so that's nice too. (Nita)[17]

In the excerpt from the report, Nita highlights the value of receiving new ideas from lurking even if one does not actively participate in posting discussion responses. A well-organized community is critical for encouraging lurkers and posters to access and respond (respectively) to information. However, since even the best organizational strategies by moderators may be puzzling to newcomers in an online community, special steps to support "newbies" can be important.

Welcome Newcomers

Newcomers are an essential part of an online community because they help to grow, expand, and enrich the community with new ideas, resources, and participation. Moreover, newcomers are critical to achieving impact at scale; "even established communities must attract a stream of new members to replace others who leave."[18] However, newcomers also present a unique challenge, as they are unfamiliar with community norms and standards of interaction. It is important that the moderator welcomes new members and helps them become acquainted with the community. Members are much more likely to engage actively with the community if they receive a meaningful response to their first post. Initial positive interactions with other community members (particularly those who are experienced professionally and in the community) increase new member retention. For example, newcomers to Usenet groups are more likely to return for subsequent visits if they receive a reply; the effects are stronger if the responses are from active users ("old-timers who have been visible in the discussion in the recent past") and if the language used is welcoming, inclusive, and uniting, such as "we" rather than "you," which can indicate a divide between responder and poster.[19] Therefore, moderators should encourage active, experienced members of the community to take on welcoming responsibilities and emphasize the use of "we" language.

In addition, new members should be prompted to complete their profiles, as self-disclosure leads to strengthened interpersonal bonds and increased commitment via social interactions. According to Mendez, "Our community profiles, which appear next to each post, provide a direct link to the person who made the post, allowing me to learn about the poster and to contact her/him via private messaging if desired. The profiles bring people together and allow for networking and relationship building, which may result in deeper and more meaningful conversation. Our advisers follow the tip of referring to people by name, and asking specific questions."[20]

In the APTC Chemistry, the moderator has created the following thread: "New to Community? If so, click here to learn how things work." As of June 2015, this thread had received 1,988 views, making it a top-rated thread (though the thread on AP Chemistry exam results received 4,747 views). In the APTC Biology, the thread "New Teacher Advice and Assistance" is incorporated into the "Help!" category, which alerts all users, not just new teachers, to burning questions. Regardless of which approach is employed, there are clear sections designated for newcomers to ask questions and receive extra support as they navigate and acclimate to the online community.

Encourage Contributions

As a moderator, it is important to serve as a facilitator—not leader—of community discussions, helping to move conversations forward and to encourage participation from the broader community. For example, the moderator should offer advice, ask clarifying questions, and introduce broader issues, all while providing space for other members in the community to step into that role as well. Moderators should not underestimate the power of referring to people by name, whether asking a question, offering praise, or providing attribution. According to one study, asking specific, direct questions (as opposed to statements or vague, open-ended questions) increases the likelihood of getting a response by 55 percent.[21] These researchers define *specific, direct questions* as those in which it is clear what the author is requesting and who is being asked to provide the information (e.g., AP Biology teachers, "Where can I purchase the Campbell textbook?" AP Chemistry teachers, "Where can I find the materials I will need for the titration and green crystal labs?"). By contrast, *vague, open-ended questions* indicate that the author is requesting something from the group but not explicitly naming the desired information (e.g., "I'm wondering if anyone has experienced this?"), making it unclear whether the author is looking for sympathy or information.

In addition, moderators should encourage reflective dialogue, not just information-seeking dialogue. These types of conversations can tease out the diversity of perspectives within the community and support the personal growth of members. In particular, moderators should reach out to specific members for contributions, particularly if the request aligns with their interests and expertise. A well-targeted request is generally more effective than a broad request to the whole community.[22] Finally, moderators should act as the memory of the community. They should connect participants with related discussions happening in other parts of the community, as well as refer people to relevant past resources and conversations.[23]

In their examination of the NSTA Learning Center, Booth and Kellogg include a quote from a user, Cody, about the importance of moderators encouraging contributions:

> When I talk to other teachers in my school about what I'm doing in my classroom, if it's different from what they're doing, sometimes it causes conflicts. To avoid conflict, I don't share what I'm doing. So the Learning Center pretty much has been my safe haven to go to if I want to share or get new ideas without the fear of someone laughing at me or throwing stones at the ideas. The conversations are very professional, which I really, really appreciate. When I post something and someone responds like, "Oh, good idea, Cody," or, "I never thought about that, Cody." It's like, oh wow, I actually connected with somebody in another part of the country and got feedback on my ideas. It is a great feeling.[24]

As Cody describes it, online communities can provide an alternate space where teachers are encouraged to contribute openly and honestly and where a variety of perspectives can be entertained, which may not be possible in a face-to-face environment. Moderators are a critical component of both creating the conditions for participants to contribute and fostering interaction and feedback at various levels of intensity (i.e., Cody being on the "light" end of the spectrum). Moderators should be encouraged to give specific and detailed feedback to promote participants' growth. Moderators should also stoke discussion by providing additional resources and/or topics for discussion.

The interchange in figure 10.2 shows how a NSTA Learning Center moderator, called a Web Accelerator, encourages contributions just ninety-seven minutes after a participant posts.

Support Top Contributors

Online communities typically follow an unbalanced participation model—that is, the majority of the contributions are made by a minority of the members.[25] With this in mind, it is important, as a moderator, to make sure that top contributors feel valued and involved. Moderators should let highly active contributors know how much they are appreciated by sending them a private note from time to time, praising them for specific and detailed things that they have done to help the community. With encouragement from the moderator, some top contributors may also begin to take on informal moderation roles by supporting the community with frequent responses to questions or reminders of norms for interaction. This support can be very valuable to the moderator, as well as to the entire community. So, when a top contributor emerges, moderators should offer mentorship and encouragement. However, moderators should also keep in mind that top contributors can be intimidating to members who contribute less frequently. Moderators should make top contributors aware of this and encourage them to use their time and presence to encourage a diversity of opinion in the community and thereby draw less frequent contributors into the discussion. An example from the NSTA Learning Center illustrates this point:

> The opportunity to take on a leadership role (called an online adviser) in the community enabled NSTA member Alana to apply the knowledge she had gained through the Learning Center to help other teachers. Alana explains:
>
>> I am very, very thankful to be able to be a part of this program of online advisers. I am very thankful that somebody on the inside of NSTA is really pushing this, not so much because of the role I play, but from what I gain from it. When I first joined the community, I literally floundered around the Learning Center for the first two years. I never knew exactly where I was going or what I was doing. And if I got to somewhere that worked for me I was thrilled but I couldn't seem to get back to those places. Now with my experience as an online adviser, I know all four corners of the room within the Learning Center. It has given me the confidence to say to other people, "Yeah, it can be very overwhelming at first but you gotta hang in there and if you're lost, click on Live Sup-

FIGURE 10.2   A Web Accelerator encourages participant contribution

by **Tammi**, Mon Nov 07, 2011 5:40 PM

I searched the Community Forums and found many references to the need for quality classroom management. I have been told of a variety of techniques and been involved with a wide variety of ages. Commonly the response is disrespectful, insubordinate or disruptive behavior. However, how fast should one respond? When should non-verbal responses be used? What are the specific behaviors that teachers today consider disrespectful and disruptive? Define a firm response as opposed to a chaotic or poor solution. I have been told that it is bad to send students constantly to the principal or office, or worse to have administrative interventions in the classroom. I have even heard it said that you have managed a classroom well when the students begin to intervene in the situation.

Tammi

SciPack
Accelerator

6

8 Posts
3930 Activity Points

[REPLY TO THIS POST]
[REPORT]

by **Arlene**, Mon Nov 07, 2011 7:17 PM

Tammi,
You ask good questions and I hope others will respond. I have been looking at some the the teaching videos on the Teachers Network.

YOu might want to check out this one of science teacher discussing and demonstrating how routine, structure and behavior expectations to engage students.

Included are the three steps she uses to deal with disruptive students. I really like what her students said about her approach. Video is about 12 minutes long.
Go to:
http://teachersnetwork.org/Videos/onlinevideoClassroomManagementSecondary.htm

Let me know what you think about her approach !

Arlene

Arlene

Web Seminar
Accelerator

10

1867 Posts
39825 Activity Points

port for help and let us know that you need assistance because you're just learning your way around the community and trying to figure out where everything is. But once you've got it and you know where you're going, there's so much there." It's such an incredible resource for science teachers . . . And then, part of my job working within the Learning Center is to read and evaluate various articles. I spend a lot of time reading articles. The process of reading and reviewing the articles also adds to my own professional qualifications because I'm widening my horizons, finding new and different ways to teach things that I can bring back to teachers at my own school.[26]

As she describes it, Alana "floundered" initially, but once she grasped the setup of the community, she found taking on a leadership role as an adviser beneficial to the online community, her face-to-face community, and herself. Encouraging top contributors helps to grow and sustain the community and the individuals within it.

Foster Commitment

Moderators should remember that an online community is diverse, and the ways in which members choose to commit will vary.[27] Therefore, the moderator should foster different forms of commitment in the community in order to build member retention, engagement, and compliance within the community. For example, the moderator might encourage the formation of small subgroups within the community that might cluster around similar goals, interests, or expertise. Promoting the development of subgroup identity (i.e., a name or tagline) that aligns with the mission of the larger community can also increase members' overall commitment levels.

Moderators should also suggest that members fill out their profile with as much personal information as they are comfortable sharing. Specifically, the inclusion of a profile picture has been shown to be of particular importance when building peer bonds in an online space.[28] Moderators should also invite members to recruit their qualified professional and social acquaintances to become members of the community. This can bolster commitment by capitalizing on existing interpersonal bonds. In addition, moderators should use intentional language to prime the members of the community to the norm of reciprocity. Phrases such as "pay it forward" or "return the favor" can activate members' altruism and promote their development of commitment to the community. To accomplish this, moderators might consider highlighting what benefits certain members have received as well as any opportunities for them to "give back" to the community that supports them.

Address Problems

Inappropriate conduct can be incredibly disruptive to the community, so it is vital that moderators take appropriate and immediate action in suppressing it. Moderators can refer to and cite community guidelines in making these decisions. Most of all, if an issue arises and the moderator is at fault, addressing the situation as quickly as possible, taking responsibility for the actions, apologizing to the community, and explaining steps that will be taken to rectify the situation are all vital actions. Other violations to community norms are best handled constructively to help ensure that the members at fault are encouraged to learn from their mistakes without being discouraged from participating in the community.[29]

It is good practice to clearly communicate the following in the event of a violation: thank the member for their contribution, explain which community guideline was disobeyed, and provide a link to the official community guidelines as a resource. In addition, moderators should give all members who are found to be at fault the opportunity to explain and argue their case, as well as the chance to make an appeal. This will help ensure a fair process and will make sure each member feels that her voice is valued in the community. Moderators should always strive to be fair, particularly when challenged. Consistent standards of moderation increase legitimacy, and therefore effectiveness, as a moderator.

According to Mendez, "Community guidelines are available at the footer of every page in the community forums. Problems have not really been an issue within the community. Perhaps the use of profiles by the posts provide the accountability needed to encourage users to have civil and respectful discussions."[30]

Model Good Behavior

Members look to the moderator for direction and guidance. Therefore, it is of utmost importance that moderators actively model the behavior that they expect to see from members. This means always upholding the community guidelines as well as enthusiastically facilitating and authentically engaging in the discourse of community. Moderators should be encouraged to have fun. Being a moderator does not mean being bland or detached. It is important for them to take the time to get to know the members and to let the members get to know them.

The APTC Biology moderator started the thread "Some Ideas for the New Year" after reading the Moderator Guide:

> I know most of you have been in the new year for a bit longer than those of us in NY have, but now that the major craziness of "opening" the year is subsiding, I thought it might be nice to share a few things I'm doing differently this year, in the hope of getting (more—since many have already) other folks to do the same. So let's begin:
>
> I decided that I wanted to base my SBG [standards-based grading] system on something a bit more thought-through on the part of my students than I did last year. So I've required them to keep a weekly reflective journal that frames the work they are doing every week against the standards in the course, and has them consider their performance critically. I've dabbled in things like this in the past, but I've always had a problem keeping on top of reading the reflections, and I would find myself at the end of a marking period doing a pile of reading, and not giving each student the time and effort they deserve for this kind of work. The major logistic issue

finally clicked this year, when I realized that in the age of GAFE [Google Apps for Education] and similar online systems, it's very easy to put all student work into an easily accessible routine. The student-facing guidelines are here [hyperlink], but on my end, I have a spreadsheet that lists each student, the URL of their journal, and the last date I checked in. This lets me pop in and read/comment on ~5 journals whenever I feel like it.

Part of the above required that I provide students with a pretty comprehensive record of the work that we are doing in class from day to day. So I took a page from Mary's BILL [Biology Interactive Learning Log] idea, and have created a daily list of activities that anyone can access from here [hyperlink]. I just update it every day. It's a nice example of how the kind of sharing of ideas in this community leads to interesting cross-pollinations.

I've changed some other things, too, but I'd be more interested to hear from you folks as to the changes you have made.

The post explicitly models the behavior (i.e., sharing reflections on what the moderator is doing differently at the start of the new year) that he hopes to elicit from other participants. It also includes links to specific resources for others to access (if they want to follow suit, modify, delve more deeply into, or discard) and explicitly acknowledges other members who have inspired and affected the moderator's own practice. This type of leadership by the moderator can evoke similar leadership in participants.

Overall, the empirical evidence collected supports the recommendations in the Moderator Guide. While the empirical evidence collected and cited here supports the current seven guidelines that comprise the Moderator Guide, the research on online moderators continues to evolve and expand based on increased comfort with digital environments and new technological activities within online communities.

RESPONSES TO THE MODERATOR GUIDE

An extended version of these recommendations, in the form of a Moderator Guide was distributed to the APTC moderators for the Biology, Chemistry, and Physics communities.[31] The APTC Biology and Chemistry moderators were interviewed in July 2013 and again in October 2014 to gauge their successes and struggles. Initial findings show that the Moderator Guide was effective at providing support and empowering moderators. Following are a few comments from the moderators.

Indeed, the tips are both useful and reassuring—not just offering new ideas but also reinforcing the usefulness of things I had already implemented.

...

For my part, I can see that I can become a bit more of an active presence in my community. I have been trying to be a neutral observer, referee, and resource, but this encouraged me to speak up a bit more.

...

After reading the "7 Tips" article, I plan to be more involved in the future, primarily through encouragement for newcomers and long-time members, and providing reinforcement for those who take the time to offer useful information and suggestions.

...

I think that it's filled with good practical suggestions, some of which are part of my practice. I especially like the idea of enlisting the experienced members and recognizing them by name as we comment on questions and suggestions.

...

Before this document, I would say to myself, should I do it this way or that way? The document reinforces some of the good things that I was doing and says, you should be doing more of this.

While some APTC moderators could recall more levels of detail than others about the Moderator Guide after several weeks has passed, all of them regarded the resource as useful. Subsequent research will focus on the extent APTC moderators act to put the recommendations from the Moderator Guide into practice, as well as their feedback on which recommendations were most helpful.

Initial research results point to the important role of moderators in online teacher professional development communities. Given the nascent role of online community moderators, training and support for moderators is an important component of developing and sustaining an online community. Also, online communities can be managed and facilitated to achieve their intended goals. Through the explained seven guidelines, among other heuristics, moderators can support the change in behavior and knowledge sharing to which an online community aspires.

CHAPTER 11

Making Online and Blended Teacher Professional Development Accessible

RAYMOND M. ROSE

The classic *New Yorker* cartoon that jests "on the Internet no one knows you're a dog" embodies the notion that personal characteristics, such as disability, might be hidden during an online experience. The misperception of online anonymity is further reinforced by the limited availability of research on interaction patterns examined by disability in online education, and specifically in online teacher professional development. Accessibility requirements address the full range of disability issues, which broadly cover vision, hearing, learning disabilities, and mobility.

This chapter aspires to bring awareness to the unique aspects of making online professional learning accessible for people with disabilities by reviewing historical background, discussing the current state of online accessibility, and providing suggestions to improve course accessibility. Whether one is a developer, funder, policy maker, or practitioner, it is useful to know and understand the guidelines and opportunities that exist for making online and blended teacher professional development more accessible for all.

BACKGROUND

The Seeing Math Project: A Case Study of Early Accessibility Issues

In *Online Professional Development for Teachers: Emerging Models and Methods*, Concord Consortium's United States Department of Education-funded Seeing Math project and collaboration with the PBS TeacherLine project was described as a model for scaling-up a national professional development program.[1] While there was an understanding that the project had an obligation to meet federal civil rights requirements related to accessibility for people with disabilities, there was no guidance available from the funding agency, the US Department of Education, about accessibility. However, the National Center for Accessible Media (NCAM) at WGBH Boston was identified as a place that might be able to produce guidance, resources, or technical assistance to make the online teacher professional development materials accessible. Although NCAM was intrigued by the challenge and idea of working with an online professional development project, by the time the organizations were able to partner, the Seeing Math project was entering its final year of funding.

NCAM was willing to caption a limited number of the project's professional development videos as a pilot with the understanding that NCAM could then use the videos as demonstrations of online teacher professional development programs. These captioned videos were part of the Seeing Math website. Interestingly, when a small sample of teachers was asked about their preferences in video, captioned or noncaptioned, all consistently reported that the captioned videos were easier to understand. Making opportunities available for some can lead to better understanding for all.

In addition to captioning, audio description makes videos usable by individuals who are blind. But because audio description can be quite distracting for sighted users, is it usually most practical to produce one version with captions and audio description and a second version with just captions.

Other Early Work in Accessibility

When the Concord Consortium created the country's first Virtual High School in 1995, a special needs policy was written that focused on involving the virtual education program in the development of an individualized education plan (IEP) for students with special needs. The focus was on ensuring that student placement was good and was not on making sure students with disabilities had the ability to acquire the same information and engage in the same interactions as students without disabilities. One of the participating schools in the Virtual High School program was a school for the deaf, and those students reportedly performed on a par with the nondisabled students. Florida Virtual School, which started at about the same time, also had participation by students from a school for the deaf. The Virtual High School reported that special needs students enjoyed the online learning experience and performed well. However, the final report from the Virtual High School project does not mention students with disabilities, an interesting indication of the state of accessibility awareness in the late 1990s and early 2000s.

At the same time, universal design for learning (UDL) was starting to gain visibility. UDL, created by CAST, a nonprofit educational research and development organization, is a "framework to improve and optimize teaching and learning for all people based on scientific insights into how people learn."[2]

As the UDL concept was gaining traction, one of the issues identified was the use of color; colors in the web-based interactive tools had not been selected in a way that ensured someone with a form of color blindness would be able to distinguish important features. These interactive tools were a significant component of the Seeing Math project's professional development experience. This internal, heightened awareness around the issue of colors led the Concord Consortium to team up with the UDL project to create practical science materials for inclusive classrooms, in particular the development of graphing software that expresses data and relationships in text and spoken form.[3]

In 2007, the North American Council for Online Learning (now the International Association of K–12 Online Learning [iNACOL]) published a report titled *Access and Equity in Online Classes and Virtual Schools*.[4] The report, however, presents only a single noncompliance finding related to online education by the US Department of Education's Office for Civil Rights (OCR), and that was for a school district that denied all special needs students access to any online course.

The Current Status of Online Accessibility

The history of current enforcement of access in online education started in 2009 with a lawsuit filed by the National Federation of the Blind and the American Council of the Blind, which charged that Arizona State University's use of Amazon Kindle e-readers for electronic textbooks was a violation of accessibility mandates, explaining that the device cannot be used by blind students. Since that time, enforcement of federal accessibility has increased, driven in part by legal action by disability advocacy groups as well as by compliance monitoring by the US Department of Justice (DOJ), which monitors enforcement of the Americans with Disabilities Act.[5] By 2015, the number of private law suits and reports, including additional findings by the DOJ, has grown to almost twenty. The findings and the issues are very consistent. The OCR defines *accessible* in at least four compliance monitoring and complaint resolutions as when "those with a disability are able to acquire the same information and engage in the same interactions—and within the same time frame—as those without disabilities."[6]

Furthermore, OCR considers links to materials outside the online course or learning management system to be a part of the course, and therefore those resources also need to conform to accessibility requirements. OCR broadly defines the course as "all content offered," including links to all ancillary resources. In a 2014 K–12 noncompliance report, OCR identified a significant number of course links outside of the learning management system that did not meet the legal accessibility standards.

Most personnel involved in online education have not had training in the importance of accessibility or in how to ensure that digital materials are accessible. Informal surveys of instructional design and teacher preparation programs across the United States found that the majority do not address digital access in any significant way.[7] Furthermore, most teacher preparation faculty seem unaware of the legal requirements for online education programs to ensure access for students with disabilities, and most higher education institutions are not compliant in serving their own online students with disabilities.

ACTIONS TO IMPROVE COURSE ACCESSIBILITY

Online courses have many different elements, so there are a number of design considerations necessary when ensuring that online courses are accessible. One way to address the variety of elements is to adopt a set of standards that describe a high-quality online course and include accessibility. Three national organizations have developed such quality standards for online courses: Quality Matters (QM) for K–12 and higher education; the Online Learning Consortium (OLC) for online courses; and iNACOL for K–12 online and blended learning. All three organizations require accessibility as a necessary component of their frameworks. Both QM and OLC standards are incorporated into a process whereby courses that fully meet the standards receive certification.

Standards help a program or organization develop online courses that are consistent in quality and address criteria to ensure that all relevant design issues are met. Online teacher professional development providers can adopt one of the existing three frameworks or create their own. If an organization opts to create its own standards, it is advised to consider the existing standards as a starting point. iNACOL's website contains its standards for quality online courses, teaching, and programs as well as standards for blended learning.[8] Although acquiring the QM and OLC standards incurs a cost, both of those organizations offer training on their standards and the process for reviewing courses to meet those standards.

GUIDELINES FOR MAKING DIGITAL CONTENT ACCESSIBLE

Derived from course standards, guidelines and checklists exist for web content developers. (Some are listed in appendixes 11A and 11B.) Because the technology changes swiftly, developers can stay abreast of the latest information by visiting the World Wide Web Consortium (W3C) and their Web Accessibility Initiative (WAI).[9] The following are current guidelines for making web content accessible; although not exhaustive, this list provides a starting point for improving the accessibility for online content.

- *Use alt tags on images.* Alt tags (alternate text) provide descriptions of images on a website or in Microsoft's PowerPoint. These are important for blind readers and others who use screen readers (audio-based applications that read text on the computer screen). The screen reader speaks the alt text, allowing the person listening to interact with the element on the page. In technical terms, an alt tag is an attribute used in HTML/XHTML to provide the descriptive alt text tag (called alt text). Alt tags should be descriptive in ways that contribute to learning. For example, rather than graphically tagging *girl,* a description can be provided as to the purpose and action that the girl is taking, along with a visual description of what the image looks like. If math equations are presented as images, it is useful to know about the Benetech MathML Cloud that will create MathML and alt text that may be used to voice the equations with TTS.[10]
- *Avoid eye candy.* Gratuitous use of graphic images to make a page look pretty may not contribute to the instructional goals. Think about what the alt text will say for these images in order to ensure the images augment the user experience.
- *Use alternatives to color.* Convey information with more than just color and make sure the colors used are distinct from each other and distinguishable by someone with a visual impairment. Attention to contrast, such as yellow on black, and avoiding red and green, colors not easily seen by those with color blindness, can ensure greater accessibility.

- *Make hyperlinks meaningful.* Hyperlinks, the text that links to web content, should be relevant, and the link should tell readers exactly what they will find when they follow the link. Any external material linked from the course must be accessible.
- *Avoid frames.* Frames, a structure for laying out content in a web page, can be challenging for those who are visually impaired because frames are difficult for screen reader software to capture. If they must be used, give frames meaningful titles and provide "no frames" information.
- *Describe charts.* Describe the information conveyed in charts for those who are unable to view charts. Long descriptions, rather than alt text, may be even more beneficial for this purpose; or data can be provided on the page so that the chart information can be read as live text.
- *Make file formats accessible.* PDF documents need to be well structured, styled, and described, just as Word files. Once PDF documents are well designed, they can be saved as graphics or in a searchable format. When a PDF is saved as a graphic, the content is not accessible to someone using a screen reader, so be sure to save in searchable formats (optical character recognition).
- *Use logical tags and proportional fonts.* Logical tags are used to convey to screen readers that there is some emphasis on text. Logical structure, fonts that can be enlarged, and links that can be navigated via the tab key are critical to making an accessible page because they allow for attention to the reading order of the links. Where possible, fonts should be sans serif, such as Arial.
- *Provide alternatives for accessing multimedia content.* Captioned videos and transcripts for podcasts and other audio content make content accessible to all users.

Accessibility Tools

It is useful for course designers to understand the tools people with disabilities use to access information on a computer.

To be considered accessible, video must be captioned and described. However, captioning is more than having a transcript; the captioning needs to match and sync with the audio stream and accurately reflect the spoken words. YouTube has added an automatic captioning tool for video, but its intent was to help producers create the captions, not to serve as the primary captioning mechanism. This tool does not meet the legal standard for use by people with disabilities, as it is currently only about 50–75 percent accurate. If uploading a video to YouTube without a transcript, then YouTube captioning is a place to start. Video owners can edit YouTube's automatic captioning, reducing the amount of work required. However, users technically cannot caption videos they did not create or have the rights to change.

A screen reader speaks text that appears on a computer screen and provides support navigating the content of a web page or website when the content is well structured. Screen readers cannot read graphics, nor can they provide a narrative for a video, so it falls to the course designer to include a way for a learner with a screen reader to interact with the content. Also, because screen readers read from left to right, the order of information and link placement are important considerations. Course designers might learn a good deal by using a screen reader to perform a basic evaluation of the accessibility of their online content. There are a variety of different screen readers available; perhaps the most widely used and known is JAWS (Job Access With Speech).[11] JAWS is not cheap, but a free trial is available that has a forty-minute limit per session, and there is no restriction on number of sessions. NVDA (NonVisual Desktop Access) is a free, open-source alternative to the JAWS screen reader.[12] It has a unique feature that is useful for sighted users: "For sighted software developers or people demoing NVDA to sighted audiences, a floating window is available that allows you to view all the text that NVDA is currently speaking."[13] WebAIM, an organization that offers a range of web accessibility service and has many free resources, features an article describing the use of VoiceOver, a screen reader that comes on Mac computers, iPhones, iPads, and iPod Touches.[14] The article is designed to help users learn the basics of VoiceOver to test web content.

There are also tools to help developers understand color perception for those affected by color blindness. Vischeck is a website that simulates colorblind vision for checking web pages.[15] Seewald Solutions has created the Android Color Blindness Correction and Simulator that uses the device's camera to show what it is like to have red, green, or blue color confusion.[16]

Accessibility Reports

There are a number of websites that can provide an accessibility report for particular web pages.[17] The free sites generally will not check a page behind a password, but ther-e are fee-based services that will. The free sites include:

- Cryptzon Cynthia Says Portal, http://CynthiaSays.com
- WAVE Web Accessibility Evaluation Tool, http://wave.webaim.com
- AMP Express–SSB BART Group, https://amp.ssbbartgroup.com/express/

Additional information about reading accessibility reports is available at:

- W3C How to Meet WCAG 2.0, http://www.w3.org/WAI/WCAG20/quickref/
- Web Accessibility Best Practices, https://www.webaccessibility.com/best_practices.php

Each service presents its report a little differently, so it can be useful to use them as a group to take advantage of the different reporting styles. When pointing out accessibility issues, having multiple sources helps an organization accept the results. It is also important to consider the need to learn about creating accessible Word, PDF, PowerPoint, EPUB, and other documents that are commonly included as downloads from the HTML pages of the course.

There are browser add-ons (listed in appendix 11B) that essentially do the same job as the free accessibility check websites, with an advantage being that they can check individual pages behind a password.

BEGIN NOW!

Given technological affordances, the time is ripe for making online professional development accessible to all. After being provided with accessibility training and information, there are a number of changes that course designers and facilitators can implement. For example, adjusting the colors and contrast to support those with visual impairment and changing the file format are possible starting points, for color blindness tools can be used to assess and correct color use and contrast. Also, PDF files can be checked, and then any that are saved as images can be converted to the searchable format (see appendix 11B). In addition, adopting a set of quality standards for online content or creating original standards will increase the awareness of accessibility for both designers and subject matter experts.

Design teams should commit to make all new courses accessible, as it is much easier to create an accessible new course than it is to retrofit accessibility into an existing course. This can be addressed by ensuring that the online platforms that are purchased are accessible and support the development and delivery of additional accessible content authored by the educational institution.

Online and blended instruction is growing fast, and it is good practice for a professional development provider to model the best in online learning. Making sure online content is accessible will benefit all participants.

APPENDIX 11A

Issues and Actions Checklist

This checklist identifies the issues and actions that help ensure online teacher professional development learning opportunities meet the legal requirements for accessibility.

Policies

Purchasing policies related to online platforms are updated to ensure consideration for accessibility right from the start.

All of the institution's courses (including those from external providers) are reviewed to ensure that they meet legal accessibility standards.

Institution has policy and activities to ensure that the organizational website meets accessibility requirements.

Institution has determined the process, responsibility, and timeline for retrofitting accessibility or replacing courses that are not accessible.

Institution has adopted, as policy, a set of quality standards to which all courses adhere.

Course Design

Color and contrast selection do not impede users with visual impairment.

Limit use of graphical eye-candy. If it must be used, it should not be made accessible by using "nul alt text," and no title attribution should be used on gratuitous image elements to ensure that they are ignored.

All content put into PDFs is searchable (if a graphic, follow requirements for graphics).

All graphics have meaningful, learning-related alt tags.

All audio is accompanied by text transcripts.

All video includes synchronized captioning and description. (Note: there is cost and time associated with implementing this appropriately.)

Course navigation is possible without the use of a mouse.

Content at all external links meets the same accessibility standards.

Courses are reviewed with access to a screen reader in mind.

APPENDIX 11B

Resources

Accessibility

Articles

Alternative Text (Alt Text) detailed tutorial with examples and recommendations
    http://webaim.org/techniques/alttext/

Guidelines for describing STEM images
    http://ncam.wgbh.org/experience_learn/educational_media/stemdx/guidelines

Definition of web accessibility and a set of resources
    http://en.wikipedia.org/wiki/Web_accessibility

White papers on making media and websites accessible using Adobe products
    http://www.adobe.com/accessibility/resources.html

Macromedia accessibility kit
    http://www.macromedia.com/accessibility

How the ADA impacts video accessibility
    http://www.3playmedia.com/2013/06/13/
    the-americans-disability-act-ada-accessible-online-video-requirements/

Web accessibility and universal design information
    http://www.dcp.ucla.edu/resources/

National Center for Accessible Media (NCAM)
    http://ncam.wgbh.org/

"Accessible Digital Media" guidelines
    http://ncam.wgbh.org/publications/adm

MAGpie (a tool for creating closed captions and audio descriptions)
    http://ncam.wgbh.org/webaccess/magpie/

Crowdsource site for captioning YouTube and Vimeo videos
    http://amara.org/en/

National Instructional Materials Access Center (NIMAS) information
    http://nimas.cast.org

Microsoft Windows guidelines
    http://www.microsoft.com/enable

IMS accessibility specs and guidelines for distance learning
    http://www.imsglobal.org/accessibility

Color Blindness Tools

Color advice for cartography
    http://colorbrewer2.org/

Vischeck (simulates color-blind vision)
    http://www.vischeck.com/
Color blindness simulator (Android only)
    http://www.seewald.at/en/2012/01/color_blindness_correction_and_simulator

Web Accessibility Resources

What not to do to make a website more accessible
    http://jimthatcher.com/whatnot.htm
Web Accessibility in Mind (WebAIM)
    http://www.webaim.org/
Web Accessibility Initiative
    http://www.w3.org/wai
Illinois Accessible Web Publishing Wizard for Microsoft Office
    http://accessiblewizards.uiuc.edu/
Four steps to readily achievable web accessibility
    http://www.hisoftware.com/why-hisoftware/thought-leadership/whitepapers/
    Readily-Achievable-Web-Accessibility.aspx
2014 roadmap to web accessibility in higher education
    http://info.3playmedia.com/wp-web-accessibility.html
Creating section 508–compliant e-learning solutions
    http://elearningindustry.com/creating-section-508-compliant-elearning-solutions
    http://www.access-board.gov/508.htm
Universal design for learning
    http://www.cast.org/

Web Accessibility Checkers

Free website accessibility tools
    http://CynthiaSays.com
    http://wave.webaim.com

Browser-Based Accessibility Tools

Accessibility evaluator for Firefox
WAVE evaluation tool for Google Chrome
List of accessibility checkers (free and fee)
    http://www.w3.org/WAI/ER/tools/complete

General Accessibility Resources

Java guidelines
    http://www-3.ibm.com/able/guidelines/java/snsjavag.html
PDF accessibility information
    http://access.adobe.com/

Creating accessible tables and data tables
  http://webaim.org/techniques/tables/
  http://webaim.org/techniques/tables/data
Apple accessibility information
  http://www.apple.com/accessibility
More accessible web video conferencing
  http://www.talkingcommunities.com/
SETDA policy brief *The Accessibility of Learning Content for All Students,
  Including Students with Disabilities*
  http://www.setda.org/wp-content/uploads/2014/03/SETDA_PolicyBrief_
  Accessibility_FNL.5.29.pdf

Screen Readers

JAWS (Job Access With Speech)
  http://www.freedomscientific.com/jaws-hq.asp
NVDA (NonVisual Desktop Access)
  http://www.nvaccess.org/
10 Free Screen Readers
  http://usabilitygeek.com/10-free-screen-reader-blind-visually-impaired-users/

Legal Resources

Information on Public Law 94-142 (now called IDEA)
  http://www.scn.org/~bk269/94-142.html
Council of Educators for Students with Disabilities, Inc., section 504 overview
  http://www.504idea.org/Council_Of_Educators/Welcome.html
US Department of Justice's Americans with Disabilities Act
  http://www.usdoj.gov/crt/ada/adahom1.htm
US Department of Education's nondiscrimination on the basis of disability in state
  and local government services
  http://www.ed.gov/policy/rights/reg/ocr/edlite-28cfr35.html
US government's website on section 508 and the 508 standards
  http://www.section508.gov/
  http://www.section508.gov/index.cfm?FuseAction=Content&ID=12
  https://www.section508.gov/index.cfm?fuseAction=Standards_Harmonization

Office of Civil Rights Findings

2013 Virtual Community School of Ohio press release
  http://www.ed.gov/news/press-releases/us-education-department-announces-
  first-its-kind-resolution-virtual-charter-school-civil-rights-investigation

2013 Virtual Community School of Ohio resolution letter
    http://www2.ed.gov/documents/press-releases/virtual-community-ohio-letter.
    doc
2013 Virtual Community School of Ohio agreement press release
    http://www2.ed.gov/documents/press-releases/virtual-community-ohio-
    agreement.doc
2014 South Carolina Virtual Charter School agreement press release
    http://www.ed.gov/news/press-releases/us-department-education-announces-
    resolution-south-carolina-virtual-charter-schools-civil-rights-investigation

Relevant OCR and Department of Education "Dear Colleague" Letters
Charter schools and civil rights legislation
    http://www2.ed.gov/about/offices/list/ocr/letters/colleague-201405-charter.pdf
ADA requirements for K–12 programs
    http://www.ed.gov/news/press-releases/department-education-issues-ada-
    amendments-act-dear-colleague-letter-provide-gui
Broadened definitions for ADA
    http://www2.ed.gov/about/offices/list/ocr/letters/colleague-201109.html
E-book readers
    http://www.ed.gov/news/press-releases/departments-education-and-justice-
    announce-continuing-commitment-accessible-tech
    http://www2.ed.gov/about/offices/list/ocr/letters/colleague-20100629.html
Questions and answers about the law, the technology, and the population affected
    (June 29, 2010)
    http://www2.ed.gov/about/offices/list/ocr/docs/504-qa-20100629.pdf
To colleges and universities on emerging technologies (May 26, 2011)
    http://www2.ed.gov/about/offices/list/ocr/letters/colleague-201105-pse.html
To school districts on emerging technologies (May 26, 2011)
    http://www2.ed.gov/about/offices/list/ocr/letters/colleague-201105-ese.html
Frequently asked questions about the June 29, 2010, letter (May 26, 2011)
    http://www2.ed.gov/about/offices/list/ocr/docs/dcl-ebook-faq-201105.html
Equal access regardless of immigration status
    http://www2.ed.gov/about/offices/list/ocr/letters/colleague-201405.pdf

PART IV

SUMMARY INSIGHTS

CHAPTER 12

Exploring Models of Online Professional Development

S. A. SCHNEIDER, K. L. LEPORI, C. E. CARROLL, A. B. RAMIREZ,
A. K. KNOTTS, M. D. SILBERGLITT, M. A. GALE, K. SALGUERO,
K. M. LUTTGEN, S. HAUK, AND C. RINGSTAFF

Online learning opportunities, including online teacher professional development, are pervasive in education. Free, disruptive technologies such as the Khan Academy are being used by millions of learners around the globe in multiple topic areas, from test preparation to immunology.[1] Disruptive technologies, unlike sustainable ones that offer incremental improvements to an already established technology, displace known technologies with groundbreaking products, often creating a completely new market.[2] The shift from the traditional face-to-face model to the newer, more innovative approach of online teacher professional development is continuing at a rapid rate. There are compelling reasons the traditional face-to-face model is preferred by many, but the reality of today's education economics means emerging technologies are pushing the field further in the direction of technology-enhanced professional development. From the grass-roots efforts on Pinterest and the Teaching Channel to professionally designed and facilitated webinars like Schools Moving Up, educators looking for an opportunity to learn readily can find something free on the Internet. But is it a good fit for the professional need? This is an important aspect of online teacher professional development design and use.

As with any good professional development design, no matter the mode of instruction, designers and planners need to ask the same goal-driven ques-

FIGURE 12.1 Tenets of good teacher professional development

Effective professional development:

- Is designed to address student learning goals and needs
- Is driven by a well-defined image of effective classroom teaching and learning
- Provides opportunities for teachers to build their content and pedagogical content knowledge and reflect on practice
- Is research based and engages teachers in the learning approaches they will use with their students
- Provides opportunities for teachers to collaborate with colleagues and other experts to improve their practice
- Helps teachers develop their professional expertise to serve in leadership roles
- Links with other parts of the education system
- Is continuously evaluated and improved

Source: S. Loucks-Horsley et al., *Designing Professional Development for Teachers of Science and Mathematics,* *3rd ed.* (Thousand Oaks, CA: Corwin Press, 2010).

tions about purpose and target outcomes (see figure 12.1).[3] In recent years, guided by these tenets, the STEM program team at WestEd has designed and implemented online teacher professional development in tailored and loose-fitting ways.

A community of developers, designers, and facilitators of teacher professional development, the authors seek to contribute usable knowledge for the field's ongoing work to build models for online teacher professional development that are informed by theory and by empirical results.[4] This chapter recounts the multithreaded story of how WestEd's traditional, face-to-face delivery is evolving into a variety of online approaches. The five cases include in-depth courses, curriculum implementation wraparounds, and hybrid and ongoing support models.

CASE 1: NATIONAL RESEARCH AND DEVELOPMENT CENTER ON COGNITION AND MATHEMATICS INSTRUCTION

The National Research and Development Center for Cognition and Mathematics Instruction (Math Center), funded by the US Department of Education's Institute for Education Sciences, has a core goal of redesigning components of a widely used middle school mathematics curriculum, Connected Mathematics Project (CMP), and evaluating the efficacy of the redesigned materials.[5] Participants were mathematics teachers experienced in using CMP. Study year 1 (2011–2012) included grades 6 and 8; study year 2 (2012–2013) focused on grade 7. In the study, teachers taught a version of the curriculum that included revisions grounded in cognitive and learning sciences research-based design principles for mathematics curriculum and instruction. An experienced WestEd team designed the Math Center professional development using its customary, face-to-face format to introduce teachers of grades 6 and 8 to these principles and provide grounding in effective implementation of the revised curriculum.

Why Online Professional Development?

Aside from the normal difficulty in recruiting teachers for a typical randomized controlled trial (RCT), the study's inclusion and exclusion restrictions (e.g., subject, grade level, prior experience implementing a specific curriculum) narrowed the pool of eligible and interested teacher participants. When the recruiting was complete, the study included participants from schools in urban, suburban, and rural districts across seventeen different states. It was neither possible nor cost effective to implement WestEd's standard practice of face-to-face professional development, so the researchers had to think outside the box. After much discussion and investigation to find an online venue that could support the key elements of high-quality professional development, the developers chose Blackboard Collaborate, an online synchronous format. They had considered using WebEx, a venue they had used previously that also supports an online synchronous format; however, after comparing the capabilities of the two platforms, they chose Collaborate due to its ability to create a learning environment and community that would support teacher participants.

Getting Started

With teachers recruited, time was of the essence, and it was imperative to get the professional development started. Due to the researchers' limited experience using an online venue, in December 2011, consultants from Collaborate translated the existing face-to-face design to the new platform. The researchers were aware that teachers needed support in learning to learn online. Effective professional development for the intervention had to offer information about the ideas behind the cognitive design principles as integrated in the Connected Mathematics Project materials, as well as include individual reflection time, activities, and time for participants to work on implementation ideas together. Through a series of back-and-forth reviews, the WestEd team and Collaborate created a plan with slots for each type of content. The prototype was a pair of five-hour sessions (two hours online, one hour offline work time, two hours online) across two days for those implementing one CMP booklet (in the first year, each teacher implemented one of four revised booklets). The prototype became a template for future two-day workshops. In this first implementation, four facilitators led the two-day workshops for a total of 107 teachers. In the second year of implementation, the existing two-day professional development plan was adapted and scaled-up to a design where each of eighty-seven teachers implemented an entirely revised curriculum (eight booklets). In this second round, the two-day workshops were offered at the beginning of the year and augmented by three, ninety-minute online sessions spaced across the remainder of the academic year.

Professional Development

The Math Center professional development focused primarily on instructional practices, assessment practices, and universal design for learning. Teachers also had an opportunity to work on mathematical knowledge for teaching as well as understanding student thinking. The program engaged teachers in a variety of learning activities, including:

- reading and discussing research summaries for each of the cognitive design principles of visual-verbal mapping, spaced practice, formative assessment, and worked examples
- working in small groups (using Collaborate breakout rooms) on math tasks and instructional practice tasks and sharing with the whole group
- viewing and discussing expert video on the design principles
- trying out new approaches in the classroom and then sharing reflections with the group in the follow-up sessions.

To a great degree, it was about sharing information with teachers to enhance their implementation of the revised CMP materials. The design engaged groups of teachers who gathered virtually on a regular basis in a synchronous environment. While this program worked with participants from across the country, the model could be applied locally by a district or regional agency to connect teachers for learning opportunities. A major challenge was scheduling for teachers in different time zones. The program designers learned quickly to offer at least two time/day options for each session. If necessary, teachers had the option of watching an archive of the session. Emerging technologies such as Zaption, can transform the passive experience of simply watching a video into an interactive learning activity. With Zaption software, instructional designers can add text, images, questions, and embedded links to any existing online video and tailor it to meet the learners' needs (in this case, the needs of the study participants). Zaption also has analytics that offer data on how viewers interact with content and understand key concepts.

Preparing Facilitators

All of the facilitators needed to understand the cognitive design principles as they were applied in CMP and the associated changes in the curriculum. Facilitators also needed to learn about Collaborate and become comfortable with the various tools and structures. The facilitation team was composed of nationally recognized professional development providers with extensive experience leading face-to-face professional development. They were apprehensive about the virtual format, wondering how they would be able to accomplish the engagement and interaction to which they were accustomed without having participants physically in the same room. To ease these concerns, all facilitators attended a two-day workshop to learn how to offer interactive learning in a Collaborate session. After the workshop, during a debriefing, facilitators said they felt comfortable and excited about the first online sessions. The teachers, too, were very positive and were no longer apprehensive about the online experience.

This marked a major turning point in how professional development in the STEM program will be offered in the future. Prior to the Math Center, all WestEd STEM professional development was offered face-to-face; now, many offerings combine face-to-face and online activities, and there are several programs that are completely online. In addition, its various funded projects, WestEd has created personal learning communities so that teacher participants have an online venue in which to share their work and support one another.

Working in the Online Environment

Many options are available in an online venue that can be difficult to do in a face-to-face environment. The virtual breakout rooms can be used for small-group work without losing time moving bodies into physical rooms. Sharing content discussed in breakout rooms is relatively easy using Collaborate, since individual whiteboards can be shared with the whole group when everyone "returns" to the main room. The entire session, including the whiteboards and chat, can be archived. But prior to the initial professional development sessions, teachers needed to become familiar with Collaborate, so WestEd professional development facilitators and tech support staff offered both a self-directed asynchronous exploration of it as well as a short, live, online "techinar." In the synchronous techinar, Collaborate-savvy staff walked participants through fifteen minutes of activities (e.g., audio setup, using the whiteboard, moving in and out of a breakout room).

Lessons Learned

The development team refined and revised the professional development based on year 1 participant feedback and facilitator reflections. To date, hundreds of teachers have been engaged in numerous online sessions. Many of these are an adaptation or scaling of the Math Center design. Experience shows that online teacher professional development is enhanced when the facilitator makes use of a variety of Collaborate features, such as the breakout rooms for small-group work and the ability to share and discuss the breakout room whiteboards in the main room with the whole group. In ongoing professional development for the facilitators, they shared ideas on increasing effective use of the whiteboard, working with small groups in breakout rooms, and devising strategies for encouraging participants to interact not only with the facilitator but also with each other.

In addition to increasing facilitators' competence and comfort with the online environment, it became clear that participants needed the same orientation. Since most of the Math Center study participants were new to the online environment, the professional development providers offered Introduction to Blackboard Collaborate techinars for participants in the days prior to engaging them in the content of the professional development; equipped each participant with a high-quality headset (under $15 each); and, during each session, supported participants who had technical difficulties.

The facilitators tested the adaptability and scalability of the design in the second round of implementation: adapting session plans to new content and scaling to a workshop, plus follow-up design supporting eighty-seven teachers for an entire year. Designers and facilitators created the templates for the workshop sessions and used follow-up webinars as frames in which to insert new course content.

WestEd invested substantially in developing facilitation capacity for online teacher professional development. Now established, it has meant online professional development, like this model, can be used sustainably. It is also possible to train new facilitators to lead sessions using the course designs and facilitator training structures already in place. Additionally, the investment in learning about Collaborate has paid off: most of the Math Center professional development facilitators have taken their new skills into other professional development projects (e.g., MAS).

Because the efficacy study did not include face-to-face professional development, no comparison of student outcomes based on type of teacher professional development can be made (e.g., student learning when teachers did online versus face-to-face professional development).

CASE 2: MAKING MATHEMATICS ACCESSIBLE FOR ALL STUDENTS

Making Middle School Mathematics Accessible for All Students (MAS) is a yearlong professional development experience that promotes culturally responsive instruction.[6] It offers strategies for helping all learners, across socioeconomic, racial, ethnic, and linguistic categories, build their understanding of mathematics content and mathematics language. The MAS experience includes attention to language development strategies drawn from *Making Mathematics Accessible to English Learners: A Guidebook for Teachers* along with related ideas in intercultural competence development.[7] Participants to date have comprised two cohorts: a pilot group of twenty-five and a second iteration of forty-eight. Each participant group had math teachers, special educators, paraeducators/aides, and teacher leaders. In learning teams, they worked to notice and support academic language during math lessons, create equitable classroom activities and assessments, and plan lessons for learners at different language development levels. The hybrid delivery structure of MAS has been a mix of an intensive six-day in-person summer institute across two weeks and online academic year follow-up.

Why Online Professional Development?

Participants worked in different schools and were spread across a three-state geographical area. After the face-to-face summer institute, to conquer the geographic dispersion of team participants and teacher leaders during the academic year, the program used Collaborate for web-based synchronous communication for gathering in the same virtual room and, to support professional peer interaction around shared artifacts, PBworks wiki, an asynchronous tool for posting and sharing artifacts. The goal was to create an accessible, useful space for professional communication and for that space to include a diversity of professional voices and experiences.

Getting Started

MAS facilitators, many of whom had worked on the Math Center project, were eager to build (more) skill with the online tools of Collaborate and a PBworks wiki. However, teacher leaders and the participants needed preparation for their roles in the online environments. Participants began preparing for online interactions during the summer institute. Across the two weeks, institute leaders set aside three blocks of time for exploration of the PBworks site and the Collaborate platform. Face-to-face professional development included time for practice with distance-delivery platforms. Gathered in a computer lab, participants logged on to Collaborate, shared documents, practiced with the control panels, and moved from the virtual main room to a breakout room and back. They also explored PBworks. These activities set the stage for the way the teams of participants would communicate throughout the school year. In summer, teams also began preparation of the plan to guide them during their online interactions, culminating in the end-of-year full-cohort webinar where teams shared their year's work with each other.

Professional Development

Together, a teacher leader and MAS staff member filled the online facilitator roles. The learning teams of five to eight participants met monthly in Collaborate. Between meetings, participants shared student work and reflections on their classroom experience on PBworks. Across both platforms, sharing by participants included professional readings, classroom tasks, and student work, all as stimuli for professional discussions. To keep attendance high, monthly one-hour learning team meetings took place late in the day (5:00 pm or later, depending on time zone). Given the summer preparation, participants had little trouble navigating the platforms and tools. The team sessions during the academic year became a support system for participants (especially valued by those who were the only person at their school site participating in the MAS project).

Working in Synchronous and Asynchronous Online Environments

Working in a combination of synchronous and asynchronous online activities during the academic year helped participants maintain enthusiasm and energy for taking calculated risks in teaching, attending to student thinking, and trying out teaching and assessment practices.

Lessons Learned

Some challenges surfaced during the pilot year. For example, some school sites did not have sufficient bandwidth, so a few participants had to find another Internet source. In the second iteration of the project, to increase inclusivity, the summer institute preparation for online work included doing an activity online (even though people were in the same room). For the monthly follow-up meetings, MAS staff liaisons worked closely with teacher leaders, providing technical support in all learning team sessions so the leader could focus on the agenda rather than technology logistics. Such support might be a challenge to scalability, but that could be addressed with "cascading up," having teacher leaders from one year matriculate into the facilitator role in a later year. In moving beyond the development phase reported here, sustainability still faces several challenges, particularly the cost in time and effort of the summer institute. While the return on investment has been high in terms of teacher and student learning, current efforts include migrating the entire MAS experience to a virtual environment—still having an intensive summer experience, but doing so online. The emerging MAS-Online design also leverages the accessibility of online interaction during the school year, and lessons learned from the Math Center work to add a Fall Intensive two-day set of sessions.

In a quasi-experimental design study, MAS teachers and their students had greater gains than comparison peer groups on several validated and reliable measures.[8] For MAS teachers, gains were statistically significantly greater than comparison groups on the Learning Mathematics for Teaching—Patterns and Functions test ($p<0.03$, Hedge's effect size $g=0.4$), and their gains approached significance on the Intercultural Development Inventory ($p=0.11$). For the students of MAS teachers, state test scores after the MAS year were significantly greater than comparison groups when controlling for teacher Learning Mathematics for Teaching (LMT) survey score and students' previous year state test scores ($p=0.00$, Hedge's effect size $g=0.3$).

CASE 3: MATH PATHWAYS & PITFALLS ANYTIME, ANYPLACE PROFESSIONAL DEVELOPMENT: PRINCIPLES TO PRACTICE

The Math Pathways & Pitfalls (MPP) Anytime, Anyplace Professional Development: Principles to Practice website contains ten online professional development modules that require approximately 90 to 120 hours of online work.[9] These modules are anchored in research-based teaching principles and proven-effective mathematics materials. The design project reported here was both about sharing information with teachers and gathering information to improve online teacher professional development. Its overarching goal was to help teachers implement Common Core mathematical practices using MPP lessons to get them started and then transferring these practices strategically to their regular lessons.

Why Online Professional Development?

A typical implementation institute for MPP takes about five days of face-to-face professional development, with each day dedicated to a MPP principle and the related practices, plus two to four follow-up sessions during the school year. The total face-to-face time required to introduce and model all of the principles and practices is approximately thirty to forty hours. The goals of this kind of sustained implementation support are to familiarize teachers with MPP lessons' structure, rationale, and strengths as well as learning about how to adapt the MPP principles and practices to the lessons they typically use for the majority of their math instruction. However, the cost to districts hindered the dissemination of the tried and proven MPP materials.

Getting Started

Whether face-to-face, online, or blended, professional development must be intellectually stimulating and provide an engaging learning environment. How to stimulate consumers intellectually, especially in a model that uses prerecorded segments, was a design challenge. That challenge was met by anchoring professional development in case-based materials. Users viewed video clips of actual MPP and non-MPP lessons-in-action in diverse classrooms among teachers with varied pedagogical, linguistic, and ethnic backgrounds. Project evaluators performed small "tests" of the modules, focusing on one module at a time. Once developed, a pilot group of 13 teachers completed 3 modules over the course of 4 months. They dedicated approximately 90 minutes of time online for each module and then spent time offline planning and teaching MPP and non-MPP math lessons. In order to get them started, project staff developed an orientation module (Module 0). For the pilot, the project director introduced the MPP teacher professional development online experience at a face-to-face kick-off meeting.

Professional Development

Each module has two parts, each with the same structures. Part 1 focuses on MPP lessons and Part 2 on "regular" lessons using a teacher's own curriculum. Each part takes between forty-five and sixty minutes of online time and is "chunked" so that teachers can leave and come back as needed. Teachers apply what they learn offline by teaching a lesson and then return to the module to reflect on it. They complete this sequence twice within a module, once with an MPP lesson and once with a lesson from their regular curriculum. This mix of minimal time commitment, scaffolds for learning, and direct application creates a powerful learning combination specifically tailored for the realities of teaching.

Preparing Facilitators

Funding is currently being sought to develop facilitator's guides for the modules. The research team also plans to develop discussion notes for facilitators to use in supporting teachers to prepare, teach, and reflect on their own lessons as well as to scaffold discussion of the video exemplars and teacher activities.

Working in the Online Environment

Like Collaborate, the Canvas online environment used for the MPP modules required minimal technology. Analytics through the Canvas platform let the research team and the teachers track progress and know what tasks were completed. This is not always possible in face-to-face professional development. Online, teachers can start and stop at will and play slideshows and videos as many times as desired when planning their lessons.

Inclusivity had to be considered in a different way for online teacher professional development. The online modules contain a mix of text, audio, and video. Anytime video is provided online; captions, which support learning for some often-marginalized audiences (e.g., the hearing impaired, English language learners), legally have to be included. Brevity is crucial. As opposed to print, the bulk of the content was conveyed in video, pictures, slideshows, and only limited text. This is an important consideration for those wishing to develop "static" courses or modules.

Lessons Learned

Conciseness proved to be very valuable. The video clips have to be short, clearly compelling, and, in six minutes or less, give a snapshot of a forty-five-minute lesson. They also have to be a recognizable example of the practice being illustrated. Pilot teachers gave rich feedback on content and quality, indicating that there are still a few concerns that need to be addressed. One issue is the smooth streaming of videos and slideshows. The Canvas platform is compatible with many computers and tablets but has functional constraints. The other concern arose from a request by teachers to show not only examples of the principles and practices being implemented successfully but also provide nonexamples—what it looked like when things did *not* go well for teachers. An open question that needs to be researched is the value of using a video case to intentionally illustrate an instructional pitfall.

This experience raises some questions for online teacher professional development developers. For example, while certainly scalable, what is the place in the landscape for stable materials that are asynchronous, where teachers works through modules on their own and then implement and reflect individually on what they learned? Does there always need to be a feature for teachers to share with each other? What are alternatives to that if the resources are not available to moderate that space? As these modules are rolled out for use with print materials, the research team is actively seeking resources that will help test out possible scenarios and addresses these questions.

Though the current focus is on pedagogical approaches that help engage students in mathematical practices, requests from test sites are prompting us to explore adaptations of modules for additional content. The research-proven MPP face-to-face professional development can run a school or district upward of $25,000 for thirty teachers. When including the cost of generating and then field-testing any model in a research and development environment, online development costs are similar to developing and field-testing print materials and face-to-face models. However, once developed, the cost of the kind of self-guided online teacher professional development modules created for MPP is far less for consumers (teachers, schools, districts).

CASE 4: PEPPER: ONLINE COMMON CORE PROFESSIONAL DEVELOPMENT FOR MATHEMATICS TEACHERS

The Pepper project is a collection of asynchronous, ten-to-twelve-hour online courses created by WestEd in partnership with Public Consulting Group and Edu2000.[10] Similar to Case 3, the goal of the project is to prepare US teachers to implement the Common Core State Standards for Mathematics (CCSSM). Districts purchase one license per teacher, which provides them access to the collection. The fees from the licenses are then used to finance the creation of new courses.

When teachers have a better understanding of both the history and underlying philosophy of the CCSSM, and of the mathematics content and practices in it, they are more likely to implement the standards well in their classrooms. Theoretically, this should, in turn, result in greater learning gains for students in mathematics.

Why Online Professional Development?

There is a nationwide need for teacher support around the Common Core. Arranging meaningful, high-quality, face-to-face professional development is not feasible for many schools and districts for a host of logistical and financial reasons. Asynchronous, online courses, however, require only an Internet connection and a compatible device.

Getting Started

The WestEd STEM math team drew on its experience with another WestEd online professional development project, Charter School Teachers Online, when developing the first Pepper course. The team outlined each course, determined the essential understandings participants would take away from the course, decided how best to parcel the content into sessions, and finally selected learning activities and resources. Some research into online course development options led to the decision to use the edX learning platform. After several rounds of revisions, the team completed the first Pepper course in December 2013. Introduction to the Standards for Mathematical Practice in Middle School went live in January 2014. It has received a great deal of positive feedback from early participants.

Professional Development

Pepper math courses focus on deepening teachers' knowledge and understanding of the Common Core math standards (see figure 12.2). There are

---

FIGURE 12.2   Pepper math courses available in late 2014

---

*The Standards for Mathematical Practice: The Heart of the Common Core

*The Standards for Mathematical Content: Clusters, Domains, and Learning Progressions

Getting Started with Operations and Algebraic Thinking

Getting Started with Number and Operations in Base Ten

Getting Started with Expressions and Equations

Implementing Expressions and Equations

Conceptual Categories in High School

---

*Three separate courses for elementary, middle, and high school.

---

strong emphases on subject matter knowledge for teaching mathematics, understanding student thinking, and mindful selection of instructional practices. In each session, teachers:

- work on math tasks
- observe and analyze classroom video
- review and analyze classroom vignettes
- examine and analyze student work
- read and respond to professional articles
- watch and respond to interviews with teachers and other subject matter experts
- plan lesson activities
- explore libraries of resources
- reflect on their learning

Facilitation

Pepper courses are self-paced. They can be augmented by face-to-face interactions with colleagues and/or a facilitator (e.g., coach or math specialist). The "For Your PLC" section of each course contains additional suggested opportunities for teachers and teacher leaders to engage and discuss an activity with a professional learning community at their school.

Working in the Online Environment

The asynchronous online teacher professional development approach makes it possible to share a wealth of information about the standards and their implementation with a considerably larger audience, and at a lower price point, than could ever be done in person. An advantage of the asynchronous model that schools and districts find attractive is that it gives teachers the ability to work on the courses at their convenience. The ability to save their progress in a portfolio at any point lets participants work at their own pace—over multiple days or weeks.

Lessons Learned

In terms of design and structure, the original plan was to organize courses according to domain and conceptual category at grade level. The first content course focused on the middle school Expressions and Equations domain and was further organized by clusters of standards. However, it seemed to isolate consideration of the work students do with expressions and equations from their work in other domains. This detracted from the message of coherence that the Common Core authors have consistently espoused.[11] Teachers needed to see the important relationships and cross-connections among different aspects of mathematics and communicate those relationships effectively to their students. Thus, the math team refined the planning process so that the goals for each course were more targeted and achievable within the ten-to-twelve-hour timeframe. What had been a single overwhelming course on the Expressions and Equations domain became two courses: an introductory Getting Started course and a course focused on a more in-depth implementation of those standards, Introduction to Implementing Expressions and Equations.

The time- and labor-intensive nature of developing new courses has been a significant challenge. With existing courses covering only a small portion of the Common Core mathematics standards, many districts are wary of investing precious professional development dollars. Yet, these dollars are necessary to support ongoing course development.

Because the model is so new, it is difficult to say what additional challenges Pepper will face. Currently, participants complete pre/post assessments, where they rate their own understanding of and confidence in implementing the ideas discussed in the course. There are also end-of-course surveys, and thus far teachers have given positive feedback. Based on that feedback, the STEM program math team has made some revisions to current courses.

Because it is asynchronous and self-paced, the Pepper approach is, by design, scalable to any size school or district and sustainable in that it is available on demand. However, any facilitation is local, so internal resources for facilitation could be a constraint on scalability, depending on the goal(s) of the user school or district. The creation of the courses is time and labor intensive to scale-up in order to have a large library from which districts or teachers may choose.

Challenges to adaptability of the model come in two shapes: (1) finding and holding onto authors who are expert in the right fields while coordinating Pepper's production schedule; (2) and selling enough licenses so the royalties cover the cost to develop new courses. The courses are inclusive in that there is a relatively low barrier to entry; all that's needed is Internet access via a computer or tablet. And as with other online models, some familiarity with basic Internet technology is required. Public Consulting Group created an introductory course that covers basic navigation, how to find and get started on a course, information on how the courses are organized and how to use the interactive features, and tips on collaboration opportunities. All videos are subtitled and are accompanied by transcripts.

CASE 5: SIMSCIENTISTS

The SimScientists program aims to design simulation environments that model dynamic science system phenomena "in action" in order to create simulation-based assessments and curriculum supplements to assess and promote the Next Generation Science Standards (NGSS). The program includes a portfolio of projects that gather evidence of impacts on science learning, the technical quality of the assessments, the feasibility of implementing them across a range of school settings, and their potential as components in a balanced state science assessment system. They integrate research on model-based learning to represent science systems in the natural and designed world in a framework that depicts the system components, interactions, and emergent system behavior.[12] The projects employ evidence-centered assessment design to link learning targets, task designs, and evidence of learning gathered.[13] Cognitive science research findings guide the design and use of representations and interactions in the tasks.

SimScientists has been providing teacher professional development to participants in research projects that use its computerized, simulation-based instructional modules and assessments.[14] Initially, professional development consisted of a one-and-a-half-day, face-to-face workshop with ongoing support via email or phone, along with a short online component to introduce middle and high school science teachers to the SimScientists modules, reports, reflection activities, and online scoring of student responses. To make the face-to-face workshop feasible and convenient, the principal investigators purposely sampled teacher recruitment from schools that were close to one another.

Why Online Professional Development?

Each current project includes professional development on three to four topics over the course of a year of instruction. Participating teachers are from many geographical areas, with only a few in each area. Online teacher professional development is now replacing the face-to-face workshops, beginning with a pilot that delivers the content online but during an in-person meeting with four teachers. This setting allows researchers to monitor the online experience in person and make adjustments as needed.

Getting Started

The move to online professional development progressed slowly. The projects that motivated the need for it started in 2012, but the first large-scale studies did not begin until 2014. During this two-year conversion, the designer evaluated several platforms, designed the content, and then tested it internally in small mock workshops, with the designer serving as a facilitator and other members of the research group serving as participants.

Professional Development

The online SimScientists professional development program is designed to provide opportunities for individual reflection during offline "assignments" and to promote greater interaction for participants during synchronous group discussions and one-on-one communication with the facilitator. These opportunities are already exceeding what was possible in the large face-to-face workshops. The web-based teacher professional development is delivered just-in-time for each facet of the SimScientists program and includes the theoretical foundations of this approach.

Teachers are asked to consider how the modules support model-based learning and how data from the modules can be used formatively in the classroom. They are asked to think of formative assessment as a process that begins with assessment embedded into instruction, that includes time for teachers and students to work together to identify gaps in students' understanding, and that closes the feedback loop when teachers use data from the embedded assessments to adjust and differentiate instruction. For example, the SimScientists curriculum-embedded assessments provide teachers with sample progress reports and ask them to identify science content and practices that students need additional help with and to discuss possible strategies for adjusting instruction to meet those needs.

While the total time a teacher interacts with the facilitator remains similar to the face-to-face workshop, eight to twelve hours, the professional development scope is broader, attending to teacher pedagogical knowledge about model-based learning and formative assessment. While these were important components of the face-to-face workshop, the online environment provides opportunities to consider how these strategies apply more broadly than SimScientists, with a focus on changes in teacher practice that go beyond the particular project.

Preparing Facilitators

One veteran teacher and one expert professional development designer currently facilitate the online experience for about forty users. Additional subject matter expertise is brought in as needed to answer specific questions that require advanced knowledge beyond the content of the SimScientists materials.

Working in the Online Environment

The web-based environment supports teachers' experiential and immersive learning about the SimScientists modules. The synchronous online environment is collaborative, giving teachers opportunities in discussion groups to share their understandings of the modules and how they can be used in the classroom. The asynchronous component asks teachers to spend individual time to reflect on the module and the discussions, followed by a wrap-up activity, such as a video that provides a useful comparison of different approaches that the developers and the participants might take in using the modules in the classroom. The online medium also allows the facilitator the opportunity for ongoing monitoring by reviewing teacher discussion and reflection to determine if and how teachers are implementing SimScientists consistently according to the plans they developed during the initial professional development session.

Lessons Learned

Because online teacher professional development is so new to the SimScientists program, there are many lessons to be learned. All teachers will take a survey on its quality and utility. Depending on the project, either the principal investigators or the external evaluator will include an additional survey at the end of the implementation to find out how well-prepared each teacher felt while they used SimScientists in their classrooms. They will use information from this evaluation to compare and contrast the intended and enacted teacher professional development and to make improvements. While the project has a proposal for design additions to support sustainability (e.g., facilitator guide), they are still in the early stages of development. Scaling-up and potential future adaptation to additional or alternate content are concerns that will be addressed in future work.

SUMMARY

Depending on its modes of delivery, scope, and project maturity, each case articulates the nature of the challenges it has faced in approaching scalability, sustainability, inclusivity, and adaptability.

The sustainability of the Math Center online model is due, in part, to its substantial initial investment in facilitator development. The sustainability of the MAS project faces several challenges. Current efforts include migrating the entire MAS experience to a virtual environment that incorporates and extends the idea of intensive experience to retreat-like two-day virtual sessions. The MPP project found online program development costs are similar to developing and field-testing print materials for traditional face-to-face professional development. However, once developed, the MPP self-guided online teacher modules provide a more cost-effective and flexible way to engage in and sustain professional development.

Many projects addressed inclusivity by introducing study participants to learning in the online platform first, before they attended the actual online professional development, with online technical assistance available during the sessions. In some cases, staff liaisons provided technical support in online sessions, another potential challenge to scalability. As noted in the MAS case, this challenge might be addressed with cascading up, by having teachers from one year matriculate into the facilitator role in a later year. The MPP and Pepper asynchronous approach is designed to be scalable to any size school or district. However, how to support the enhancement of local facilitation could be a constraint on scalability, depending on the goal(s) of the user school or district. In all of the cases, only the Math Center project implemented an adaptation: using templates developed in the first year of the project to create new online teacher professional development in the second year with new content.

Among the biggest challenges the online teacher professional development designer and provider encounter is staying current with the dynamic nature of technological advancement. This chapter illustrates the diversity in approaches taken and exemplifies the time and effort it takes to accomplish different goals and outcomes. Backward mapping from the goals for what teachers will know and be able to do after completing the professional development drives the variety of these models. Major decisions that the design teams made factored in cost, potential impact to meet the goals, and the convenience and feasibility of the intervention to the end user (the teacher). Part of that is deciding if the professional development will include any traditional face-to-face component (i.e., hybrid model) or if it will take place completely online and, if so, if that online delivery will be synchronous, asynchronous, or both.

WestEd is still learning about creating rich, engaging, and effective online teacher professional development, and technologies will continue to complicate the choices surrounding its delivery. The future of online professional development in teacher and student learning will be enhanced with simulations, game-based learning, and other promising technologies. Some developers are incorporating the learning sciences in their products to enhance their impact. All of these innovations need to have the companion research in place so that those in the field are informed about what works in different contexts to accomplish the explicit goals and outcomes of the intended online teacher professional development.

Insights and Next Steps

CHRIS DEDE AND ARTHUR EISENKRAFT

The final chapter of this book focuses on insights the coeditors have gained through studying the professional development models presented in the book. First, an analysis is presented of four cross-cutting themes the authors were asked to address: scalability, adaptability, sustainability, and inclusivity/accessibility. Next, core tensions in improving the models are identified. Finally, an aspirational vision for the next five years is described and recommended next steps for various stakeholders are delineated.

CROSS-CUTTING THEMES

For each model of professional development, the authors were encouraged to consider four cross-cutting themes: scalability, adaptability, sustainability, and inclusivity/accessibility. Scalability refers to the extent a model can be implemented in many types of settings and populations with varying levels of resources, not just in contexts similar to where it was first developed. Adaptability refers to how readily a model can be modified to fit local conditions without losing its effectiveness. Sustainability refers to how a model is designed to be self-sustaining over time in terms of resources. Inclusivity refers to accessibility across cultures, technical divides, diversity, physical challenges, and a host of other equity issues.

Scalability

In general, web-based delivery of online and blended professional development keeps costs down, which is important for scalability. As an example, electronic teacher guides for curricula are cheaper to deliver and more accessible than the print versions, which increases scalability of that model. Electronic guides also increase the capability of individual teachers to personalize their guide, which aids in creating a sense of ownership, again increasing scalability. That said, at some school sites, bandwidth problems for webinars, streaming video, and other intensive digital experiences impact online delivery. In other schools, websites that could be a useful part of the professional development model (e.g., YouTube) are blocked.

The type of professional development most strongly associated with massive delivery methods is massive open online courses (MOOCs), which attempt to reach large numbers of participants inexpensively. Authors note that most MOOCs do not have the instructional design characteristics necessary for good professional development, as illustrated by low rates of participation and completion. However, the MOOC-Eds Glenn Kleiman and Mary Ann Wolf describe in chapter 3 are a notable exception, illustrating the potential of this approach if done well. The NSTA Learning Center is a different model that has achieved massive levels of participation, which it has done in part by partnering with those who offer professional development either in districts or universities. Finding ways to recruit and train new moderators for professional learning communities such as this is one of the keys to scalability for this type of model, especially if the community is massive.

Many of the professional development models presented have been tested with teachers across a range of settings (urban, suburban, rural) and characteristics (varied years of experience, subject matter knowledge), which is a good method to design for scalability. Some models have also shown that "flexible fidelity" in implementation does not undercut effectiveness, which is another important aspect of scalability across settings, as variation in implementation allows for more widespread use of the model without losing its integrity.

Adaptability

Online professional development models face several types of challenges related to adaptability. Some challenges stem from translating student activities learned in professional development for use in specific classrooms under the constraints of that setting. Other challenges come from the need to modify professional development models for different subjects and for teachers who are working at various grade levels. As an example of design for adaptability, Talk Science focuses on strategies and skills transferable to other disciplines and to a range of student developmental levels. As another illustration, the Active Physics model has proven its adaptability by extending to the Active Chemistry curriculum.

Some models emphasize combining online experiences with face-to-face work among local colleagues as a way of tailoring professional development to a specific setting. In general, blended models that can adjust the mix of online and face-to-face to match the needs of a particular context are more adaptable than online only or face-to-face only professional development. However, blended programs that require a particular local resource (e.g., the American Museum of Natural History) are limited in their adaptability.

Professional development about a specific curriculum builds teachers' knowledge of strategies for adaptability, since that is the focus of what they are learning. Also, moderating teacher learning communities to be responsive to their participants and to be driven by participants' priorities fosters adaptability of learning across a range of contexts.

Sustainability

Sustainability of online professional development models has several dimensions. One is generating a continuing stream of resources (e.g., financial, administrative, substantive) to support the model over time. Providing external resources as part of the content aids with substantive sustainability. The NSTA Learning Center's fee for access by districts or universities is a mechanism for financial sustainability, while at the same time individual teacher learning is free.

Another dimension of sustainability relates to participants' commitment: feeling that involvement in this form of teacher learning is worth the time and effort, finding others with whom one shares interests so that individual strengths can be amplified, and developing a feeling of ownership of the model as one adapts it to a particular situation. Effective moderators in learning communities can aid with all these dimensions of commitment.

Some of the models in this book have achieved financial sustainability, but others currently have no path to continue their services indefinitely. In addition, professional learning communities require a critical mass of participants, which is a potential challenge for some models, particularly those that use synchronous formats. Models tied to participating teachers being at the same stage in implementing a particular curriculum (e.g., Active Physics) also face the challenge of having enough participants to be effective in sharing their strategies and insights.

In chapter 1, Barry Fishman describes how design-based implementation research can aid with factors necessary for sustainability, including a focus on persistent problems of practice from multiple stakeholders' perspectives and a concern with developing capacity for sustaining change in systems. The American Museum of Natural History's programs have achieved impressive sustainability across two decades, but this has required continuing evolution of its model while retaining fidelity to the basic elements of the program.

Inclusivity/Accessibility

The emergence of mobile infrastructure and social media, which together enable interaction with online professional development anytime and anywhere, has greatly improved access compared to a decade ago. That said, professional development approaches that use video require captioning to make them fully accessible and inclusive, a feature that many models currently lack. In chapter 11, Raymond Rose describes a variety of other accommodations in professional development necessary for full inclusivity; even the best professional development at this time falls short of that ambitious goal.

Varying discussion formats (e.g., online forums and scheduled synchronous Twitter chats) provide different ways for participants to engage in conversation. The design principle of multiple voices promotes inclusivity by enabling participants to consider a rich set of varied perspectives from other educators, students, researchers, and experts from the field. Providing private interactions can help with inclusivity for participants who don't want to publicly reveal challenges they are facing. Moderators reaching out to specific users to encourage their participation also can support inclusivity.

Expert panels provide participants access to expertise to which they might typically not have access, and resource collections provide equitable access to resources. However, programs that involve a substantial financial commitment by participants are less accessible and inclusive than programs with free services or a low cost. That said, lack of a funding stream can undercut sustainability, and it also means that few resources are available to create inclusivity accommodations.

Simultaneous Application of Cross-Cutting Themes

The interactions among these four themes illustrate tradeoffs in designing professional development. For example, raising the price aids with resources for inclusivity and sustainability but undercuts accessibility. Digital media requiring Internet bandwidth, like video and electronic teacher guides, can increase adaptability and scalability but undercut some types of inclusivity/ accessibility. Bootstrapping is required to get professional learning communities to scale because their adaptability and sustainability is limited at the beginning when they are small in size. Narrowly focused professional development aids teachers in adapting what they are studying, but the limited scope can restrict scale and sustainability. These and other tradeoffs illustrate the complexity of designing and evolving online and blended professional development.

CORE TENSIONS IN ONLINE AND BLENDED PROFESSIONAL DEVELOPMENT

Almost a decade ago, the final chapter in *Online Professional Development for Teachers* identified four core tensions in evolving these models: design for incremental learning versus design for transformation; tensions among stakeholders' agendas; customization vs. generalizability; and research versus program evaluation.[1] Discussed here are three of these perennial tensions relative to the professional development models in this book. (Customization vs. generalizability has already been covered in the prior discussion about adaptability.)

Design for Incremental Learning vs. Design for Transformation

Incremental learning versus transformational learning is a continuum rather than a dichotomy. At one end of the spectrum, professional development may focus on small enhancements to instructional strategies teachers are already using. At the other end, teachers may be asked to "unlearn" most aspects of their practice (as discussed in the introduction) and learn different methods of instruction and assessment. In this book, the professional development models were selected to encourage transformational change, in keeping with the calls for pervasive shifts in education.

Barry Fishman and Chris Dede describe the distinction between incremental and transformational technology-enhanced teaching:

We view this as a dichotomy between using technology to *do conventional things better* versus using technology to *do better things*.[2] While there is value in doing things better (i.e., more efficiently and effectively), we believe that the deeper value in technology for teaching lies in rethinking the enterprise of schooling in ways that unlock powerful learning opportunities and make better use of the resources present in the twenty-first century world. Doing better things includes preparing students to be more responsive to the opportunities and challenges of a global, knowledge-based, innovation-centered civilization.[3]

Other dimensions of transformational professional development include better addressing the changing nature of learners, reconceptualizing assessments, and rethinking learning as an activity that connects various aspects of students' lives rather than as fragmented experiences that isolate learning by subject area and portions of the day or year.

Exemplary curriculum, assessment, and instruction of the future will require exemplary professional development. Exemplary professional development, in turn, can inspire new visions and practices for curriculum, assessment, and instruction.

Tensions Among Stakeholders' Agendas

Tensions among stakeholders can lead to different perceived goals of professional development, including disjunctions between incremental and transformational learning. For example, in communities of practice based primarily on peer learning but enriched by experts, giving teachers what they need (e.g., deep knowledge about what scientific inquiry is) as opposed to what they want (a simple-steps lab to do the next morning with their students) is sometimes a challenge.

That said, the richest forms of professional learning acknowledge these tensions and richly combine theoretical and research-based insights with the wisdom of practice. These can foster ownership by practitioners through providing some autonomy while also enabling deep impacts on instruction via expert modeling of innovative practices coupled with teacher-led discussions about overcoming challenges in implementation. Various chapters in this book illustrate a range of approaches by which professional development models can foster this type of rich interaction.

Even the best professional development and teacher learning models, however, cannot resolve larger tensions inherent in society's current attitudes about education.[4] An illustrative, but not exhaustive list of these tensions follows.

- Researchers push for teachers to move toward more active forms of student learning than teaching-by-telling and learning-by-listening. At the same time, a broad, shallow curriculum and high-stakes tests that narrowly assess both students' learning outcomes and teachers' performance for accountability drive teachers to use presentational/assimilative instructional methods.
- Funders' time horizons for teacher learning and system change are typically short, with limited resources, sometimes faddish approaches, and occasionally ideologically driven goals. At the same time, both research and experience provide compelling evidence that lasting change in professionals and systems takes long periods of time, a steady focus on desired outcomes, and substantial funding.
- Teachers are told how important professional development is for their own practice and for school improvement, yet time for this learning is often not provided, and teachers who move toward transformation may find themselves out of step with the majority of their colleagues and outside the culture of their school.

The challenge is bringing together a truly representative group of stakeholders—teachers, educational leaders, regulators, funders, policy makers, teacher unions, parents, and community—to talk through these tensions in agendas.

Research vs. Program Evaluation

The questions asked by external funders, policy makers, and regulators about the *effectiveness* of professional development are different than those asked by researchers, educational leaders, and teachers themselves about the *impact* of professional development.[5] Effectiveness is defined by questions of scalability, sustainability, and cost benefit. Scalability and sustainability were discussed earlier; cost benefit deals with participants' assessment that the costs (time, effort, money) provide sufficient benefit to their practice and professional status to make the involvement worthwhile.

In contrast, impact is defined primarily by teacher learning and teacher change. Core questions include: Are teachers learning new skills, concepts, pedagogies, resources, and knowledge? Are teachers then altering their instructional practices with students? Is student achievement improving as a result of these shifts in teaching/learning? In short, impact is more about outcomes for teachers and students, while effectiveness is more about the attributes of the professional development program.

Both of these perspectives are important, and the coeditors asked the contributing authors to provide whatever findings are currently available from research or evaluation. Evidence was an important criterion in selecting which models to include in the book, as was a perspective balanced between effectiveness and impact. One challenge is that it is less difficult to measure effectiveness than impact, and less expensive, so program evaluation tends to dominate research.

AN ASPIRATIONAL FIVE-YEAR VISION FOR ONLINE AND BLENDED PROFESSIONAL DEVELOPMENT

A report from the Computing Research Association, *New Technology-Based Models of Postsecondary Learning: Conceptual Frameworks and Research Agendas,* describes the shift in types of knowledge and skills students need for the twenty-first century:

- moving from thinking about expertise as something an expert "knows" and can articulate to a complex mix of tacit (i.e., nonconscious) and conscious competencies; simply asking experts to "teach" whatever comes to mind, whether in an online format available to millions or in their own classrooms, is not enough to efficiently bring many students to expert performance levels.
- moving from knowledge and skills localized in a student's mind to distributed understandings and performances; understanding how to apply distributed knowledge and skills in real-world and novel contexts requires demonstrations via sophisticated, authentic performances adapting to complex situations, rather than traditional rote recall of a small amount of what experts comprehend and do in routine situations.
- moving from a focus on memorizing and applying facts, simple concepts, and straightforward procedures to "higher-level" conceptual and analytical capabilities deployed adaptively in diverse contexts; higher-level problem solving, complex decision making, and learner-based experimentation and exploration are key to the development of expertise and promotion of innovation that, in turn, lead to an expanding economy

prepared to meet the many rapidly evolving science and technology challenges of the future.

- recognizing how, beyond the conceptual and procedural aspects of learner competencies (often described as "cognitive"), complementary aspects of learner competencies ("noncognitive" factors") are instrumental to successful postsecondary learning, work, and citizenship; extensive research from social and developmental psychology has documented how learner orientations such as persistence/grit, engagement, mind-set about intelligence (as either improvable through effort or as a nonmalleable personal attribute), stereotype threat, and related constructs are consequential for learning.[6]

Consistent with this perspective on student outcomes and with the 2012 National Research Council report *Education for Life and Work*, the 2010 National Education Technology Plan (NETP) offers a different vision of teaching as one of its primary themes.[7] While teaching has long been characterized as an isolated or isolating activity, the central assertion of the NETP is that, to meet the demands of teaching in an interconnected world, isolation is no longer possible and may represent poor practice.[8] The NETP describes the new role of teaching as "connected teaching" and depicts teachers at the center of a network that begins in their own classroom and extends outward to include the surrounding school, community, and broader world of connected resources. Far from relying solely on their own resources behind closed classroom doors, effective teachers in a networked world manage connections between themselves and their students, from student to student, to parents, to other teachers and youth development workers inside and outside the school, and with far flung data, resources, and experts.

We chose to place Fishman's chapter regarding the future of professional development as the lead chapter so that the present models could be compared with that vision. Fishman states that "online teacher professional development is professional development." In the future, we do not expect providers to differentiate between online, hybrid, and face-to-face models, much the same way that we no longer make distinctions between landlines and cell phones in terms of contacting individuals. We ask people to call us and we do not care what device they are using as long as they can connect to the device we are using. Similarly, *face-to-face* may come to mean communication among teachers using an online video platform, no longer meaning people being in the same room.

Professional development is arguably the best hope we have for positive sustainable change in curriculum, assessment, and instruction. If we know and can articulate all the changes we desire in education, then we can use the resources available to us to create professional development opportunities to support teachers in meeting the demands of new curriculum, assessment, and instruction. Advances in technology can lead to new professional development models as illustrated in this volume.

Fishman describes a future where the professional development is assembled by teachers and precisely meets their needs. Glimpses of this personalization of professional development may be seen in some of the models presented here. Specifically, teachers can decide to selectively participate in online communities, use resources that are specific to the curriculum they are teaching, or seek out the content that they require. He also predicts the increasing use of gamelike elements in learning environments. In some of the NSTA resources, we see the use of badges as an incentive for teachers to engage in professional development.

Teachers and educational systems must also alter their practices as the types of students they serve shift. As global populations shift and migrate, in part to follow work opportunities, the language and cultural diversity of classrooms shifts commensurately.[9] This presents classroom teachers with a much more challenging environment in which to teach. Most teachers are not prepared to develop these kinds of sophisticated knowledge and skills in this wide range of students, yet the demands of a rapidly changing society call for such understandings and performances to become integrated across traditional content areas.

Managing changing contexts, students, and resources calls for the development of teachers' skills in the areas of communication, coordination, and collaboration.[10] Such skills have always been important in teaching, but these take on increased importance and new meanings in connected teaching. Connectedness extends to teacher professional learning as well, both for preservice and in-service teachers. Conceptions of professional learning based in collaborative and ongoing networks are powerful and consistent with general thinking about effective professional development design.[11]

This aspirational vision for society, education, and teachers is transformational on a number of levels. Even the best professional development now falls short in preparing teachers to play a pivotal role in realizing such a future. What steps are needed in the next few years to evolve current professional development models toward empowering such a shift?

NEXT STEPS IN EVOLVING PROFESSIONAL DEVELOPMENT AND TEACHER LEARNING

Almost a decade ago, the final chapter in *Online Professional Development for Teachers* made recommendations for various stakeholders to evolve professional development at that time.[12] Many of those priorities for action still hold true today, and the following recommendations build on them.

Funders should support both the refinement of sophisticated research methodologies and related empirical research on current and new models. These studies should aim to provide evidence of both effectiveness and impact, so funders should embed program evaluation and empirical research in requests-for-proposals and encourage mixed-methods studies that develop deep understanding of complex program dynamics. Most important, funders should focus on transformational professional development that develops teachers' professional capacities consistent with the vision discussed earlier. For example, almost all the models in this book focus on preparing teachers to enhance classroom learning, yet their life-wide, connected learning is very important as well and should be a focus of innovative new forms of professional development. Dede's research team works with virtual worlds and augmented realities that are exciting new media for professional development and for student learning.[13]

Policy makers and regulators should recognize that school reform cannot succeed without an ongoing investment in transformational teacher professional development. Policies for school funding should be refined to enable sustained investment in human capacity building. Developing flexible policies for teacher compensatory time, release days, industry externships, and summer work is important in providing incentives that promote teacher participation in comprehensive professional development.

Administrators and school leaders should view professional development as a vital element of comprehensive, transformational change. They should not only challenge teachers to improve practice but also provide institutional and structural supports that encourage teacher risk taking, reflection, collaboration, and leadership. As part of teacher supervision, administrators and school leaders should focus on individualized learning plans for teachers, holding teachers accountable for pursuing, applying, and demonstrating their own learning as well as creating a culture that supports groups of teachers engaging in professional development. Administrators and school leaders should develop incentives for individual participants in professional development to disseminate what they have learned throughout the school.

Developers and researchers should build on the innovative, effective models discussed in this book, evolving their designs as new insights are generated by research and as emerging digital tools and media offer innovative ways to enhance teacher learning. The visions, themes, tensions, and tradeoffs discussed here provide useful direction for creating next-generation models.

Parents and community should play a greater role in shaping the goals of their local school districts, asserting that children should be educated with knowledge and skills appropriate for a global, knowledge-based, innovation-centered economy. In this, they should recognize that teachers are the biggest single influence on shaping students' educational outcomes but that families, communities, and informal educators have important roles to play in life-wide connected learning and teaching.

Finally, *teachers, as stakeholders, should assume more power and responsibility over their own learning.* Not only should they demand professional development that has the characteristics listed above, but they should also recognize that they must invest substantial time and effort to achieve transformational changes in their own practice.

Discussion Questions

Chapter 1

What are the necessary features of professional development for teachers? How can technology support these? What unique features of the technology (online communications) can be used to support and/or improve professional development?

Roschelle and colleagues argued that there are essentially two directions one can go in designing with technology: to do existing things better or to do better things. Discuss examples of each with respect to online professional development.

Define *personalized learning*. How do you think personalized learning will advance in the next five years? Ten years? Twenty years?

In discussing design-based implementation research, Fishman states that the most important question is not what the designer is trying to accomplish but what teachers who participate in professional learning perceive as their needs. How are the perceived needs of teachers dependent on different stakeholder groups (e.g., students, administrators, parents)?

Chapter 2

Doubler and Paget indicate that although this professional development model is about science talk, "the strategies, skills, and professional development model are applicable for learning in other disciplines." Which strategies developed in this professional development model would be most adaptable to the social studies curriculum? To math? To reading/language arts?

Scaling-up involves teachers modifying the approach to local conditions, then sharing their insights about adaptation with other teachers and with developers. This leads to *shift* (teachers feeling ownership of the approach, which is important for scale) and *evolution* (developers gaining new insights from users). How can shift and evolution be maximized in Talk Science?

How might Talk Science approaches change as technologies such as social media advance?

How can the videos be updated over time to reflect the shifting realities of classroom practice, technology infrastructures, and student learning needs and preferences?

Chapter 3

What conditions are necessary for successful implementation of this model?

In what ways might the business strategies that empower sustainability for Seminars on Science be adopted and applied by MOOC-Ed developers?

How do the design principles impact participants' learning?

What are some of the benefits and drawbacks to using this type of professional development?

Chapter 4

Based on what you read in the teachers' comments and in the course description, where do you see evidence of any of the four dimensions of Reading Apprenticeship (social, personal, cognitive, and knowledge building) and the metacognitive conversation being enacted?

What strikes you as significant in the authors' discussion of the "translation" trade-offs between face-to-face and online professional development?

What role do you think synchronous participation played in teachers' positive and negative reactions to this course (peer-to-peer interaction, whole-group accountability, commitment, depth of content and pedagogical learning, and engagement)?

How does the length of an online course (six weeks versus a year) change what is required to get participants' complete commitment and engagement? What strategies do you think work best for longer-term (yearlong) courses?

Chapter 5

What do you see as the benefits and tradeoffs of the three versions of Seminars on Science (blended, online, and MOOCs)?

With Seminars on Science, how do you see the relationship between accessibility (or inclusivity) and scale?

How does the fact that Seminars on Science is run by a well-regarded museum impact the program? What would be different about a similar program that was not run by such an established institution? Do you think it would be successful?

How have partnerships contributed to the success of this model?

Chapter 6

Levy and Eisenkraft describe the difficulty of scaling-up a professional development model that requires a critical mass of participants all working in the same part of the curriculum at the same time. What workarounds could be developed if there is not enough critical mass?

The Share window of the APTC uses a moderator, an experienced physics teacher and moderator of online forums. Do you envision a Share window that might not require a moderator? What might be the benefits, other than cost savings, of creating a space without a moderator?

Lurkers posed an issue for the Share and Compare windows, since they did not contribute substantive content and comments in the windows. How sustainable is an online professional development model in which new, substantive content and comments are not posted? Other than mandated participation, how can teachers be supported to transform from lurkers into content creators?

This intervention relies on teachers' own self-analysis and assessment about what is working. What are potential challenges to that approach?

Chapter 7

What additional features are needed in order for teachers to continue find the eTG useful in improving their instruction?

What evaluation tool features would help teachers objectively determine that they are optimizing their practice?

The teachers who pilot-tested the eTG participated in a learning community to share their feedback, artifacts, and questions. How could offering an eTG online community or tools to set up a local community (online, F2F, or blended) support increased teacher use and understanding of the materials, strategies, and tools? How might the eTG learning community be designed to support implementation, sustainability, and scalability of the curriculum?

In the second case study, after using the reflection tool, the science teacher realized he lacked sufficient content knowledge. How could an eTG help teachers identify and address their content gaps prior to teaching the material?

Chapter 8

The goal of focusing on multiple conceptually rich investigations seems consistent with best practice. Many professional development models have focused on higher-order instruction and deep, meaningful content knowledge growth, but they have been unsuccessful. What about this professional development will overcome the challenges experienced in other similar trainings?

Zahm and Demery note several scalability issues with the initial model: short supply of experienced workshop leaders, large-scale delivery of effective workshops, affordability of face-to-face workshops, and inability to offer ongoing professional development during an implementation cycle. What other rationale is there for scaling a professional development model through online delivery?

The authors note that this model is now being adapted for the Interactive Mathematics Program's CyberPD system. Do you assume that the model will remain the same? What changes could be incorporated to address any concerns the authors noted with the initial rollout?

The authors indicate that their primary goal is for teachers to be able to make independent instructional decisions as they implement the curriculum with fidelity. Penuel and colleagues, in a recent *American Educational Research Journal* article, show that making independent instructional decisions is important and different than other types of professional development that focus on increasing content knowledge or making pedagogical changes.[1] If the goal is creating adaptive implementers, what are implications for the content and quality of online professional development?

Chapter 9

The authors use Anderson's equivalency interaction theorem, but this may seem like a justification to suggest that content-focused professional development can be weak on interaction. Is there any evidence that this is true? What about online learning works or doesn't work, and how is that integrated into this model?

What seem to be missing are practice, observation, and feedback. How do these work with this model?

The authors include just-in-time learning, which the professional development literature has shown to be important. To what extent are self-identified needs versus externally identified needs useful in driving such professional development?

The authors prefer to use the term *professional learning* as opposed to *professional development*. Prior to the adoption of the term *professional development,* the literature often used *teacher training*. Does it matter which term is adopted? Would all stakeholders favor the same term?

Chapter 10

The seven tips for the moderators are: (1) facilitate organization, (2) welcome newcomers, (3) encourage contributions, (4) support top contributors, (5) foster commitment, (6) address problems, and (7) model good behavior. Which of these would you rank as the most important? Which of these would you rank as least important? What additional tips do you have for online moderators to be successful?

The authors noted that a quick, short response to a post is more valuable than a delayed longer response. Under what circumstances do you think this is true? When do you think that the delayed longer response is more valuable?

What should be included in a community norms or guidelines statement? How should these norms and guidelines be generated?

When and why might synchronous activities be included in an online community?

Chapter 11

Consider the strengths and weaknesses in providing equitable access to online professional development. Have the legal requirements gone too far or not far enough?

Is there an economic limit to accessibility? When does the cost of accessibility impact the creativity of what can be done on a site that would benefit others? How is this decided?

How do knowledge and awareness of learning disabilities impact issues of accessibility?

What benefits do people without disabilities accrue from the modifications made to sites to make them accessible?

Chapter 12

Figure 12.1 lists qualities of effective professional development. In general, are some of these more important than others? Are some of these qualities defined differently for online professional development?

What are the opportunities and challenges of facilitated and self-paced professional learning?

In what ways does video support online professional learning? What purposes should video serve, and what video designs serve those purposes? How can developers address the access and accessibility issues for video and virtual meetings?

What suggestions do you have to provide effective and cost-effective online facilitator training to enable facilitated online professional developments programs to scale?

Notes

Introduction

1. H. Borko, J. Jacobs, and K. Koellner, "Contemporary Approaches to Teacher Professional Development," in *International Encyclopedia of Education*, ed. P. L. Peterson, E. Baker, and B. McGaw (New York: Elsevier, 2010), 548–556; L. Darling-Hammond et al., *Professional Learning in the Learning Profession: A Status Report on Teacher Development in the United States and Abroad* (Palo Alto, CA: National Staff Development Council and the School Redesign Network, Stanford University, 2009).

2. A. Kurz, "Alignment of the Intended, Planned, and Enacted Curriculum in General and Special Education and Its Relation to Student Achievement," *Journal of Special Education* 44, no. 3 (2010): 131–145.

3. C. Dede, "Reinventing the Role of Information and Communications Technologies in Education," in *Information and Communication Technologies: Considerations of Current Practice for Teachers and Teacher Educators, NSSE Yearbook*, ed. L. Smolin, K. Lawless, and N. Burbules (Malden, MA: Blackwell, 2007), 11–38.

4. National Council of Chief State School Officers and National Governors Association, *Common Core State Standards*, 2010, http://www.corestandards.org; H. Sweingruber, T. Keller, and H. Quinn, ed., *A Framework for K–12 Science Education: Practices, Crosscutting Concepts, and Core Ideas* (Washington, DC: National Academies Press, 2012); NGSS Lead States, *Next Generation Science Standards: For States, by States* (Washington, DC: National Academies Press, 2013).

5. C. Dede, *The Role of Technology in Deeper Learning. Students at the Center: Deeper Learning Research Series* (Boston: Jobs for the Future, 2014).

6. National Research Council, *Education for Life and Work: Developing Transferable Knowledge and Skills in the 21st Century* (Washington, DC: National Academies Press, 2012).

7. C. Dede, ed., *Online Professional Development for Teachers: Emerging Models and Methods* (Cambridge, MA: Harvard Education Press, 2006), 1–2.

8. Darling-Hammond et al., *Professional Learning*.

9. J. Mehta, "Why American Education Fails—and How Lessons from Abroad Could Improve It," *Foreign Affairs* 92, no. 3 (2013): 105–116.

10. Darling-Hammond et al., *Professional Learning*.

11. Dede, *Online Professional Development*.

12. A. Eisenkraft, *Active Physics: A Project-Based Inquiry Approach* (Armonk, NY: It's About Time, 2010). See also chapter 6 in this volume.

13. K. Frumin and C. Dede, "The Importance of Moderators," chapter 10 in this volume.

14. B. Fishman et al., *Professional Development for the Redesigned AP Biology Exam: Teacher Participation Patterns and Student Outcomes* (Philadelphia: American Educational Research Association, 2014).

Chapter 1

1. See, for example, H. Borko, "Professional Development and Teacher Learning: Mapping the Terrain," *Educational Researcher* 33, no. 8 (2004): 3–15; H. Borko, R. Elliot, and K. Uchiyama, "Professional Development: A Key to Kentucky's Educational Reform Effort," *Teaching and Teacher Education* 18, no. 8 (2002): 969–987.

2. M. Fullan, *The New Meaning of Educational Change*, 4th ed. (New York: Teachers College Press, 2007); J. A. Supovitz and H. M. Turner, "The Effects of Professional Development on Science Teaching Practices and Classroom Culture," *Journal of Research in Science Teaching* 37, no. 9 (2000): 963–980; B. Fishman et al., "Linking Teacher and Student Learning to Improve Professional Development in Systemic Reform," *Teaching and Teacher Education* 19, no. 6 (2003): 643–658.

3. C. Dede et al., "A Research Agenda for Online Teacher Professional Development," *Journal of Teacher Education* 60, no. 1 (2009): 9; Fullan, *New Meaning*.

4. US Department of Education, *Transforming American Education: Learning Powered by Technology; National Education Technology Plan 2010* (Washington, DC: US Department of Education, Office of Educational Technology, 2010), https://www.ed.gov/sites/default/files/netp2010.pdf.

5. R. E. Clark, "Reconsidering Research on Learning from Media," *Review of Educational Research* 53, no. 4 (1983): 445–459; R. B. Kozma, "Will Media Influence Learning? Reframing the Debate," *Educational Technology Research and Development* 42, no. 2 (1994): 7–19.

6. J. M. Roschelle et al., "Changing How and What Children Learn in School with Computer-Based Technologies," *The Future of Children: Children and Computer Technology* 10, no. 2 (2000): 76–101.

7. C. Vrasidas and G. V. Glass, "Teacher Professional Development: Issues and Trends," in *Online Professional Development for Teachers*, ed. C. Vrasidas and G. V. Glass (Greenwich: Information Age, 2004), 1–11. There are notable exceptions, including early efforts at using synchronous online environments such as MUDs or MOOs to support professional learning. See, for example, P. Curtis and D. A. Nichols, "MUDs Grow up: Social Virtual Reality in the Real World," in *Compcon Spring '94 Digest of Papers* (San Francisco: IEEE, 1994). However, these environments only rarely involve K–12 teachers.

8. R. Tinker and S. Haavind, "Netcourses and Netseminars: Current Practice and New Designs," *Journal of Science Education and Technology* 5, no. 3 (1996): 217–223.

9. E. Wenger, *Communities of Practice: Learning, Meaning, and Identity* (Cambridge, UK: Cambridge University Press, 1998); R. W. Marx et al., "New Technologies for Teacher Professional Development," *Teaching and Teacher Education* 14, no. 1 (1998): 33–52.

10. M. S. Schlager, J. Fusco, and P. Schank, "Evolution of an Online Education Community of Practice," in *Building Virtual Communities: Learning and Change in Cyberspace*, ed. K. A. Renninger and W. Shumar (New York: Cambridge University Press, 2002), 129–158.

11. M. S. Wiske and D. E. Spicer, "Teacher Education as Teaching for Understanding with New Technologies," in *International Encyclopedia of Education*, ed. P. L. Peterson, E. Baker, and B. McGaw (Toronto: Elsevier, 2008).

12. K. A. Renninger and W. Shumar, "The Centrality of Culture and Community to Participant Learning at and with the Math Forum," in *Designing for Virtual Communities in the Service of Learning*, ed. S. Barab, R. Kling, and J. Gray (Cambridge, UK: Cambridge University Press, 2004), 181–209.

13. Fishman et al., "Linking Teacher and Student Learning."

14. L. Desimone, "Improving Impact Studies of Teachers' Professional Development: Toward Better Conceptualizations and Measures," *Educational Researcher* 38, no. 3 (2009): 181–199. The core features of professional developmented listed here are as defined in M. S. Garet et al., "What Makes Professional Development Effective? Results from a National Sample of Teachers," *American Educational Research Journal* 38, no. 4 (2001): 915–945.

15. B. Fishman and C. Dede, "Teaching and Technology: New Tools for New Times," *Handbook of Research on Teaching*, 5th ed., ed. D. Gitomer and C. Bell (Washington, DC: American Educational Research Association, forthcoming).

16. National Research Council, *Rising above the Gathering Storm* (Washington, DC: National Academy of Sciences, National Academy of Engineering, Institute of Medicine, 2007); National Research Council, *Rising above the Gathering Storm, Revisited* (Washington, DC: National Academy of Sciences, National Academy of Engineering, Institute of Medicine, 2010); T. L. Friedman, *The World Is Flat: A Brief History of the Twenty-First Century*, 1st ed. (New York: Farrar, Straus & Giroux, 2005).

17. National Research Council, *Education for Life and Work: Developing Transferable Knowledge and Skills in the 21st Century* (Washington, DC: National Academies Press, 2012).

18. US Department of Education, *Transforming American Education*. Chris Dede and Barry Fishman were part of the technical working group that produced the 2010 National Education Technology Plan and helped shape the teaching section of the document in particular.

19. See, for example, D. Lortie, *Schoolteacher: A Sociological Study* (Chicago: University of Chicago Press, 1975).

20. J. Banks et al., *Learning in and out of School in Diverse Environments: Life-Long, Life-Wide, Life-Deep* (Seattle: NSF LIFE Center and University of Washington Center for Multicultural Education, 2006); M. Ito et al., *Connected Learning: An Agenda for Research and Design* (Irvine, CA: Digital Media and Learning Research Hub, 2013).

21. See, for example, H. Borko, J. Jacobs, and K. Koellner, "Contemporary Approaches to Teacher Professional Development," in *International Encyclopedia of Education*, ed. P. L. Peterson, E. Baker, and B. McGaw (Toronto: Elsevier, 2008), 548–556; T. A. McMahon, *From Isolation to Interaction? Computer-Mediated Communications and Teacher Professional Development* (Bloomington: Indiana University Press, 1996); R. Putnam and H. Borko, "What Do New Views of Knowledge and Thinking Have to Say About Research on Teacher Learning?" *Educational Researcher* 29, no. 1 (2000): 4–15; R. R. Ruopp et al., *LabNet: Toward a Community of Practice* (Hillsdale, NJ: Erlbaum, 1993).

22. See, for example, D. F. McCaffrey et al., "Models for Value-Added Modeling of Teacher Effects," *Journal of Educational and Behavioral Statistics* 29, no. 1 (2004): 67–101.

23. Vrasidas and Glass, "Teacher Professional Development."

24. See, for example, T. Walker, "No More 'Sit and Get': Rebooting Teacher Professional Development," *National Education Association* (blog), April 29, 2013, http://neatoday.org/2013/04/29/no-more-sit-and-get-getting-serious-about-effective-professional-development/; Fullan, *New Meaning*.

25. Putnam and Borko, "New Views of Knowledge and Thinking"; National Research Council, *Education for Life and Work*.

26. The characterization of constructivist pedagogy as "more demanding" than behaviorist or cognitivist pedagogies is not intended as a value judgment. Rather, it is an observation that constructivist learning environments tend to have many moving parts that require coordination and are thus more difficult to enact successfully or congruently with their original designer's intent.

27. Putnam and Borko, "New Views of Knowledge and Thinking."

28. J. S. Brown, A. Collins, and P. Duguid, "Situated Cognition and the Culture of Learning," *Educational Researcher* 18, no. 1 (1989): 32–42; J. Lave and E. Wenger, *Situated Learning: Legitimate Peripheral Participation* (Cambridge, UK: Cambridge University Press, 1991).

29. Desimone, "Improving Impact Studies"; C. Lewis, R. Perry, and A. Murata, "How Should Research Contribute to Instructional Improvement? The Case of Lesson Study," *Educational Researcher* 35, no. 3 (2006): 3–14; J. Stigler, *The Teaching Gap: Best Ideas from the World's Teachers for Improving Education in the Classroom,* 1st ed. (New York: Free Press, 2009)

30. E. A. Davis and J. S. Krajcik, "Designing Educative Curriculum Materials to Promote Teacher Learning," *Educational Researcher* 34, no. 3 (2005): 2–14.

31. A. Eisenkraft, *Active Physics* (Armonk, NY: It's About Time, 2010).

32. Lave and Wenger, *Situated Learning*; Wenger, *Communities of Practice*; A. Collins, J. S. Brown, and S. Newman, "Cognitive Apprenticeship: Teaching the Crafts of Reading, Writing, and Mathematics," in *Knowing, Learning, and Instruction: Essays in Honor of Robert Glaser*, ed. L. Resnick (Hillsdale, NJ: Erlbaum, 1989), 453–494; S. Barab and T. M. Duffy, "From Practice Fields to Communities of Practice," in *Theoretical Foundations of Learning Environments*, ed. D. Jonassen and S. Land (Mahwah, NJ: Erlbaum, 1999), 25–55.

33. Fishman et al., "Linking Teacher and Student Learning"; B. Kubitskey and B. Fishman, "A Role for Professional Development in Sustainability: Linking the Written Curriculum to Enactment," in *7th International Conference of the Learning Sciences*, vol. 1 (Mahwah, NJ: Erlbaum, 2006), 363–369.

34. B. Kubitskey et al., "Curriculum-Aligned Professional Development for Geospatial Education," in *Teaching Science and Investigating Environmental Issues with Geospatial Technology,* ed. J. MaKinster, N. Trautmann, and M. Barnett (Dordrecht, Germany: Springer, 2014), 153–171.

35. B. Fishman et al., "Comparing the Impact of Online and Face-to-Face Professional Development in the Context of Curriculum Implementation," *Journal of Teacher Education* 64, no. 5 (2013): 426–438.

36. Renninger and Shumar, "The Centrality of Culture and Community"; M. S. Schlager and J. Fusco, "Teacher Professional Development, Technology, and Communities of Practice:

Are We Putting the Cart Before the Horse?" in *Designing for Virtual Communities in the Service of Learning*, ed. S. Barab, R. Kling, and J. Gray (Cambridge, UK: Cambridge University Press, 2004), 120–153; Ruopp et al., *LabNet*.

37. J. D. Bransford et al., "Anchored Instruction: Why We Need It and How Technology Can Help," in *Cognition, Education, and Multimedia: Exploring Ideas in High Technology*, ed. D. Nix and R. Spiro (Hillsdale, NJ: Erlbaum, 1990), 115–141.

38. Cognition and Technology Group at Vanderbilt, *The Jasper Project: Lessons in Curriculum, Instruction, Assessment, and Professional Development* (Mahwah, NJ: Erlbaum, 1997).

39. V. Richardson and R. S. Kile, "Learning from Videocases," in *Who Learns What from Cases and How? The Research Base for Teaching and Learning with Cases*, ed. M. A. Lundeberg, B. B. Levin, and H. L. Harrington (Mahwah, NJ: Erlbaum, 1999), 121–136.

40. T. Chaney-Cullen and T. M. Duffy, "Strategic Teaching Frameworks: Multimedia to Support Teacher Change," *Journal of the Learning Sciences* 8, no. 1 (1998): 1–40.

41. Putnam and Borko, "New Views of Knowledge and Thinking."

42. R. D. Pea, "Practices of Distributed Intelligence and Designs for Education," in *Distributed Cognitions: Psychological and Educational Considerations*, ed. G. Salomon (New York: Cambridge University Press, 1993), 47–87.

43. M. Consalvo, "Cheating Can Be Good for You: Educational Games and Multiple Play Styles," *On the Horizon* 13, no. 2 (2005): 95–100.

44. G. Salomon, D. N. Perkins, and T. Globerson, "Partners in Cognition: Extending Human Intelligence with Intelligent Technologies," *Educational Researcher* 20, no. 3 (1991): 2–9.

45. L. Johnson et al., *NMC Horizon Report: 2014 Higher Education Edition* (Austin, TX: the New Media Consortium, 2014); L. Johnson et al., *NMC Horizon Report: 2014 K–12 Education Edition* (Austin, TX: the New Media Consortium, 2014).

46. A. McAuley et al., "The MOOC Model for Digital Practice," 2010, https://oerknow ledgecloud.org/sites/oerknowledgecloud.org/files/MOOC_Final_0.pdf; Vrasidas and Glass, "Teacher Professional Development."

47. McAuley et al., "MOOC Model."

48. I. Bogost, "MOOCs and the Future of the Humanities (Part One)," *Ian Bogost* (blog), June 14, 2013, http://bogost.com/writing/moocs_and_the_future_of_the_hu/.

49. W. G. Bowen et al., *Interactive Learning Online at Public Universities: Evidence from Randomized Trials* (New York: Ithaka S+R, 2012); R. Murphy et al., *Blended Learning Report* (Menlo Park, CA: Michael & Susan Dell Foundation and SRI International, 2014).

50. See https://www.mooc-list.com/tags/teacher-education for a curated list of MOOCs and MOOC-like offerings aimed at teachers.

51. W. Harlen and S. J. Doubler, "Can Teachers Learn Through Enquiry On-Line? Studying Professional Development in Science Delivered On-Line and On-Campus," *International Journal of Science Education* 26, no. 10 (2004): 1247–1267.

52. Schlager and Fusco, "Teacher Professional Development."

53. Garet et al., "What Makes Professional Development Effective?"; W. R. Penuel et al., "What Makes Professional Development Effective? Strategies That Foster Curriculum Implementation," *American Educational Research Journal* 44, no. 4 (2007): 921–958.

54. J. Moon et al., "Beyond Comparisons of Online Versus Face-to-Face PD Commentary in Response to Fishman et al., 'Comparing the Impact of Online and Face-to-Face Profes-

sional Development in the Context of Curriculum Implementation,'" *Journal of Teacher Education* 65, no. 2 (2014): 172–176, doi: 10.1177/0022487113511497.

55. J. A. Supovitz and S. G. Zeif, "Why They Stay Away," *Journal of Staff Development* 21, no. 4 (2000): 24–28.

56. L. Takeuchi and S. Vaala, *Level Up Learning: A National Survey on Teaching with Digital Games* (New York: Joan Ganz Cooney Center at Sesame Workshop, 2014).

57. National Research Council, *Learning Science: Computer Games, Simulations, and Education* (Washington, DC: Board on Science Education, Division of Behavioral and Social Sciences and Education, 2011).

58. R. Christensen et al., "SimSchool: An Online Dynamic Simulator for Enhancing Teacher Preparation," *International Journal of Learning Technology* 6, no. 2 (2011): 201–220.

59. A. Arici and S. Barab, "Quest2Teach: Digitally Bridging Educational Theory to Practice," in *Proceedings of the Games, Learning, and Society Conference*, vol. 4, ed. A. Ochsner et al. (Pittsburgh: ETC Press, 2014); S. Barab et al., "Transformational Play as a Curricular Scaffold: Using Videogames to Support Science Education," *Journal of Science Education and Technology* 18, no. 4 (2009): 305–320.

60. A. T. Hayes et al., "Ludic Learning: Exploration of TLE TeachLivE and Effective Teacher Training," *International Journal of Gaming and Computer-Mediated Simulations* 5, no. 2 (2013): 20–33.

61. I. Bogost, "Gamification Is Bullshit," *Ian Bogost* (blog), August 8, 2011, http://www.bogost.com/blog/gamification_is_bullshit.shtml.

62. K. Langdon, "Thinking About Classroom Dojo—Why Not Just Tase Your Kids Instead?" *TeachingAce* (blog), August 31, 2013, http://www.teachingace.com/thinking-about-classroom-dojo-why-not-just-tase-your-kids-instead/2013.

63. C. Haskell, "3D GameLab: Quest-Based Pre-Service Teacher Education," in *Cases on Digital Game-Based Learning: Methods, Models, and Strategies*, ed. Y. Baek and N. Whitton (Hershey, PA: IGI Global, 2013), 302–340.

64. S. Aguilar, C. Holman, and B. Fishman, "Game-Inspired Design: Empirical Evidence in Support of Gameful Learning Environments." *Games and Culture* (in press), doi:10.1177/1555412015600305.

65. S. Rigby and R. M. Ryan, *Glued to Games: How Video Games Draw Us in and Hold Us Spellbound* (Santa Barbara, CA: Praeger, 2011); R. M. Ryan and E. L. Deci, "Self-Determination Theory and the Facilitation of Intrinsic Motivation, Social Development, and Well-Being," *American Psychologist*, 55, no. 1 (2000): 68–78.

66. A. Collins and R. Halverson, *Rethinking Education in the Age of Technology: The Digital Revolution and Schooling in America* (New York: Teachers College Press, 2009).

67. Ito et al., *Connected Learning*; D. Thomas and J. S. Brown, *A New Culture of Learning: Cultivating the Imagination for a World of Constant Change* (North Charleston, SC: Create Space, 2011).

68. US Department of Education, *Transforming American Education*.

69. M. M. Riconscente, A. Kamarainen, and M. Honey, *STEM badges: Current Terrain and the Road Ahead* (New York: New York Hall of Science, 2013).

70. D. Hickey, "Recognizing, Supporting, and Attracting Adult Learners with Digital Badges," *EvoLLLution* (blog), November 20, 2012, http://www.evolllution.com/program_planning/recognizing-supporting-and-attracting-adult-learners-with-digital-badges/.

71. G. Siemens, "Learning Analytics: The Emergence of a Discipline," *American Behavioral Scientist* 57, no. 10 (2013): 1380–1400, doi: 10.1177/0002764213498851.

72. J. R. Anderson et al., "Cognitive Tutors: Lessons Learned," *Journal of the Learning Sciences* 4 (1995): 167–207.

73. R. D. Pea, *The Learning Analytics Workgroup: A Report on Building the Field of Learning Analytics for Personalized Learning at Scale* (Palo Alto, CA: Stanford University, 2014).

74. Putnam and Borko, "New Views of Knowledge and Thinking."

75. Moon et al. "Beyond Comparisons"; Ito et al., *Connected Learning*.

76. G. Collison et al., *Facilitating Online Learning: Effective Strategies for Moderators* (Madison, WI: Atwood, 2000).

77. C. Dede et al., "A Research Agenda for Online Teacher Professional Development," *Journal of Teacher Education* 60, no. 1 (2009): 8–19.

78. Ibid., 13.

79. A. L. Brown, "Design Experiments: Theoretical and Methodological Challenges in Creating Complex Interventions in Classroom Settings," *Journal of the Learning Sciences* 2, no. 2 (1992): 141–178; Design-Based Research Collective, "Design-Based Research: An Emerging Paradigm for Educational Inquiry," *Educational Researcher* 32, no. 1 (2003): 5–8.

80. P. Cobb et al., "Design Experiments in Educational Research," *Educational Researcher* 32, no. 1 (2003): 10.

81. B. Fishman et al., "Creating a Framework for Research on Systemic Technology Innovations," *Journal of the Learning Sciences* 13, no. 1 (2004): 43–76.

82. B. Fishman et al., *Design-Based Implementation Research: Theories, Methods, and Exemplars. National Society for the Study of Education Yearbook*, vol. 2 (New York: Teachers College Record, 2013).

83. W. R. Penuel et al., "Organizing Research and Development at the Intersection of Learning, Implementation, and Design," *Educational Researcher* 40, no. 7 (2011): 332.

84. Supovitz and Zeif, "Why They Stay Away."

Chapter 2

1. R. D. Pea, "Practices of Distributed Intelligence and Designs for Education," in *Distributed Cognitions: Psychological and Educational Considerations*, ed. G. Salomon (New York: Cambridge University Press, 1993), 47–87; E. Hutchins, "Distributed Cognition," in *The Routledge Handbook of Language and Professional Communication*, ed. V. Bhatia and S. Bremner (New York: Routledge, 2000), http://www.artmap-research.com/wp-content/uploads/2009/11/Hutchins_DistributedCognition.pdf; J. G. Greeno, "Learning in Activity," in *The Cambridge Handbook of the Learning Sciences*, ed. R. K. Sawyer (New York: Cambridge University Press, 2006), 79–96.

2. National Research Council, *A Framework for Science Education, Practices, Crosscutting Concepts, and Core Ideas* (Washington, DC: National Academies Press, 2012).

3. A. Collins, J. Brown, and A. Holum, "Cognitive Apprenticeship: Making Thinking Visible," *American Educator* 15, no. 3 (1991): 6–11.

4. M. Knowles, E. Holton, and R. Swanson, *The Adult Learner* (Burlington, VT: Elsevier, 2005).

5. To view the case, go to http://www.inquiryproject.terc.edu/prof_dev/pathway/pathway5. cfm?pathway_step=step6&pathway_substep=substep3.

6. J. S. Brown, A. Collins, and P. Duguid, "Situated Cognition and the Culture of Learning," *Educational Researcher* 18, no. 1 (1989): 32–42.

7. These ideas, concepts, and challenges are also found in the aligned readings by Tobin, *The Scientist*, http://inquiryproject.terc.edu/curriculum/curriculum5/child_and_scientist/roger5_3. cfm, and by Smith, *The Child*, http://inquiryproject.terc.edu/curriculum/curriculum5/ child_and_scientist/carol5_3.cfm.

8. See http://inquiryproject.terc.edu/prof_dev/resources/video_cases/video_case.cfm?case_ type=sc&case_grade=5&case_num=3&case_return=ip_5_3.

9. See http://inquiryproject.terc.edu/research/talk_science/.

10. S. Michaels et al., *Accountable Talk: Classroom Conversation That Works* (Pittsburgh: University of Pittsburgh Press, 2002).

11. D. Barnes, *From Communication to Curriculum*, 2nd ed. (Portsmouth, NH: Heineman, 1992); J. L. Lemke, *Talking Science: Language, Learning, and Values* (Norwood, NJ: Ablex, 1993); R. Alexander, *Culture and Pedagogy: International Comparisons in Primary Education* (Oxford, UK: Blackwell, 2001); C. Cazden, *Classroom Discourse: The Language of Teaching and Learning* (Portsmouth, NH: Heinemann, 2001).

12. C. Wallace, "Overview of the Role of Teacher Beliefs in Science Education," in *The Role of Science Teachers' Beliefs in International Classrooms*, ed. R. Evans et al. (Rotterdam: Sense, 2014).

13. J. Lave and E. Wenger, *Situated Learning: Legitimate Peripheral Participation* (Cambridge, UK: Cambridge University Press, 1991), 101.

14. Ibid., 102.

Chapter 3

The authors thank Alex Brier, Dave Frye, Mark Samberg, and Blythe Tyron for their many contributions to the overall Friday Institute MOOC-Ed initiative, along with Lauren Acree, Tamar Avineri, Sherry Booth, Suzanne Brannon, Natasha Elliott, Nicole Fonger, Abbey Futrell, Abbey Graham, Teresa Gibson, Lisa Hervey, Alex Kaulfuss, Shea Kerkhoff, Shaun Kellogg, Verna Lalbeharie, Hollylynne Lee, John Lee, Erin Lyjak, Brittany Miller, Benjamin Robinson, Hiller Spires, Jaclyn Stevens, Isaac Thompson, Dung Tran, and Eric Wiebe, all from the Friday Institute, for their contributions to the development of the MOOC-Eds and the related research program. They also thank North Carolina governor Bob Wise, Sara Hall, and the Alliance for Excellent Education team for their collaboration on the Digital Learning Transition MOOC-Ed, along with the many colleagues and consultants from other organizations who have contributed to this initiative. The work reported in this chapter has been supported by the Hewlett Foundation, the Oak Foundation, Lenovo, Google, and the State of North Carolina.

1. The National Center for Education Statistics reports 3.5 million teachers in the United States. See http://nces.ed.gov/fastfacts/display.asp?id=28.

2. R. C. Wei, L. Darling-Hammond, and F. Adamson, *Professional Development in the United States: Trends and Challenges* (Dallas: National Staff Development Council, 2010).

3. L. Darling-Hammond et al., *Professional Learning in the Learning Profession: A Status Report on Teacher Development in the United States and Abroad* (Dallas: National Staff Development Council, 2009).

4. G. M. Kleiman and B. Treacy, "EdTech Leaders Online: Building Organizational Capacity to Provide Effective Online Professional Development," in *Online Professional Development for Teachers: Emerging Models and Methods*, ed. C. Dede (Cambridge, MA: Harvard Education Press, 2006).

5. L. M. O'Dwyer et al., "E-Learning for Educators: Effects of On-Line Professional Development on Teachers and Their Students: Findings from Four Randomized Trials," 2010, http://www.bc.edu/research/intasc/PDF/EFE_Findings2010_Report.pdf; S. Dash et al., "Impact of Online Professional Development or Teacher Quality and Student Achievement in Fifth Grade Mathematics," *Journal of Research on Technology in Education* 45, no. 1 (2012): 1–26; R. de Kramer et al., "The Effects of Online Teacher Professional Development on Seventh Grade Teachers' and Students' Knowledge and Practices in English Language Arts," *Teacher Educator* 47, no. 3 (2012): 236–259.

6. R. Carey et al., "Online Courses for Math Teachers: Comparing Self-Paced and Facilitated Cohort Approaches," *Journal of Technology, Learning, and Assessment* 7 no. 3 (2008); M. Russell et al., "Comparing Self-Paced and Cohort-Based Online Courses for Teachers," *Journal of Research on Technology in Education* 41, no. 4 (2009): 443–466.

7. S. E. Booth and S. B. Kellogg, "Value Creation in Online Communities for Educators," *British Journal of Educational Technology* (May 2014), doi: 10.1111/bjet.12168; S. Kellogg, S. Booth, and K. Oliver, "A Social Network Perspective on Peer Supported Learning in MOOCs for Educators," *International Review of Research in Open and Distance Learning* 15, no. 5 (2014): 264–289.

8. Darling-Hammond et al., *Professional Learning*; iNACOL, *National Standards for Quality Online Teaching* (Vienna, VA: iNACOL, 2011).

9. H. A. Spires et al., "Relating Inquiry to Disciplinary Literacy: A Pedagogical Approach," 2014, MOOC-Ed.org, http://www.mooc-ed.org/wp-content/uploads/2014/10/Literary_discipline_9.28.14.pdf.

10. P. Mishra, M. J. Koehler, and D. Henriksen, "The 7 Trans-Disciplinary Habits of Mind: Extending the TPACK Framework Towards 21st Century Learning," *Educational Technology* (2010); R. R. Puentedura, "The SAMR Model: Background and Exemplars," *Hippasus* (blog), August 23, 2012, http://wiki.milaca.k12.mn.us/sandbox/groups/samr/wiki/welcome/attachments/9dbda/SAMR%20Geography%20Examples.pdf?sessionID=ea21d61e21160d01b883c2e38459e65c40e052d0.

11. Completed research has already been reported in G. M. Kleiman, M. A. Wolf, and D. Frye, *The Digital Learning Transition MOOC for Educators: Exploring a Scalable Approach to Professional Development* (Washington, DC: Alliance for Excellent Education, 2013); and in Kellogg, Booth, and Oliver, "Social Network Perspective."

Chapter 4

1. B. Fishman et al., "Comparing the Impact of Online and Face-to-Face Professional Development in the Context of Curriculum Implementation," *Journal of Teacher Education* 64, no. 5 (2013): 426–438; B. Treacy, G. Kleiman, and K. Peterson, "Successful Online Professional Development," *Learning and Leading with Technology* 30, no. 1 (2002): 42–49.

2. C. Greenleaf et al., "Integrating Literacy and Science in Biology: Teaching and Learning Impacts of Reading Apprenticeship Professional Development," *American Educational Research Journal* 48, no. 3 (2011): 647–717.

3. National Assessment of Educational Progress, *The Nation's Report Card: Reading 2007* (No. NCES 2007-496) (Washington, DC: National Center for Education Statistics, 2007); J. Snipes and A. Horwitz, *Advancing Adolescent Literacy in Urban Schools. Research Brief* (Washington, DC: Council of the Great City Schools, 2007).

4. National Council of Chief State School Officers and National Governors Association, *Common Core Standards for English Language Arts and Literacy in History/Social Studies and Science*, 2010, http://www.corestandards.org.

5. National Research Council, *Literacy for Science: Exploring the Intersection of the Next Generation Science Standards and Common Core for ELA Standards: A Workshop Summary* (Washington, DC: National Research Council, 2014); NGSS Lead States, *Next Generation Science Standards: For States, by State*s (Washington, DC: National Academies Press, 2013).

6. L. D. Yore et al., "New Directions in Language and Science Education Research," *Reading Research Quarterly* 39, no. 3 (2004): 347–352.

7. C. Greenleaf and R. Schoenbach, "Building Capacity for the Responsive Teaching of Reading in the Academic Disciplines: Strategic Inquiry Designs for Middle and High School Teachers' Professional Development," in *Improving Reading Achievement Through Professional Development*, ed. D. Strickland and M. L. Kamil (Norwood, NJ: Christopher-Gordon, 2004); P. D. Pearson, E. Moje, and C. Greenleaf, "Literacy and Science: Each in the Service of the Other," *Science* 328, no. 5977 (2010): 459–463; T. Shanahan and C. Shanahan, "Teaching Disciplinary Literacy to Adolescents: Rethinking Content-Area Literacy," *Harvard Educational Review* 78, no. 1 (2008): 40–60.

8. G. N. Cervetti et al., "Reading and Writing in the Service of Inquiry-Based Science," in *Linking Science and Literacy in the K–8 Classroom*, ed. R. Douglas, M. Klentshy, and K. Worth (Arlington, VA: National Science Teachers Association Press, 2006), 221–244; C. H. Weiss et al., *Looking Inside the Classroom: A Study of K–12 Mathematics and Science Education in the United States* (Chapel Hill, NC: Horizon Research, 2003).

9. C. S. Dweck and D. Molden, "Self-Theories: Their Impact on Competence Motivation and Acquisition," in *Handbook of Competence and Motivation*, ed. A. Elliot and C. S. Dweck (New York: Guilford Press, 2005); M. L. Kamil et al., *Improving Adolescent Literacy: Effective Classroom and Intervention Practices; A Practice Guide* (Washington, DC: National Center for Education Evaluation and Regional Assistance, Institute of Education Services, 2008); Pearson, Moje, and Greenleaf, "Literacy and Science."

10. R. Schoenbach, C. Greenleaf, and L. Murphy, *Reading for Understanding: How Reading Apprenticeship Improves Disciplinary Learning in Secondary and College Classrooms*, 2nd ed. (San Francisco: Jossey-Bass, 2012).

11. S. R. Goldman and G. Bisanz, "Toward a Functional Analysis of Scientific Genres: Implications for Understanding and Learning Processes," in *The Psychology of Science Text Comprehension*, ed. J. Otero, J. A. León, and A. C. Graesser (Mahwah, NJ: Erlbaum, 2002), 19–50; P. van den Broek, "Using Texts in Science Education: Cognitive Processes and Knowledge Representation," *Science* 328, no. 5977 (2010): 453–456.

12. M. W. Conley, "Cognitive Strategy Instruction for Adolescents: What We Know About the Promise, What We Don't Know About the Potential," *Harvard Educational Review* 78, no. 1 (2008): 84–106; R. A. Duschl and J. Osborne, "Supporting and Promoting Argumentation Discourse in Science Education," *Studies in Science Education* 38, no. 1 (2002):

39–72; S. P. Norris and L. M. Phillips, "How Literacy in Its Fundamental Sense Is Central to Scientific Literacy," *Science Education* 87, no. 2 (2003): 224–240.

13. R. Schoenbach and C. Greenleaf, "Fostering Adolescents' Engaged Academic Literacy," in *Handbook of Adolescent Literacy Research*, ed. L. Christenburg, R. Bomer, and P. Smagorinsky (New York: Guilford Press, 2009).

14. Greenleaf et al., "Integrating Literacy and Science."

15. Schoenbach, Greenleaf, and Murphy, *Reading for Understanding*.

16. See http://readingapprenticeship.org/research-impact/research-results-tools/randomized-controlled-studies/.

17. D. Ball and D. Cohen, "Developing Practice, Developing Practitioners: Toward a Practice-Based Theory of Professional Education," in *Teaching as the Learning Profession: Handbook of Policy and Practice*, ed. L. Darling-Hammond and G. Sykes (San Francisco: Jossey-Bass, 1999), 3–32; D. A. Schon, *The Reflective Turn* (New York: Teachers College Press, 1991); L. S. Shulman, "Knowledge and Teaching: Foundations of the New Reform," *Harvard Educational Review* 57, no. 1 (1987): 1–23.

18. C. E. Coburn, "Rethinking Scale: Moving Beyond Numbers to Deep and Lasting Change," *Educational Researcher* 32, no. 6 (2003): 3–12; L. Darling-Hammond and N. Richardson, "Research Review/Teacher Learning: What Matters," *Educational Leadership* 66, no. 5 (2009): 46–53.

19. Grant U411C120094, 2012–2016, was funded by the US Department of Education's Office of Innovation and Improvement.

20. By the last year of the project, in June 2017, three cohorts of teachers and two cohorts of instructors-in-training will have participated in iRAISE. Teachers are paid for participation in the professional development; participants are also eligible to receive university credit.

21. These grants were National Science Foundation grant 0440379, 2005–2008; IES grant R305M05003, 2006–2010; and Office of Innovation and Improvement i3 Validation grant U396B100255 2010–2015.

22. The core iRAISE design team included the four coauthors of this article as well as two WestEd colleagues who specialize in web-based learning design, Bob Montgomery and Kurt Larsen. In addition, two meetings with an advisory group of teachers and Barbara Treacy, a national expert in online professional development, provided important input for the core design team.

23. The facilitators were Reading Apprenticeship staff and chapter coauthors Willard Brown and Heather Howlett. The other facilitator, Curtis Refior, is a longtime Reading Apprenticeship teacher and consultant.

24. Schoenbach, Greenleaf, and Murphy, *Reading for Understanding*.

25. M. Toby, A. Schellinger, A. Jaciw, and Empirical Education, Inc., *iRAISE Final Internal Feedback Report* (Palo Alto, CA: Empirical Education, 2014).

26. M. Toby, M. A., Schellinger, A., Jaciw, and Empirical Education, Inc., *iRaise Final Report Evaluation Report* (Palo Alto, CA: Empirical Education, forthcoming), available at http://empirical education.com/pdfs/iRAISE-FR.pdf.

27. R. J. Mislevy and J. P. Sabatini, "How Research on Reading and Research on Assessment are Transforming Reading Assessment (or If They Aren't, How They Ought to)," in *Measuring Up: Advances in How We Assess Reading Ability*, ed. J. P. Sabatini, E. Albro, and T.

O'Reilly (Lanham, MD: Rowman & Littlefield, 2012). As of 2015, neither teacher implementation nor student assessments for the study year 2014–2015 are reported. Empirical Education will be publishing the *iRAISE Evaluation Report* in the winter of 2016.

28. S. E. Booth, "Cultivating Knowledge Sharing and Trust in Online Communities for Educators," *Journal of Educational Computing Research* 47, no. 1 (2012): 1–31.

Chapter 5

1. L. Stokes et al., *Results from the Independent Evaluation of the Seminars on Science* (Inverness, CA: Inverness Research, 2007).
2. C. Dede, ed., *Online Professional Development for Teachers: Emerging Models and Methods* (Cambridge, MA: Harvard Education Press, 2006).
3. D. Randle, "An Analysis of Interactions and Outcomes Associated with an Online Professional Development Course for Science Teachers" (PhD diss., Teacher College, Columbia University, 2013).
4. H. Quinn, T. Keller, and H. Schweingruber, eds., *A Framework for K–12 Science Education: Practices, Crosscutting Concepts, and Core Ideas* (Washington, DC: National Academies Press, 2012); NGSS Lead States, *Next Generation Science Standards: For States, by States* (Washington, DC: National Academies Press, 2013).
5. C. Dede, *Online Professional Development for Teachers.*
6. G. Collison et al., *Facilitating Online Learning: Effective Strategies for Moderators* (Madison, WI: Atwood, 2000).
7. Stokes et al., *Results.*
8. Inverness Research, *The AMNH* Seminars on Science *Project: Lessons Learned from Phase I 1992–2002* (Inverness, CA: Inverness Research, 2002), 13.
9. Stokes et al., *Results*, 1.
10. Ibid.
11. Ibid.
12. Ibid., 4.
13. Ibid.
14. Ibid., 5.
15. Inverness Research, *AMNH Seminars on Science*, 37.
16. Ibid., 9.
17. Inverness Research, *Evaluation for AMNH Seminars on Science: I. The Climate Change Course, Year 2 and II. The Pilot PoLAR Curricular Unit Plan Repository* (Inverness, CA: Inverness Research, 2012), 2.
18. Inverness Research, *Evaluation*, 15.
19. Randle, "Analysis of Interactions."
20. C. Dede, P. Whitehouse, and T. Brown-L'Bahy, "Designing and Studying Learning Experiences That Use Multiple Interactive Media to Bridge Distance and Time," in *Current Perspectives on Applied Information Technologies: Distance Education and Distributed Learning*, ed. C. Vrasidas and G. Glass (Charlotte, NC: Information Age Press, 2002), 1–30; M. Bullen, "Participation and Critical Thinking in Online University Distance Education," *Journal of Distance Education* 13, no. 2 (1998): 1–32.
21. D. R. Garrison, T. Anderson, and W. Archer, "Critical Thinking, Cognitive Presence, and Computer Conferencing in Distance Education," *American Journal of Distance Education* 15, no. 1 (2001): 7–23.

22. T. McKlin, S. W. Harmon, W. Evans, and M. G. Jones, "Cognitive Presence in Web-Based Learning: A Content Analysis of Students' Online Discussions," *ITFORUM*, March 21, 2002, http://it.coe.uga.edu/itforum/paper60/paper60.htm; K. A. Meyer, "Face-to-Face Versus Threaded Discussions: The Role of Time and Higher-Order Thinking," *Journal of Asynchronous Learning Networks* 7, no. 3 (2003): 55–65; N. Vaughn and D. R. Garrison, "Creating Cognitive Presence in a Blended Faculty Development Community," *Internet and Higher Education* 8, no. 1 (2005): 1–12; Garrison, Anderson, and Archer, "Critical Thinking"; P. Celentin, "Online Education: Analysis of Interaction and Knowledge Building Patterns Among Foreign Language Teachers," *Journal of Distance Education* 21, no. 3 (2007): 39–58; K. A. Meyer, "Evaluating Online Discussions: Four Different Frames of Analysis," *Journal of Asynchronous Learning Networks* 8, no. 2 (2004): 101–114.

23. A. Picciano and R. Steiner, "Bridging the Real World of Science to Children: A Partnership of the American Museum of Natural History and the City University of New York," *Journal of Asynchronous Learning Networks* 12, no. 1 (2008): 69–84.

24. E. Miele, D. Shanley, and R. Steiner, "Online Teacher Education: A Formal-Informal Partnership Between Brooklyn College and the American Museum of Natural History," *The New Educator* 6, no. 3 (2010): 247–264.

25. Relevant academic and administrative challenges, local funding opportunities, and course adoptions are detailed in Miele, Shanley, and Steiner, "Online Teacher Education"; and in E. Miele and W. G. Powell, "Science and the City: Community Cultural and Natural Resources at the Core of a Place-Based Science Teacher Preparation Program," *Journal of College Science Teaching* 40, no. 2 (2010): 18–22.

26. Inverness Research, *AMNH Seminars on Science*.

27. National Center for Education Statistics, http://nces.ed.gov/fastfacts/display.asp?id=28.

Chapter 6

This material is based on work supported by the National Science Foundation (grant 733268). Any opinions, findings, and conclusions or recommendations expressed in this material are those of the authors and do not necessarily reflect the views of the National Science Foundation.

1. A. Eisenkraft, "Expanding the 5E Model," *The Science Teacher* 70, no. 6 (2003): 56–59.

2. J. L. Kolodner et al., "Problem-Based Learning Meets Case-Based Reasoning in the Middle-School Science Classroom: Putting Learning by Design into Practice," *Journal of the Learning Sciences* 12, no. 4 (2003): 495–547; R. Schneider et al., "Student Learning in Project-Based Science Classrooms," *Journal of Research in Science Teaching* 39, no. 5 (2002): 410–422.

3. National Research Council, *A Framework for K–12 Science Education: Practices, Crosscutting Concepts, and Core Ideas* (Washington, DC: National Academies Press, 2012); NGSS Lead States, *Next Generation Science Standards: For States, by States* (Washington, DC: National Academies Press, 2013).

4. C. Dede, ed., *Online Professional Development for Teachers: Emerging Models and Methods* (Cambridge, MA: Harvard Education Press, 2006).

5. Because the APTC and ACTC platforms follow the same design, this description will refer only to APTC for brevity.

6. C. Lewis, "Chapter 14: Lesson Study," in *Powerful Designs for Professional Learning*, ed. L. Easton (Oxford, UK: National Staff Development Council, 2004), 135–148.

7. D. K. Cohen and H. C. Hill, *Learning Policy: When State Education Reform Works* (New Haven, CT: Yale University Press, 2001); M. S. Garet et al., "What Makes Professional Development Effective? Results from a National Sample of Teachers," *American Educational Research Journal* 38, no. 4 (2001): 915–945.

8. S. Dash et al., "Impact of Online Professional Development on Teacher Quality and Student Achievement in Fifth Grade Mathematics," *Journal of Research on Technology in Education* 45, no. 1 (2012): 1–26; J. Duncan-Howell, "Teachers Making Connections: Online Communities as a Source of Professional Learning," *British Journal of Educational Technology* 41, no. 2 (2010): 324–340; B. Fishman et al., "Comparing the Impact of Online and Face-to-Face Professional Development in the Context of Curriculum Implementation," *Journal of Teacher Education* 64, no. 5 (2013): 426–438; B. Treacy, G. Kleiman, and K. Peterson, "Successful Online Professional Development," *Learning and Leading with Technology* 30, no. 1 (2002): 42–49.

9. B. Holmes, "Online Communities for Teachers' Professional Development," *Brian Holmes' Research Blog*, July 2010, http://holmesbrian.blogspot.com/2010/07/online-communities-for-teachers.html; P. Whitehouse, E. McCloskey, and D. Ketelhut, "Online Pedagogy Design and Development: New Models for 21st Century Online Professional Development," in *Online Learning Communities and Teacher Professional Development: Methods for Improved Education Delivery*, ed. J. Lindberg and A. Ologsson (Hershey, PA: IGI Global, 2010), 247–262.

10. C. L. McNamara, "K–12 Teacher Participation in Online Professional Development" (EdD diss., University of California, San Diego, and California State University, San Marcos, 2010); H. So, "Designing an Online Video Based Platform for Teacher Learning in Singapore," *Australasian Journal of Educational Technology* 25, no. 3 (2009): 440–457.

11. A. Palmer, S. Hudson, and Q. Huo, "Critical Mass as an Antecedent to Stability in Online Communities" (paper presented at the International Days of Statistics and Economics conference, University of Economics, Prague, 2011); D. R. Raban, M. Moldovan, and Q. Jones, "An Empirical Study of Critical Mass and Online Community Survival," in *Proceedings of the 2010 ACM Conference on Computer Supported Cooperative Work* (New York: ACM Press, 2010), 71–80.

12. L. Desimone, "How Can We Best Measure Teachers' Professional Development and Its Effects on Teachers and Students?" *Educational Researcher* 38, no. 3 (2009): 184.

13. R. K. Blank and N. de las Alas, *Effects of Teacher Professional Development on Gains in Student Achievement: How Meta-Analysis Provides Scientific Evidence Useful to Education Leaders* (Washington, DC: Council of Chief State School Officers, 2009); L. Darling-Hammond, *Professional Learning in the Learning Profession: A Status Report on Teacher Development in the United States and Abroad* (Palo Alto, CA: National Staff Development Council and the School Redesign Network, Stanford University, 2009); L. Desimone et al., "Improving Teachers' In-Service Professional Development in Mathematics and Science: The Role of Postsecondary Institutions," *Educational Policy* 17, no. 5 (2003): 613–649; Garet et al., "What Makes Professional Development Effective?"

Chapter 7

1. C. Borgman et al., *Fostering Learning in the Networked World: The Cyberlearning Opportunity and Challenge* (Arlington, VA: National Science Foundation, 2008); C. Dorsey,

"Perspective: Prepare and Inspire; A Watershed Report," @*Concord* 14, no. 2 (2009): 2–3; President's Council of Advisors on Science and Technology, *Prepare and Inspire: K–12 Education in Science Technology, Engineering, and Math (STEM) for America's Future* (Washington, DC: President's Council of Advisors on Science and Technology, 2010); National Research Council, *Education for Life and Work: Developing Transferable Knowledge and Skills in the 21st Century* (Washington, DC: National Academies Press, 2012).

2. W. H. Schmidt, H. C. Wang, and C. McKnight, "Towards Coherence in Science Instruction: A Framework for Science Literacy," *Journal of Curriculum Studies* 37, no. 5 (2005): 525–559; F. M. Newman et al., "Instructional Program Coherence: What It Is and Why It Should Guide School Improvement Policy," *Education Evaluation and Policy Analysis* 23, no. 4 (2001): 297–321; J. Gess-Newsome and J. Taylor, "Impacting Teacher Knowledge, Teacher Practice, and Student Achievement: The Role of Educative Curriculum and Professional Development" (paper presented at the annual meeting of the National Association for Research in Science Teaching, Baltimore, April 1, 2008).

3. National Research Council, *America's Lab Report: Investigations in High School Science* (Washington, DC: National Academies Press, 2006); NRC, *Education for Life*.

4. R. A. Duschl et al., *Taking Science to School: Learning and Teaching Science in Grades K–8* (Washington, DC: National Academies Press, 2007).

5. E. Davis and J. Krajcik, "Designing Educative Curriculum Materials to Promote Teacher Learning," *Educational Researcher* 34, no. 3 (2005): 3–14; C. Drake, T. J. Land, and A. M. Tyminski, "Using Educative Curriculum Materials to Support the Development of Prospective Teachers' Knowledge," *Educational Researcher* 43, no. 3 (2014): 154–162; R. Schneider and L. Krajcik, "Supporting Science Teacher Learning: The Role of Educative Curriculum Materials," *Journal of Science Teacher Education* 13, no. 3 (2002): 221–245.

6. R. Tinker, email message to Jacqueline S. Miller, April 4, 2013.

7. Unpublished field test data from Education Development Center, Inc., Foundation Science: Biology, July 2006, NSF annual report (grant 0439443).

8. Unpublished field test data from Education Development Center; J. Carlson and B. Nagle, email message to Jacqueline S. Miller, 2006.

9. Davis and Krajcik, "Designing Educative Curriculum Materials"; Drake, Land, and Tyminski, "Using Educative Curriculum Materials."

Chapter 8

1. President's Council of Advisors on Science and Technology, *Prepare and Inspire: K–12 Education in Science, Technology, Engineering, and Math (STEM) for America's Future* (Washington, DC: Executive Office of the President, 2010).

2. C. L. Borgman et al., "Fostering Learning in the Networked World: The Cyberlearning Opportunity and Challenge," *A 21st Century Agenda for the National Science Foundation: Report of the NSF Task Force on Cyberlearning*, 2008, http://www.nsf.gov/pubs/2008/nsf08204/index.jsp.

3. E. A. Davis and J. S. Krajcik, "Designing Educative Curriculum Materials to Promote Teacher Learning," *Educational Researcher* 34, no. 3 (2005): 3–14.

4. National Research Council, *A Framework for K–12 Science Education: Practices, Crosscutting Concepts, and Core Ideas* (Washington, DC: National Academies Press, 2011).

5. Ibid.
6. National Research Council, *How People Learn: Brain, Mind, Experience, and School* (Washington, DC: National Academies Press, 1999).
7. M. Gick and K. Holyoak, "Analogical Problem Solving," *Cognitive Psychology* 12 (1980): 306–355; J. L. Kolodner, "Educational Implications of Analogy: A View from Case-Based Reasoning," *American Psychologist* 51, no. 1 (1997): 57–66; NRC, *How People Learn.*
8. J. S. Krajcik et al., "Instructional, Curricular, and Technological Supports for Inquiry in Science Classrooms," in *Inquiry into Inquiry: Science Learning and Teaching*, ed. J. Minstell and E. Van Zee (Washington, DC: American Association for the Advancement of Science Press, 2000).
9. R. Driver, P. Newton, and J. Osborne, "Establishing the Norms of Scientific Argumentation in Classrooms," *Science Education* 84, no. 3 (2000): 287–312.
10. K. L. McNeill, D. J. Lizotte, J. Krajcik, and R. W. Marx, "Supporting Students' Construction of Scientific Explanations by Fading Scaffolds in Instructional Materials," *Journal of the Learning Sciences* 15, no. 2 (2006): 153–191.
11. J. B. Kahle, J. Meece, and K. Scantlebury, "Urban African American Middle School Science Students: Does Standards-Based Teaching Make a Difference?" *Journal of Research in Science Teaching* 37, no. 9 (2000): 1019–1041; R. W. Marx et al., "Inquiry Based Science in the Middle Grades: Assessment of Learning in Urban Systemic Reform," *Journal of Research in Science Education* 41, no. 10 (2004): 1063–1080; C. Wilson et al., "The Relative Effects of Inquiry-Based and Commonplace Science Teaching on Students' Knowledge, Reasoning and Argumentation," *Journal of Research in Science Teaching* 47, no. 3 (2010): 276–301.
12. J. Taylor, P. Van Scotter, and D. Coulson, "Bridging Research on Learning and Student Achievement: The Role of Instructional Materials," *Science Educator* 16 no. 2 (2007): 44–50.
13. J. S. Krajcik et al., "A Collaborative Model for Helping Middle Grade Science Teachers Learn Project-Based Instruction," *Elementary School Journal* 94, no. 5 (1994): 483–497; J. S. Krajcik et al., "Inquiry in Project-Based Science Classrooms: Initial Attempts by Middle School Students," *Journal of the Learning Sciences* 7, nos. 3 & 4 (1998): 313–350.
14. J. S. Krajcik et al., "Inquiry in Project-Based Science Classrooms."
15. M. Schneider and J. S. Krajcik, "Supporting Science Teacher Learning: The Role of Educative Curriculum Materials," *Journal of Science Teacher Education* 13, no. 3 (2002): 221–245.
16. M. S. Garet et al., "What Makes Professional Development Effective? Results from a National Sample of Teachers," *American Educational Research Journal* 38, no. 4 (2001): 915–945; Schneider and Krajcik, "Supporting Science Teacher Learning"; S. Loucks-Horsley and K. E. Stiles, "Professional Development Designed to Change Teaching and Learning," in *Professional Development Planning and Design*, ed. J. Rhoton and P. Bowers (Arlington, VA: NSTA Press, 2001), 13–24; W. R. Penuel and B. Means, "Implementation Variation and Fidelity in an Inquiry Science Program: An Analysis of GLOBE Data Reporting Patterns," *Journal of Research in Science Teaching* 41, no. 3 (2004): 294–315; W. R. Penuel et al., "What Makes Professional Development Effective? Strategies That Foster Curriculum Implementation," *American Educational Research Journal* 44, no. 4 (2007): 921–958; W. R. Penuel et al., "Teaching for Understanding in Earth Science: Comparing Impacts on Planning and Instruction in Three Professional Development Designs

for Middle School Science Teachers," *Journal of Science Teacher Education* 20, no. 5 (2009): 415–436; G. D. Borman, A. Gamoran, and J. Bowdon, "A Randomized Trial of Teacher Development in Elementary Science: First-Year Achievement Effects," *Journal of Research on Educational Effectiveness* 1, no. 4 (2008): 237–264; National Staff Development Council, "Professional Learning in the Learning Profession: A Status Report on Teacher Development in the United States and Abroad," 2009, http://www.learning forward.org/news/NSDCstudy2009.pdf.

17. C. Mitchell and L. Sackney, *Profound Improvement: Building Capacity for a Learning Community* (Lisse, the Netherlands: Swets & Zeitlinger, 2000); J. C. Toole and K. S. Louis, "The Role of Professional Learning Communities in International Education," in *Second International Handbook of Educational Leadership and Administration*, ed. K. Leithwood and P. Hallinger (Dordrecht, Germany: Kluwer Academic, 2002).

Chapter 9

1. J. D. Bransford et al., ed., *How People Learn: Brain, Mind, Experience, and School* (Washington, DC: National Academies Press, 2000); A. Byers et al., "Developing a Web-Based Mechanism for Assessing Teacher Science Content Knowledge," *Journal of Science Teacher Education* 22, no. 3 (2011): 273–289; Council of Chief State School Officers, *State Indicators of Science and Mathematics Education* (Washington, DC: CCSSO, 2007); L. Darling-Hammond, "Constructing 21st-Century Teacher Education," *Journal of Teacher Education* 57, no. 3: (2006): 300–314; D. Goldhaber, "The Mystery of Good Teaching," *Education Next* 2, no. 1 2002): 50–55; S. Mundry, "Changing Perspectives in Professional Development," *Science Education* 14, no. 1 (2005): 9–15; S. M. Wilson, R. E. Floden, and J. Ferrini-Mundy, "Teacher Preparation Research: An Insider's View from the Outside," *Journal of Teacher Education* 53, no. 3 (2002): 190–204.

2. The NSTA estimates that nearly 2 million public and private educators teach science in the US, including 1.6 million teachers at the elementary level who teach science with those who teach science at other levels. http://www.nsta.org/about/clpa/faq.aspx. The Framework for K–12 Science Education espouses the importance of learning science at the elementary grade levels. See http://www.nsta.org/about/clpa/faq.aspx#3 and http://www.nap.edu/catalog/13165/a-framework-for-k-12-science-education-practices-crosscutting-concepts. The National Center for Education Statistics reports that there are 3.5 million K–12 teachers in the US. http://nces.ed.gov/fastfacts/display.asp?id=28.

3. US Department of Education, *Transforming American Education: Learning Powered by Technology* (Washington, DC: Office of Educational Technology, 2010), 114.

4. M. Honey, G. Pearson, and H. Schweingruber, ed., *STEM Integration in K–12 Education: Status, Prospects, and an Agenda for Research* (Washington, DC: National Research Council, 2014); US Department of Education, *Evaluation of Evidence-Based Practices in Online Learning: A Meta-Analysis and Review of Online Learning Studies* (Washington, DC: Office of Planning, Evaluation, and Policy Development, 2010), 53.

5. US Department of Education, *Transforming American Education.*

6. US Department of Education, *Evaluation of Evidence-Based Practices.*

7. K. Fulton and T. Britton, *STEM Teachers in Professional Learning Communities: From Good Teachers to Great Teaching* (Washington, DC: National Commission on Teaching and America's Future, 2011), 32.

8. The NSTA Learning Center, "SciPacks," 2008, http://learningcenter.nsta.org/products/sci-packs.aspx.

9. G. Wiggins and J. McTighe, *Understanding by Design* (Alexandria, VA: ASCD, 2005); W. Dick, L. Carey, and J. O. Carey, *The Systematic Design of Instruction, 8th ed.* (New York: Pearson, 2014).

10. NSTA, "NGSS@NSTA," 2014, http://www.nsta.org/ngss; NSTA and Achieve, "EQuIP Rubric for Lessons & Units: Science," 2014, http://www.nextgenscience.org/resources.

11. The NSTA Learning Center, home page, 2009, http://learningcenter.nsta.org; The NSTA Learning Center, "Resources and Opportunities," 2014, http://learningcenter.nsta.org/products/default.aspx.

12. Byers et al., "Web-Based Mechanism."

13. A YouTube video describes this vision. See https://www.youtube.com/watch?v=AlLXfE4YVec.

14. C. Gamrat, "Personalized Workplace Learning: An Exploratory Study on Digital Badging Within a Teacher Professional Development Program," *British Journal of Educational Technology* 45, no. 6 (2014): 1136–1148.

15. H. Berger, B. S. Eylon, and E. Bagno, "Professional Development of Physics Teachers in an Evidence-Based Blended Learning Program," *Journal of Science Education and Technology* 17, no. 4 (2008): 399–409.

16. See http://www.ed-msp.net/.

17. The NSTA Learning Center, "Research and Evaluation Studies," 2014, http://learningcenter.nsta.org/research; C. L. O'Connor, K. L. Chadwick, and D. Samanta, "Evaluation of the National Science Teachers Association SciPacks in the Houston Independent School District During School Year 2009–2010," 2010, http://learningcenter.nsta.org/research/#eval; G. Sherman, A. Byers, and S. Rapp, "Evaluation of Online, On-Demand Science Professional Development Material Involving Two Different Implementation Models," *Journal of Science Education and Technology* 17, no. 1 (2008), 19–31.

18. T. R. Guskey, "What Makes Professional Development Effective?" *Phi Delta Kappan* 84, no. 10 (2003): 748–750.

19. NSTA Learning Center, "E-Textbooks That Engage Pre-Service Teachers," 2014, http://learningcenter.nsta.org/group/etextbook.aspx. For a list of the colleges and universities that incorporate the NSTA LC as part of their strategic efforts, see http://learningcenter.nsta.org/group/etextbook.aspx.

20. A. Tweed, *Designing Effective Science Instruction: What Works in Science Classrooms* (Arlington, VA: NSTA Press, 2009).

21. V. Nolet, "Preparing Sustainability-Literate Teachers," *Teachers College Record* 111, no. 2 (2009): 409–442.

22. G. E. O'Brien and K. G. Sparrow, "Using an Historical Lens and Reflection to Establish Our Vision of Teaching Pre-Service Elementary Teachers Content and Methods of Science," in *Structuring Learning Environments in Teacher Education to Elicit Dispositions as Habits of Mind: Strategies and Approaches Used and Lessons Learned*, ed. E. S. Dottin, L. D. Miller, and G. E. O'Brien (Lanham, MD: University Press of America, 2013), 171–207.

23. NGSS Lead States, *Next Generation Science Standards: For States, By States* (Washington, DC: National Academies Press, 2013); S. Sarkar and R. Frazier, "Place-Based Inquiry: Advancing Environmental Education in Science Teacher Preparation," in *The Inclusion of*

Envioronmental Education Science Teacher Education, ed. A. M. Bodzin, B. S. Klein, and S. Weaver (Dordrecht, Germany: Springer, 2010), 159–172.

24. Nolet, "Sustainability-Literate Teachers."
25. G. E. O'Brien and K. G. Sparrow, "Using an Historical Lens."
26. J. D. Bransford et al., *How People Learn.*
27. "*The Lorax* TV Special," YouTube, 2015, https://www.youtube.com/watch?v=8V06ZO Quo0k.
28. D. Llewellyn and S. Johnson, "Teaching Science Through a Systems Approach," *Science Scope* 31, no. 9 (2008): 21–26.
29. G. Monbiot, "SustainableMan.org: How Wolves Can Alter the Course of Rivers" (paper presented at TED Global, July 2013), 2015, http://blog.ted.com/video-how-wolves-can-alter-the-course-of-rivers/.
30. National Research Council, *How Students Learn: History, Mathematics, and Science in the Classroom* (Washington, DC: National Academies Press, 2005); J. Gess-Newsome, "Secondary Teachers' Knowledge and Beliefs about Subject Matter and Their Impact on Instruction," in *Examining Pedagogical Content Knowledge: The Construct and its Implications for Science Education,* vol. 6, ed. J. Gess-Newsome and N. G. Lederman (Boston: Kluwer Academic, 1999), 51–94; M. F. Pajares, "Teachers' Beliefs and Educational Research: Cleaning up a Messy Construct," *Review of Educational Research* 62, no. 3 (1992): 307–332; D. Pomeroy, "Implications of Teachers' Beliefs about the Nature of Science: Comparison of the Beliefs of Scientists, Secondary Teachers, and Elementary Teachers," *Science Education* 77, no. 3 (1993): 261.
31. S. Koba and A. Tweed, *Hard-to-Teach Biology Concepts: Designing Instruction Aligned to the NGSS,* 2nd ed. (Arlington, VA: NSTA Press, 2014).
32. P. Keeley, *Uncovering Student Ideas in Primary Science,* Vol. 1: *25 New Formative Assessment Probes for Grades K–2* (Arlington, VA: NSTA Press, 2013).
33. E. Morgan and K. Ansberry, *Even More Picture-Perfect Science Lessons: Using Children's Books to Guide Inquiry, K–5* (Arlington, VA: NSTA Press, 2013).
34. R. del Valle and T. Duffy, "Online Learning: Learner Characteristics and Their Approaches to Managing Learning," *Instructional Science* 37, no. 2 (2009): 129–149; S. Lowes, L. Peiyi, and W. Yan, "Studying the Effectiveness of the Discussion Forum in Online Professional Development Courses," *Journal of Interactive Online Learning* 6, no. 3 (2007): 181–210; S. Whitaker et al., "Use and Evaluation of Web-Based Professional Development Services across Participant Levels of Support," *Early Childhood Education Journal* 34, no. 6 (2007): 379–386; NRC, *How Students Learn;* Gess-Newsome, "Secondary Teachers' Knowledge"; Pajares, "Teachers' Beliefs"; Pomeroy, "Implications of Teachers' Beliefs"; Fulton and Britton, *STEM Teachers.*
35. A. Byers, "Examining Learner-Content Interaction Importance and Efficacy in Online, Self-Directed Electronic Professional Development in Science for Elementary Educators in Grades Three–Six" (PhD diss., Virginia Polytechnic Institute and State University, 2010); D. Cambridge and K. Perez-Lopez, "First Steps Towards a Social Learning Analytics for Online Communities of Practice for Educators" (paper presented at the Learning Analytics and Knowledge Conference, Vancouver, April 2012); K. Perez-Lopez, D. Cambridge, and A. Byers, "Simple and Computational Heuristics for Forum Management in the NSTA Learning Center: A Role for Learning Analytics in Online Communities of Practice Sup-

porting Teacher Learning" (paper presented at the Hawaii International Conference on System Sciences, Maui, 2012); S. G. Strauss et al., "VOSS—Use of Web 2.0 Technologies to Build Distributed Communities of Practice among K–12 Science Educators," *National Science Foundation* 399, no. 564 (2011): 63; S. G. Strauss et al., "Sociotechnical Capital and Situated Knowledge in Online Communities of Practice" (paper presented at the Eighth Annual INGRoup Conference, Atlanta, 2013).

36. Byers, "Examining Learning-Content Interaction"; O'Connor, Chadwick, and Samanta, "Evaluation of . . . SciPacks"; G. Sherman, A. Byers, and S. Rapp, "Evaluation of Online, On-Demand Science Professional Development Material Involving Two Different Implementation Models," *Journal of Science Education and Technology* 17, no. 1 (2008): 19–31.

37. NSTA Learning Center, "NSTA Learning Center Impact," 2015, http://learningcenter.nsta.org/impact.

38. T. R. Guske, *Evaluating Professional Development* (Thousand Oaks, CA: Corwin Press, 2000).

39. R. Bayor, "What Do Teachers Want from Their Professional Development?" *Digital Promise,* 2015, http://www.digitalpromise.org/blog/entry/what-do-teachers-want-from-their-professional-development; D. T. Hickey, T. A. Kelley, and X. Shen, "Small to Big Before Massive: Scaling Up Participatory Learning Analytics" (paper presented at Learning Analytics and Knowledge '14: The 4th International Conference, Indianapolis, 2014).

40. D. T. Hickey and F. Soylu, "Wikifolios, Reflections, and Exams for Online Engagement, Understanding, and Achievement," *Journal of Teaching and Learning with Technology* 1, no. 1 (2012): 64–71; X. Wei, W. Chen, and K. Zhu, "Motivating User Contributions in Online Knowledge Communities: Virtual Rewards and Reputation" (paper presented at the 48th Hawaii International Conference on System Sciences, Maui, 2015); C. Gamrat et al., "Personalized Workplace Learning: An Exploratory Study on Digital Badging Within a Teacher Professional Development Program," *British Journal of Educational Technology* 45, no. 6 (2014): 1136–1148.

41. For a list of the current badges, levels, and point structures, see http://www.learningcenter.nsta.org/help/activity_awards.aspx.

Chapter 10

This research is funded by the National Science Foundation under grant DRL-1221861 awarded to the University of Massachusetts Boston. The opinions expressed here are those of the authors and do not necessarily reflect those of NSF.

1. College Board website, 2014, http://www.collegeboard.org.

2. B. Fishman et al., *Professional Development for the Redesigned AP Biology Exam: Teacher Participation Patterns and Student Outcomes* (Philadelphia: American Educational Research Association, 2014).

3. The authors are working to determine the extent to which this may be due to the community itself or instead to some other attribute that people who participate in online communities have in common (e.g., seeking help from other teachers).

4. S. E. Booth, "Cultivating Knowledge Sharing and Trust in Online Communities for Educators," *Journal of Educational Computing Research* 47, no. 1 (2012): 24.

5. See http://tinyurl.com/moderatorguide. The Moderator Guide was developed with assistance from Katherine McConachie, then a master's student at the Harvard Graduate School of Education.

6. E. Wenger, R. McDermott, and W. Snyder, *Cultivating Communities of Practice: A Guide to Managing Knowledge* (Boston: Harvard Business School Press, 2002), 34.

7. S. A. Barab, J. G. MaKinster, and R. Scheckler, "Designing System Dualities: Characterizing a Web-Supported Professional Development Community," *Information Society* 19, no. 3 (2003): 238.

8. C. Dede, ed., *Online Professional Development for Teachers: Emerging Models and Methods* (Cambridge, MA: Harvard Education Press, 2006).

9. B. Fishman and C. Dede, "Teaching and Technology: New Tools for New Times," *Handbook of Research on Teaching*, 5th ed., ed. D. Gitomer and C. Bell (Washington, DC: American Educational Research Association, forthcoming).

10. R. Putnam and H. Borko, "What Do New Views of Knowledge and Thinking Have to Say About Research on Teacher Learning?" *Educational Researcher* 29, no. 1 (2000): 4–15; M. S. Schlager and J. Fusco, "Teacher Professional Development, Technology, and Communities of Practice: Are We Putting the Cart Before the Horse?" in *Designing for Virtual Communities in the Service of Learning*, ed. S. Barab, R. Kling, and J. Gray (Cambridge, UK: Cambridge University Press, 2004), 120–153; K. A. Renninger and W. Shumar, "Community Building with and for Teachers at The Math Forum," in *Building Virtual Communities: Learning and Change in Cyberspace*, ed. K. A. Renninger and W. Shumar (Cambridge, UK: Cambridge University Press, 2002), 60–95; E. Wenger, *Communities of Practice: Learning, Meaning, and Identity* (Cambridge, UK: Cambridge University Press, 1998).

11. US Department of Education, *Transforming American Education: Learning Powered by Technology; National Education Technology Plan 2010* (Washington, DC: US Department of Education, Office of Educational Technology, 2010), https://www.ed.gov/sites/default/files/netp2010.pdf.

12. Fishman and Dede, "Teaching and Technology."

13. D. Maltese and K. Naughter, "Taking Down Walls: An International Wiki Creates a Community of Thinkers," *Voices from the Middle* 18, no. 1 (2010): 17–25; G. Sheehy, "The Wiki as Knowledge Repository: Using a Wiki in a Community of Practice to Strengthen K–12 Education," *TechTrends: Linking Research and Practice to Improve Learning* 52, no. 6 (2008): 55–60.

14. M. Ranieri, S. Manca, and A. Fini, "Why (and How) Do Teachers Engage in Social Networks? An Exploratory Study of Professional Use of Facebook and Its Implications for Lifelong Learning," *British Journal of Educational Technology* 43, no. 5 (2012): 754–769; A. K. Roach and J. J. Beck, "Before Coffee, Facebook: New Literacy Learning for 21st Century Teachers," *Language Arts* 89, no. 4 (2012): 244–255.

15. J. B. Fisher et al., "Effects of a Computerized Professional Development Program on Teacher and Student Outcomes," *Journal of Teacher Education* 61, no. 4 (2010): 301–312; B. Fishman et al., "Comparing the Impact of Online and Face-to-Face Professional Development in the Context of Curriculum Implementation," *Journal of Teacher Education* 64, no. 5 (2013): 426–438.

16. C. Dede et al., "A Research Agenda for Online Teacher Professional Development," *Journal of Teacher Education* 60, no. 1 (2009): 8–19.

17. S. E. Booth and S. B. Kellogg, "Value Creation in Online Communities for Educators," *British Journal of Educational Technology* (2014): 3, doi:10.1111/bjet.12168.

18. R. E. Kraut and P. Resnick, *Building Successful Online Communities: Evidence-Based Social Design* (Cambridge, MA: MIT Press, 2011), 3.

19. Kraut and Resnick, *Online Communities*, 207.

20. Flavio Mendez, personal communication, January 13, 2015.

21. M. Burke, R. E. Kraut, and E. Joyce, "Membership Claims and Requests: Some Newcomer Socialization Strategies in Online Communities," *Small Group Research* 4, no. 1 (2010): 27.

22. Ibid.

23. M. Alber, E. Leep, and B. Werner, *Best Practices for Community Engagement* (Redwood Shores, CA: Oracle, 2012).

24. Booth and Kellogg, "Value Creation in Online Communities for Educators," 6.

25. Kraut and Resnick, *Online Communities*.

26. Booth and Kellogg, "Value Creation," 7.

27. Kraut and Resnick, *Online Communities*.

28. Ibid.

29. Alber, Leep, and Werner, *Best Practices*.

30. Flavio Mendez, personal communication, January 13, 2015.

31. See http://tinyurl.com/moderatorguide.

Chapter 11

1. C. Dede, ed., *Online Professional Development for Teachers: Emerging Models and Methods* (Cambridge, MA: Harvard Education Press, 2006).

2. See http://www.cast.org/our-work/about-udl.html; http://www.udlcenter.org/.

3. See http://concord.org/projects/udl.

4. R. Rose and R. Blomeyer, *Research Committee Issues Brief: Access and Equity in Online Classes and Virtual Schools* (Vienna, VA: iNACOL, 2007).

5. Americans with Disabilities Act, http://www.usdoj.gov/crt/ada/adahom1.htm; section 508, http://www.section508.gov/.

6. OCR Compliance Review 11-11-2128, 06121583, paraphrased from 11-13-5001, 10122118, 11-11-6002.

7. R. M. Rose, *Access and Equity for All Learners in Blended and Online Education* (Vienna, VA: iNACOL, 2014).

8. See http://iNACOL.org.

9. W3C, http://www.w3.org/WAI/.

10. See http://benetech.org/our-programs/literacy/born-accessible/mathml-cloud/.

11. See http://www.freedomscientific.com/Products/Blindness/JAWS.

12. See http://www.nvaccess.org/.

13. See http://community.nvda-project.org/documentation/userGuide.html?#toc78.

14. See http://webaim.org/articles/voiceover/.

15. See http://www.vischeck.com/.

16. See http://www.seewald.at/en/2012/01/color_blindness_correction_and_simulator.

17. See http://www.w3.org/WAI/ER/tools/complete.

Chapter 12

1. M. Noer, "One Man, One Computer, 10 Million Students: How Khan Academy Is Reinventing Education," *Forbes*, November 2012, http://www.forbes.com/sites/michaelnoer/2012/11/02/one-man-one-computer-10-million-students-how-khan-academy-is-reinventing-education.

2. J. L. Bower and C. M. Christensen, "Disruptive Technologies: Catching the Wave," *Harvard Business Review Video* 73, no. 1 (1995): 506–520.

3. S. Loucks-Horsley et al., *Designing Professional Development for Teachers of Science and Mathematics*, 3rd ed. (Thousand Oaks, CA: Corwin Press, 2010).

4. C. Dede et al., "A Research Agenda for Online Teacher Professional Development," *Journal of Teacher Education* 60, no. 1 (2008): 8–19.

5. The research reported here was supported by the Institute of Education Sciences, US Department of Education, grant R305C100024. The opinions expressed are those of the authors and do not represent views of the Institute or the US Department of Education.

6. The research reported here was supported by the Institute of Education Sciences, US Department of Education, grant R305A100454. The opinions expressed are those of the authors and do not represent views of the Institute or the US Department of Education.

7. John Carr, Cathy Caroll, Sarah Cremer, Mardi Gale, and Rachel Lagunoff, *Making Mathematics Accessible to English Learners: A Guidebook for Teachers* (San Francisco: WestEd, 2009).

8. Learning Mathematics for Teaching online, http://sitemaker.umich.edu/lmt/about; Intercultural Development Inventory (IDI) online, http://idiinventory.com.

9. This material is based on work supported by the National Science Foundation under grant 0918834. Any opinions, findings, and conclusions or recommendations expressed in this material are those of the authors and do not necessarily reflect the views of NSF.

10. The authors acknowledge the contributions of WestEd's partners, Public Consulting Group and Edu2000, and their collaboration in the development and distribution of Pepper courses.

11. Common Core State Standards Initiative, "Key Shifts in Mathematics," http://www.corestandards.org/other-resources/key-shifts-in-mathematics.

12. B. C. Buckley, "Model-Based Learning," in *Encyclopedia of the Sciences of Learning*, ed. N. Seel (New York: Springer, 2012), 2300–2303; J. D. Gobert and B. C. Buckley, "Introduction to Model-Based Teaching and Learning in Science Education," *International Journal of Science Education* 22, no. 9 (2000): 891–894.

13. R. J. Mislevy et al., "On the Structure of Educational Assessments," *Measurement: Interdisciplinary Research and Perspectives* 1 (2003): 3–67.

14. This material is based on work supported by grants awarded to WestEd from the National Science Foundation (DRL-0733345, -1020264, -1221614, -0814776) and the US Department of Education (R305A080225, R305A120390, R305A080614, R305A130160) and by a grant awarded to the Nevada Department of Education from the US Department of Education (09-2713-126). Any opinions, findings, conclusions, or recommendations expressed in this material are those of the authors and do not necessarily reflect the views of NSF or the US Department of Education.

Conclusion

1. C. Dede, ed., *Online Professional Development for Teachers: Emerging Models and Methods* (Cambridge, MA: Harvard Education Press, 2006).

2. J. M. Roschelle et al., "Changing How and What Children Learn in School with Computer-Based Technologies," *The Future of Children: Children and Computer Technology* 10, no. 2 (2000): 76–101.

3. B. Fishman and C. Dede, "Teaching and Technology: New Tools for New Times," *Handbook of Research on Teaching*, 5th ed., ed. D. Gitomer and C. Bell (Washington, DC: American Educational Research Association, forthcoming).

4. D. J. Ketelhut et al., "Core Tensions in the Evolution of Online Teacher Professional Development," in Dede, ed., *Online Professional Development for Teachers*, 237–264.

5. Ibid.

6. Working Group on Postsecondary Learning, *New Technology-Based Models of Postsecondary Learning: Conceptual Frameworks and Research Agendas* (Washington, DC: Computing Research Association, 2013), 2–3.

7. US Department of Education, *Transforming American Education: Learning Powered by Technology: National Education Technology Plan 2010* (Washington, DC: US Department of Education, Office of Educational Technology, 2010), https://www.ed.gov/sites/default/files/netp2010.pdf.

8. Fishman and Dede, "Teaching and Technology."

9. L. Darling-Hammond, *The Flat World and Education: How America's Commitment to Equity Will Determine Our Future* (New York: Teachers College Press, 2009).

10. Fishman and Dede, "Teaching and Technology."

11. H. Borko, J. Jacobs, and K. Koellner, "Contemporary Approaches to Teacher Professional Development," in *International Encyclopedia of Education*, ed. P.L. Peterson, E. Baker, and B. McGaw (New York: Elsevier, 2010), 548–556.

12. Ketelhut et al., "Core Tensions."

13. C. Dede. *The Role of Technology in Deeper Learning: Students at the Center; Deeper Learning Research Series* (Boston: Jobs for the Future, 2014).

Appendix

1. W. R. Penuel et al., "What Makes Professional Development Effective? Strategies That Foster Curriculum Implementation," *American Educational Research Journal* 44, no. 4 (2007); 921–958.

About the Editors

Chris Dede is the Timothy E. Wirth Professor in Learning Technologies and former chair of the Learning and Teaching department at the Harvard Graduate School of Education. He was one of the key contributors on the 2010 National Education Technology Plan and has published several books about implementing technology in schools. He is active in policy initiatives, including creating a widely used State Policy Framework for Assessing Educational Technology Implementation and studying the potential of developing a scalability index for educational innovations.

Dede is a member of the National Academy of Sciences Committee on Foundations of Educational and Psychological Assessment, a member of the US Department of Education's Expert Panel on Technology, and an International Steering Committee member for the Second International Technology in Education Study. He also serves on advisory boards and commissions for PBS TeacherLine, the Partnership for 21st Century Skills, the Pittsburgh Science of Learning Center, and several federal educational labs and regional technology centers and is a member of the board of directors of the Boston Tech Academy, an experimental small high school in the Boston Public School system funded by the Gates Foundation.

Dede was the editor of the 1998 Association for Supervision and Curriculum Development (ASCD) yearbook, *Learning with Technology,* and co-editor (with James P. Honan and Laurence C. Peters) of the volume *Scaling Up Success: Lessons Learned from Technology-based Educational Innovation* (Jossey-Bass, 2005). He is also the editor of *Online Professional Development for Teachers: Emerging Models and Methods* (Harvard Education Press, 2006).

Arthur Eisenkraft is the Distinguished Professor of Science Education, professor of physics, and director of the Center of Science and Mathematics in Context (COSMIC) at the University of Massachusetts Boston. He is past president of the National Science Teachers Association (NSTA) and is currently chair of the Science Academic Advisory Committee of the College Board. He is project director of the National Science Foundation-supported Active Physics and Active Chemistry projects, introducing high quality project-based science to all students. He is chair and cocreator of the Toshiba/NSTA ExploraVision Awards, involving fifteen thousand students annually. He leads the Wipro Science Education Fellowship program which is bringing sustainable change to fifteen districts in Massachusetts, New Jersey, and New York.

His current research projects include investigating the efficacy of a second generation model of distance learning for professional development; a study of professional development choices that teachers make when facing a large scale curriculum change and assessing the technological literacy of K–12 students.

Eisenkraft has received numerous awards recognizing his teaching and related work including the Presidential Award for Excellence in Science Teaching, the American Association of Physics Teachers Millikan Medal, the Disney Corporation's Science Teacher of the Year, and the NSTA Robert Carleton Award. He is a fellow of the American Association for the Advancement of Science, holds a patent for a laser vision testing system, and was awarded an honorary doctorate from Rennssalaer Polytechnic Institute.

Kim Frumin is a doctoral candidate and Harvard Innovation Lab Fellow at the Harvard Graduate School of Education. Her research focuses on educational technology and new K–12 school designs. Frumin was a founding member of the New York City Department of Education's Office of Innovation (iZone) and served as Senior Director of Professional Development and Practice for iZone360, a whole-school redesign effort. Previously, she managed educational content, research, and outreach for international Sesame Street co-productions in Israel and Northern Ireland and served as an instructional coach in New York City public schools through Teaching Matters. Additionally, Frumin was a Fulbright Scholar in Israel, where she implemented an original photography and writing program with Bedouin youth.

Alex Hartley received her master's in secondary education in 2015 from the College of Education and Human Development at University of Massachusetts Boston. She works in a kindergarten classroom at a Boston Public School, helping the classroom teacher design and implement engineering and STEM lessons. She has taught at the South End Technology Center, with Breakthrough Collaborative, and at a number of other schools and community centers in the Boston area.

About the Contributors

Sherry Booth is a research associate at the Friday Institute for Educational Innovation and an adjunct assistant professor in the College of Education at North Carolina State University. Her professional interests center on the development and evaluation of innovative uses of technology to support teaching and learning. Currently, she leads the research for the Connected Educators project funded by the US Department of Education. She is also involved in the evaluation of North Carolina's implementation of its federal Race to the Top grant. Specifically, her work focuses on the evaluation of online professional development initiatives. Before coming to the Friday Institute, Booth had extensive experience as a curriculum developer. At the JASON Foundation for Education, she served as senior curriculum developer for online mathematics professional development courses for teachers, and through her work at Education Development Center in Newton, MA, she developed, implemented, and evaluated numerous technology-enhanced curriculum projects and professional development programs.

Al Byers is an assistant executive director of e-Learning and Government Partnerships at the National Science Teachers Association (NSTA). He serves in a strategic capacity with mission-based government agencies, state and local departments of education, universities, and education foundations to develop high-quality blended professional development solutions, resources, and opportunities (onsite, online, synchronous, and asynchronous) for science educators across the United States. Byers steers the design, development, implementation, and evaluation of large-scale blended professional development and e-learning endeavors that are now being consumed by more than 92,000 educators daily, primarily through the NSTA's award-winning Learning Center. He serves on the primary technical working group for the US Department of Education's online communities of practice efforts, was a 2008 delegate for the US Department of Education at the Asian Pacific Economic Cooperation Summit, and is an expert panelist for the National Assessment of Education Progress Science Framework Prioritization working group. Byers is a sponsored speaker at both the national and international levels and shares his research on online professional development through peer-reviewed research articles and conference presentations.

Rachel Connolly is completing her PhD in science education at Columbia University and is serving as the director of STEM education for NOVA at WGBH in Boston. Previously she served as the director of the planetarium at the University of Louisville, as the astrophysics education manager at the American Museum of Natural History, and as a high school physics teacher in New York City. Connelly considers it her life's mission to find new ways to make complex concepts accessible.

Ruta Demery was a member of the development team of the NSF-funded *Overcoming Obstacles to Scaling-Up with a Cyberlearning Professional Development Model* (*PBIS CyberPD Project*). She received her degree in science from the University of Toronto (U of T) and her degree in Education from the Ontario Institute of Studies in Education at U of T. She has been involved in education as a middle and high school teacher, a teacher's college associate, and a curriculum developer and writer of numerous middle and high school science and mathematics programs. Recently, she has been the product development editor and a contributing writer for many of It's About Time's middle and high school science programs.

Laura Desimone studies how national, state, district, and school-level policies can better promote changes in teaching that lead to improved student achievement and to closing the achievement gap between advantaged and disadvantaged students. Her research examines policy effects on teaching and learning, policy implementation, and the improvement of methods for studying policy effects and implementation. She studies all levels of the system and focuses on three policy areas at the forefront of education reform: standards-based reform, comprehensive school reform, and teacher quality initiatives.

Susan J. Doubler is the coleader of the Center for Science Teaching and Learning at TERC and an associate professor of science education at Lesley University. She is currently the principal investigator of the Inquiry Project, a National Science Foundation–funded project to develop a learning progression for grades 3–5 that lays the foundation for understanding the particulate model of matter in middle school. The project involves curriculum development, professional development, and a longitudinal study of student learning. Doubler is also the principal investigator of the Talk Science Project, a NSF-funded project to improve classroom science discussions, and is co-PI of the Fulcrum Leadership Institute, a math and science partnership with Tufts University. She recently led the development and implementation of a fully online master's program in science education for K–8 teachers. Doubler's work focuses on the interface between science education and technology with the aim of using technology to help further inquiry-based science learning. Before coming to TERC, she was an instructional specialist and teacher in the Winchester, MA, Public Schools.

Joni Falk codirects the Center for School Reform at TERC, a nonprofit research and development institution aimed at improving mathematics and science teaching and learning. Much of her recent work has focused on creating and researching electronic learning communities. She is currently the principal investigator of MSPnet.org, the electronic learning community that supports National Science Foundation's Math and Science Partnership Program, and of IGERT.org, the collaborative community created for the NSF's flagship IGERT (Interdisciplinary Graduate Education and Research Traineeship) program. In addition to developing and researching e-communities for leaders engaged in educational reform, she is also co-PI of two research projects that are studying the effects of technology infusion on science teaching and learning, Researching Science in the Wireless High School and Infusing Web-Based Digital Resources into the Middle School Science Classroom: Strategies and Challenges. Falk has a particular interest in science inquiry at the middle school level. She was PI of Eyes to the Future, a NSF-funded telementoring project that connects middle school girls with high school role models and women scientists, and also a PI of the Inquiry-Based Classroom in Context, a research project studying the gap between teachers' practices and policy mandates.

Erica Fields is a research associate at Education Development Center (EDC), Inc. She has over twenty years of experience in the field of education as a researcher and a practitioner, with over ten years of experience conducting research and evaluation focused on science and mathematics programs. Her particular interests and skills include an emphasis on qualitative research and analysis, instrument development, early childhood education, and the development of resilience in students. She received her master's degree in early childhood/elementary education from Bank Street College of Education, and her bachelor's degree in English from Amherst College. Before coming to EDC, she was a preschool teacher in New York City. She is also a certified CLASS observer, preK.

Barry Fishman is a professor of learning technologies in the University of Michigan School of Information and School of Education. His research focuses on video games as models for learning environments, teacher learning and the role of technology in supporting teacher learning, and the development of usable, scalable, and sustainable learning innovations through design-based implementation research (DBIR), which he helped establish. He is the creator of GradeCraft, a game-inspired learning management system, and is the principal investigator of the A-GAMES project, which studies the ways teachers employ video games to support formative assessment practices. Fishman currently serves as the associate steward for teaching and learning on the Information Technology Council at the University of Michigan. He was coauthor of the Obama administration's 2010 National Education Technology Plan and served as associate editor of the *Journal of the Learning Sciences* from 2005 to 2012. He is the 2010 recipient of the University of Michigan's Provost's Teaching Innovation Prize, the 2003 Pattishall Junior Faculty Research Award, and the 2001 Jan Hawkins Award for Early Career Contributions to Humanistic Research and Scholarship in Learning Technologies.

Glenn M. Kleiman is a professor and the executive director of the Friday Institute for Educational Innovation at the North Carolina State University College of Education. His work in education has spanned basic and applied research, curriculum development, software development, professional development for teachers and administrators, policy analyses, and consulting for school districts and state departments of education. Prior to joining NC State in July 2007, Kleiman, a cognitive psychologist, was vice president and senior research scientist at Education Development Center, Inc. (EDC), in Newton, MA, where he directed the Center for Online Professional Education and codirected the Northeast and Islands Regional Education Lab. He has been the principal investigator on several National Science Foundation–funded projects, including the one that developed the MathScape middle school curriculum and a research project on the effectiveness of online professional development for mathematics teachers. He was also on the faculty of the Harvard Graduate School of Education from 1995 to 2007 and was education chair of the Harvard/EDC Leadership and the New Technologies Institutes. He was a member of Governor Perdue's Education Transformation Commission and the North Carolina eLearning Commission, for which he served as chair of the Teaching and Learning Subcommittee. Kleiman recently played a lead role in the development of the North Carolina Race to the Top proposal, which received $400 million of funding from the US Department of Education. Currently he is leading the Friday Institute's Massive Online Open Courses for Educators (MOOC-Ed) initiative and serves on the Virtual Charter School study group for the North Carolina state board of education.

Jason Lange is CEO of BloomBoard, Inc., an online evaluation, observation, and professional development platform founded in 2010 to use technology to take the principles of differentiated instruction for students and apply them to teacher development. BloomBoard actively aggregates all types of professional development through a single channel to effectively scale innovation. The platform is based on research showing that learning is social, should be mastery based, should occur in short intervals, and should be initiated through personal empowerment.

Kathleen Lepori is the senior program coordinator for WestEd's STEM program, with her primary focus being on the integration of the use of technologies and how they augment student learning. Lepori has extensive experience in the STEM field, having worked on high-level projects such as WestEd's National Center on Cognition and Mathematics Instruction (Math Center), where she served as the management coordinator. She also has expertise with implementing online distance delivery, including its innovative use for teacher professional development.

Abigail Jurist Levy has more than twenty-two years' experience in the fields of public K–12 education and adult workforce development. She has managed teams of researchers in multiyear and multisite research and evaluation studies focusing on professional development, science teaching and learning, teaching workforce and workplace issues, and the sustainability of education reform in grades K–20. Levy is the coauthor of the report "Researching the Sustainability of Reform: Factors That Contribute to or Inhibit Program Endurance" published by the Center for Science Education at Education Development Center, Inc. She has published her findings in journals such as *Phi Delta Kappan* ("The Science of Professional Development") and *Science Educator* ("No Teacher Left Unqualified: How Teachers and Principals Respond to the Highly Qualified Mandate" and "Models of Providing Science Instruction in the Elementary Grades: A Research Agenda to Inform Decision Makers"). In 2010 she coauthored an article with Daphne D. Minner and Jeanne Century in the *Journal of Research in Science Teaching* ("Inquiry-Based Science Instruction—What Is It and Does it Matter?") that received the National Association for Research in Science Teaching's 2011 Outstanding Paper Award. More recently, she coauthored with Kim Kastens an *Education Week* Commentary that advocated for a phased-in approach to implementing the Next Generation Science Standards.

Jacqueline S. Miller has decades of experience designing innovative, rigorous science curricula that align with national standards, get students excited about science, and prepare students for college and careers. In the more than twenty years she has worked at EDC, she has led the development of a wide array of highly acclaimed online and print instructional resources. Recently, Miller led a team in designing the Foundation Science curricula: four introductory courses in physics, chemistry, biology, and earth science that build grade 9–12 students' science knowledge and literacy skills through challenging inquiry, writing assignments, and rich discussions. In the Electronic Teacher Guide, she is developing a prototype digital teacher guide using the genetics unit of Foundation Science. In the Taking Foundation Science to Scale Digitally project, she is working with a publisher to transform Foundation Science: Biology and Chemistry print materials to the digital environment.

Katherine F. Paget has studied science teaching and learning for more than twenty years and has extensive experience in research and evaluation. Recently, she designed formative and summative assessment items for the free, web-based Universal Design for Learning (UDL) Toolkit developed by EDC, CAST, and the University of Michigan. She has also designed assessments for Foundation Science, EDC's comprehensive four-year high school curriculum. With EDC colleagues, Paget played a lead role in developing the Exploring Bioethics curriculum supplement funded by the National Institutes of Health. Currently, she is carrying out research and evaluation for EDC's Electronic Teacher Guide. She has served as the formative evaluator for more than twenty projects funded by the National Science Foundation and by the National Aeronautics and Space Administration.

Liz Pape has over twenty years of experience in online education. Liz has been part of The Virtual High School (VHS) since its inception in 1995, served as CEO for ten years until her retirement in 2012, and successfully transitioned the company from grant funding to a self-sustaining nonprofit. An award-winning online education expert, Liz is a renowned author and speaker, working to help K–12 schools to develop a twenty-first-century learning model. Liz has written for and been quoted in numerous publications and journals including the *American School Board Journal, School Administrator, USDLA Distance Learning* magazine, *Boston Globe, Investor's Business Daily, New York Times,* and *USA Today.* Liz has presented to the National Education Summit, the American Association of School Administrators, the Association of Supervisors and Curriculum Developers, and the National School Board Association.

Raymond M. Rose has been involved in online education since the mid-1990s, when he first began defining and building a method of creating online learning communities. Helping envision, create, and administer the first virtual high school in the country, he was a pioneer in the use of computers in education and raised concerns about equity in technology use early in the education technology movement. He works with college and university programs, policy makers, and leaders in online learning from nonprofit organizations and institutions. He has helped shape the nature of e-learning efforts and supports the radical transformation of US education.

Gerhard Salinger, recently retired, has been a program director in the Instructional Materials Development program in the Division of Elementary, Secondary and Informal Education at the National Science Foundation since 1989. In this position he recommended the funding of proposals to develop nationally disseminated instructional materials and support for educational reform in mathematics, science, and technology education in K–12 classrooms. He is also a colead director of the Advanced Technological Education program, which supports technician education at the two-year college level and preparation for that at the secondary schools. He contributed to the policy development for both programs. Prior to joining the NSF, Gerhard was a professor in the physics department at Rensselaer Polytechnic Institute, which he served as chair for eleven years.

Steve Schneider is the senior program director of the STEM program at WestEd. He also serves as the principal investigator of the National Science Foundation's Center for Assessment and Evaluation of Student Learning, directs the National Center on Cognition and Mathematics Instruction, and serves as the PI and content expert for the Science Review Team for the US Department of Education's What Works Clearinghouse. Schneider has published numerous articles on science, mathematics, and technology education; professional development; and teacher preparation. In 2004 he received WestEd's Paul D. Hood Award for Distinguished Contributions to the Profession for his creation of collaborative partnerships that have advanced math and science education in the nation, including curricula, professional development, assessment, and evaluation. In 2006 he, along with his fellow National Assessment of Educational Progress Framework Team members, received this award again.

Ruth Schoenbach is codirector of the Strategic Literacy Initiative (SLI), which she cofounded in 1995 and has nurtured into a vital force for improving subject area literacy in middle school, high school, and community college. Her early work in the San Francisco school system as a teacher, curriculum developer, and humanities and language development project director has informed her leadership and contributed to the development of the Reading Apprenticeship Instructional Framework that is the core of all SLI work. Schoenbach also serves as codirector of the five-year scale-up RAISE project that is bringing the Reading Apprenticeship curriculum to 600,000 high school students and their teachers in five states. Funding for RAISE is provided by a federal Investing in Innovation (i3) grant. She also directs a second i3 grant, iRAISE, to translate face-to-face Reading Apprenticeship science professional development into an online course for STEM teachers.

Robert V. Steiner directs online teacher education at the American Museum of Natural History, including its signature Seminars on Science program. His focus is on the design, development, implementation, and evaluation of accessible, innovative, and effective online and blended programs. The Museum's partnerships with higher education institutions and other organizations have provided cutting-edge science to more than six thousand teachers across the United States and around the world during the past decade. Steiner has published and presented widely on online science education at the national and international levels, authoring or coauthoring more than forty scientific publications. He also teaches at both the City University of New York and Columbia Teachers College. Steiner is passionate about the purposeful use of educational technologies.

Barbara Treacy is a nationally recognized leader in online learning and director of EdTech Leaders Online (ETLO), the Education Development Center's national, capacity-building online learning program that enables state departments of education, school districts, virtual schools, colleges and universities, and other educational organizations to establish successful online learning programs for teachers, administrators, and students. Since ETLO's inception in 1999, Treacy has led teams of online curriculum developers, instructors, media developers, and technical specialists to provide graduate-level training programs in online and blended learning, a catalog of more than seventy online courses for teachers and administrators, a national forum for online specialists implementing local online programs, and custom online development and consulting services. ETLO is the 2010 winner of the International Association of K–12 Online Learning Award for most innovative online learning program. Treacy directed EDC's collaboration with e-Learning for Educators, a ten-state consortium funded by the US Department of Education to establish statewide online professional development programs in each state. Research conducted in the program demonstrated significant impact of ETLO courses and training on teachers' content knowledge and instructional practices and on their students' achievement.

Mary Ann Wolf has fifteen years' experience in education and education technology, having worked closely with federal, state, and local education leaders; policy makers and with organizations on connecting policy and practice for innovative education reform, digital learning, and instructional practices. Wolf developed and cofacilitated the Digital Learning Transition MOOC for Educators through the Friday Institute at North Carolina State University and the Alliance for Excellent Education. She is also the lead researcher on the National Science Foundation and Project Tomorrow Teachers' Readiness to Adopt and Adapt Content (TRAAC) project, which includes in-person and virtual focus groups with education leaders and teachers.

Barbara Zahm has been the principal investigator on several NSF-funded projects and is currently serving in that role on the *PBIS CyberPD Project*. After teaching in the City University of New York system from 1980 to 1982, she became a full-time documentary film and video producer/director for public television and educational distribution. She has received multiple awards including the Earth Watch/National Geographic Society Award, the American Film Festival Blue Ribbon Award, and several Cine Golden Eagles awards. In addition, she was field producer for the Emmy Award-winning television series *Big Blue Marble* and *3-2-1 Contact*. In 1998, she joined It's About Time (IAT) as the Director of Product Development and Grants, and she has supervised the publication of all IAT print, video, and multimedia products since that time including *Active Physics, Active Chemistry, Active Biology, MathConnections, Investigating Earth Systems, Interactive Math Project (IMP)–2015, InterActions in Physical Science* and *Project-Based Inquiry Science (PBIS)*.

Index